TRANSITIONS

D0556969

TRANSITIONS

Legal Change, Legal Meanings

Edited by
Austin Sarat

THE UNIVERSITY OF ALABAMA PRESS
Tuscaloosa

Copyright © 2012
The University of Alabama Press
Tuscaloosa, Alabama 35487-0380

The following chapters are all used with permission of their authors:
"Midnight Deregulation" by Jack M. Beermann
"Midnight Rulemaking and Congress" by Nina Mendelson
"Reconstructing the Republic: The Great Transition of the 1860s" by Akhil Reed
   Amar, Lindsey Ohlsson Worth, and Joshua Alexander Geltzer
"Transitional Disclosures: What Transitional Justice Reveals about 'Law'" by David
   Gray
"Global Transitions, New Perspectives on Legality, and Judicial Review" by Ruti
   Teitel

All rights reserved
Manufactured in the United States of America

Typeface: Caslon

∞
The paper on which this book is printed meets the minimum requirements of
American National Standard for Information Sciences—Permanence of Paper for
Printed Library Materials, ANSI Z39.48-1984.

Library of Congress Cataloging-in-Publication Data

Transitions : legal change, legal meanings / edited by Austin Sarat.
     p. cm.
   Includes bibliographical references and index.
   ISBN 978-0-8173-5690-3 (quality paper : alk. paper) — ISBN 978-0-8173-8593-4
(ebook) 1. Transitional justice. 2. Law—Political aspects. 3. Justice, Administration
of—Political aspects. 4. Rule of law. 5. Judicial review. I. Sarat, Austin.
   K487.P65T73 2012
   34-100'.115—dc23

                                                              2011048691

Cover image: First Lady Michelle Obama and President Barack Obama escort
former President George W. Bush and former first lady Laura Bush as the Bushes
prepare to depart the Capitol Building at the conclusion of the 56th Presidential
Inauguration, Washington, D.C., Jan. 20, 2009. Photo by Petty Officer 1st Class
Chad J. McNeeley, USN.

Cover design: Michele Quinn.

Dedication
To BJS, with love and gratitude for the person you are
and the person you will become

Contents

Acknowledgments

This volume is the product of a symposium held at The University of Alabama School of Law on January 29, 2010. I want to thank the colleagues, students, and staff who helped make that such a successful event. I am grateful for the financial support of The University of Alabama Law School Foundation. A special word of thanks to Dean Ken Randall for his unstinting support, for sharing the vision of legal scholarship reflected in these pages, and for making me feel so at home at the law school.

TRANSITIONS

What Transitions Mean to and for Law

An Introduction

Austin Sarat

In a world of change law often is thought to provide an island of stability. When everything is in flux, the regular procedures of law, its remove, its distant impartiality, provide reassurance that change can be managed, that order can be preserved, that transition will not disintegrate into chaos.[1] "Control or denial of this danger," Gretchen Craft argues, "motivates much of human effort in . . . law."[2] Yet law itself can be an instrument of change, fostering transitions from one form of behavior to another, inside and outside of formal institutions.[3] And, perhaps far from providing reassurance in the face of change, law may be unsettled by it. Legal inventiveness and ingenuity may be strained, legal conventions and understandings may be called into question, legal knowledge found wanting. Far from managing transitions, law may scurry to keep up with changes it can barely understand, let alone cope with adequately.

Generally, when the words law and change are linked, attention is directed to the way in which social change presses in and is reflected in changes in law[4] or, alternatively, the question of whether law is a valuable instrument of social change.[5] These outside-in and inside-out perspectives have so dominated the scholarly literature that more basic questions about what moments of legal change mean for law itself or how legal institutions bring about and respond to times of transition in legal arrangements largely have been neglected. *Transitions: Legal Change, Legal Meanings* addresses these questions.

Moments of transition pose great challenges for law, whether they are between regime types or transitions from one government to another within a single regime. In these moments law may seem absent or in suspension or to be a tool of, rather than a way of controlling and regulating, politics.

Yet law may provide a broad framework for moving from one status to another. It may provide the language for distinguishing legitimate from illegitimate transitions or setting the terms on which new understandings will be negotiated. Confronting the problem of identifying law in times of transition is an immensely consequential issue in both legal theory and jurisprudence as well as in private and administrative law.

One of the most storied of all transitions in political and legal theory is, of course, the transition from the state of nature to organized society, a change from a life that was imagined to be "nasty, brutish, and short" to a life rendered secure by a sovereign and a framework of law. The mechanism of transition, the metaphorical bridge from one condition to another, was, in the writings of Hobbes, Locke, and Rousseau, itself a legal device, a social contract.[6] While they each had a different understanding of the terms of the social contract, they all wrote about the contract's binding status. Critics of social contract theories, like David Hume, have noted the contract's status as a convenient fiction. As Hume put it, "as no party, in the present age can well support itself without a philosophical or speculative system of principles annexed to its political or practical one; we accordingly find that each of the factions into which this nation is divided has reared up a fabric of the former kind, in order to protect and cover that scheme of actions which it pursues."[7] Yet fictional or not, metaphorical or literal, some legal idea is in the social contract tradition a necessary prerequisite to the transition from chaos to order and to the foundation of legal order itself.

The centrality of transitions to the study of law is also signaled in H. L. A. Hart's classic book, *The Concept of Law*.[8] Writing in response to John Austin's *Province of Jurisprudence Determined*, H. L. A. Hart worried that Austin's account of sovereignty, namely that the sovereign is that person or persons who is habitually obeyed by the bulk of the population and who habitually obeys no other human, could not account for transitions from one sovereign to another. As Hart observed, if one king were to die and the king's son were to begin issuing orders, "the mere fact that there was a general habit of obedience to Rex I in his lifetime does not by itself even render probable that Rex II will be habitually obeyed." On Austin's account, "we shall not be able to say of Rex II's first order . . . that it was given by one who was sovereign and was therefore law."[9] Hart noted that legal systems typically respond to this problem by developing rules of succession, rules that regulate the succession "in advance, naming or specifying in general terms the qualifications of and mode of determining the law giver."[10] Here Hart portrays law as providing devices to avert "crisis" in the face of transition, as providing means of assuring continuity in the face of change.

In January 2009 the administration by Chief Justice John Roberts to President Barack Obama of an oath whose words were mangled brought home the significance of Hart's observations.[11] Though Article II, Section I of the Constitution contains the language of the oath, it does not require that a president-elect take an oath as a condition of assuming office.[12] Nonetheless, as Paul Horwitz observes, the presidential transition as a "constitutional moment" is instantiated in the act of "the taking of the presidential oath."[13]

The custom of administering an oath is so strong that Roberts re-administered it a day later. As the White House explained at the time, "We believe that the oath of office was administered effectively and that the President was sworn in appropriately yesterday. But the oath appears in the Constitution itself. And out of an abundance of caution, because there was one word out of sequence, Chief Justice Roberts administered the oath a second time."[14] The transition from one administration to another could not be secured from challenge until all the formalities and rituals of legal transfer had been played out correctly.

There is, of course, a robust literature on presidential transitions in the United States of the kind marked by the inauguration of Barack Obama.[15] That literature pays particular attention to behavior in outgoing administrations that raises issues of legal legitimacy. In the final weeks of their presidencies incumbents typically produce more regulations than at any other time during their term in office. This is due to what Jay Cochran identifies as the "Cinderella Constraint."[16] As Cochran explains: "Simply put, as the clock runs out on an administration's term in office, would-be Cinderellas—including the President, Cabinet officers, and agency heads—work assiduously to promulgate regulations before they turn back into ordinary citizens at the stroke of midnight. Executive branch term limits are periodically binding constraints that may cause an individual's focus on the deadline to increase as it draws nearer. In other words, as the term-in-office deadline approaches, a rush ensues to get regulations out the door in order to achieve the executive's ends (or to indulge his preferences) before that deadline arrives."[17]

Scholars have paid particular attention to problems that so-called midnight regulations cause for incoming administrations and to questions they raise about the legitimacy of the legal process.[18] While technically valid, do such actions represent an abuse of power or its proper use? As Jack M. Beermann explains,

> As a matter of principle, the actions of an aggressive outgoing administration are within the powers recognized under the Constitution and are part of this country's political process. The outgoing administration's actions may be legitimate attempts to enhance the outgoing party's political power and advance its performance in subsequent elections. . . . However, rules imposed very late in the President's term appear to be aimed primarily at the next administration. Other late-term action may entail a significant outlay of government resources without hope of actually coming to fruition in government policy, as when an administration initiates a long-term regulatory process at the very end of a term even though it is clear that the incoming administration has a different view on the matter involved. Some late-term action appears designed merely to embarrass the incoming administration. The outgoing administration may impose rules in a politically charged area, such as abortion or the environment, that it knows the incoming administration will dismantle.[19]

In response to the problem of midnight regulation, Beermann urges courts to afford a new administration great latitude in amending rules passed during a transition period.[20] Doing so would afford "a new administration the freedom to revise or rescind midnight rules when the record would support such a change."[21] Beermann also urges Congress to support allowing a new administration to suspend midnight regulations.[22] Other scholars have examined the problem of presidential transitions from the viewpoint of the incoming, not the outgoing, administration. Thus Nina Mendelson describes "three possibilities for increasing the president-elect's power during the transition period."[23] The three options—voluntary collaboration with the outgoing administration, required participation in the passing of regulations, or "president-elect concurrence in significant agency decisions"[24]—are all examples of ways in which transitions between presidential administrations might be made less problematic. In contrast to Beermann, who proposes (albeit tentatively) changes that would limit the power of the outgoing president, Mendelson seeks ways that transitions might be facilitated without limiting the authority of the incumbent president.[25]

Another kind of legal transition, one which in the United States is rare, though enormously consequential, is the process of constitutional amendment. Through the amendment process, legal regimes specify mechanisms and procedures for altering legal arrangements, defining or identifying rights, or providing new forms of legal recognition.[26] Occasionally, as Bruce Ackerman argues, amendments are so consequential as to represent a break from the existing constitutional order and the start of a new one.[27]

If we look beyond the national Constitution to state constitutions the amendment process is neither as rare nor as consequential.[28] Amendments to state constitutions often resemble the ordinary lawmaking process where groups press their interests or seek to undo legislative changes with which they profoundly disagree.[29] One can, of course, ask whether the constitutional amendment process represents an extraordinary or ordinary legal moment and how the frequency or infrequency of its use affects the framework of constitutional governance.[30]

Generally the study of transitions from one administration to another within an ongoing political and legal order or the meaning and significance of the amendment process within constitutional orders have been isolated from the burgeoning literatures on transitions from illiberal to liberal regimes and legal transitions in the global order. At the global level, this book inquires about the significance of the development and institutionalization of new legal institutions. How do they reflect and influence transitions from national to supra-national political orders?

With respect to transitional justice, much of the writing on the role of law in these sorts of transitions takes up the problem of responding to dramatic abuses of power and crimes committed under the prior regime.[31] How can officials be held accountable without seeming to impose legal standards in an *ex post facto* manner? How can law itself be rehabilitated as an instrument of justice when the prior regime used the forms of law for oppressive or unjust aims? Does judgment and punishment of high officials and bureaucrats from an authoritarian regime help establish the legitimacy of a new legal order?

For Simon Stacey, transitional justice focuses primarily on the question: "What should be done with the leaders of the ousted regime . . . for the abuses they inflicted upon the nation?"[32] Stacey argues that the Lockean "law of nature" that "justifies hoodwinking and eliminating deposed-regime members" does not mesh with contemporary views of universal human rights.[33] The question Stacey addresses is the status of these perpetrators of violence in light of modern developments in human-rights theory. He concludes that "Locke does not respect individual rights as deeply as he ought to" and that an acknowledgment of the limits of Lockean transitional justice might give us a "better idea of what a full satisfactory approach to transitional justice would need to take into account."[34]

Scholars like Ruti Teitel explain that in situations of transition from illiberal to liberal regimes "adjudications of the rule of law reflect understandings of legitimacy; criminal justice establishes wrongdoing; and transitional constitutionalism defines the state's political identity—all in a liberalizing direction."[35] She notes law's role is "to advance the construction of political change, transitional legal manifestations are more vividly affected by political values in regimes in transition than they are in states where the rule of law is firmly established."[36] Nonetheless, Teitel reminds us that even in times of regime transition "numerous diverse forms" of reparatory justice[37] may exist, forms that do the work that more formal legal institutions would otherwise perform.

Because scholars see law straddling the transition period as either the catalyst that incites regime change or the endpoint of a "liberal revolution," they ignore what Teitel describes as "the phenomenology of law in liberalization as a discrete subject of analysis."[38] An adequate theory of transitional justice, she contends, must include a vocabulary applicable to the specificities of what she labels the "transformative continuum."[39] She concedes that transitional justice "both stabilizes and destabilizes,"[40] but it does so in a way that evokes and respects the *rationalism* that underlies the "liberal rule of law."[41]

Today in response to the alleged abuses of power and crimes of the Bush administration, scholars are asking how, if at all, the lessons of transitional justice can be applied to the American context.[42] Indeed, within ongoing liberal legal orders questions of political identity are negotiated through such adaptations and also through explicit legal changes in the ongoing constitutional order; for example, through constitutional amendments. Here the work of Ackerman and others asks us to think about how liberal regimes reconstruct and reconstitute themselves through processes of orderly legal transitions.

The purpose of this book is to bring together scholars of different kinds of transitions, to see what we can learn about law itself by studying the role of law and the way law is used in times of transition. While there are other kinds of transitions that might be considered in a fully comprehensive treatment of the subject, this book represents the beginning of a scholarly exploration. Here we ask what challenges do different types of transitions pose for law? When and why do moments of transition encourage and nurture legal ingenuity and resourcefulness? When and why do they precipitate crises and breakdown in legal authority?

Transitions: Legal Change, Legal Meanings is the product of an integrated series of symposia at the School of Law at The University of Alabama. These symposia bring leading scholars into colloquy with faculty at the law school on subjects at the cutting edge of interdisciplinary inquiry in law. That colloquy is represented here in the commentaries that accompany each chapter.

This book begins with Jack M. Beermann's "Midnight Deregulation." Beermann's chapter examines the possible differences between midnight regulation and deregulatory measures brought into effect in the last months of a president's term. It provides an overview of presidential transitions and then briefly outlines the phenomenon of midnight regulation as well as midnight deregulation by the outgoing Bush administration in 2008–2009. Beermann argues that, although it is impossible to determine certainly, midnight deregulation might be influenced by negative politics even more than midnight regulation.

Beermann begins by outlining the possible reasons behind midnight regulation. First, some midnight regulation may be the harmless result of the human propensity to work to deadline. Midnight regulations may also be more illegitimately motivated by an outgoing administration's desire to project their policy agenda into the future. "Waiting" is another familiar reason for midnight regulation that is fundamentally political. By waiting until late in the term to act, an administration can maximize expected positive political impact or minimize the negative political impact of an unpopular action. Beermann considers "waiting" in terms of midnight regulation as a "defect in our constitutional structure" because it is an obvious example of politics conflicting with public interest and good government.

Beermann suggests that Bush's midnight regulation suffered from several defects. These actions left the incoming administration with a large volume of regulatory material to review before moving forward, risked the expenditure of unnecessary political capital, and reflected the political agenda of the outgoing administration. He argues that Bush-era midnight deregulation demonstrates how deregulation may exacerbate the worst tendencies of the midnight regulation phenomenon, because it uses legal procedures to achieve purely political aims to similar kinds of legitimacy problems.

Following this assertion, Beermann analyzes two deregulatory actions taken during the midnight period between the Bush and Obama administrations: an Endangered Species Act (ESA) consultation rule and an animal waste pollution reporting rule. Both actions were anti-environmentalist, publicly unpopular, and probably unnecessary. Neither could claim to advance the public interest. The ESA rule was also the product of a rushed regulatory process. This rule was withdrawn within the first months of Obama's presidency. The animal waste pollution rule, although less controversial, is another example of waiting to take politically sensitive action in order to avoid negative public reaction. In the end, Beermann concludes that midnight deregulation is more threatening to legality because it "reflect(s) favors to special interests" and "reflect(s) narrow interests that were defeated in the public-regarding initial regulatory push."

In "Midnight Rulemaking and Congress," Nina Mendelson argues that midnight rulemaking provides an opportunity to strengthen law and legal legitimacy. As she sees it, midnight rulemaking can present a unique opportunity to create an interbranch dialogue between the executive and the Congress as well as to engage the public in thinking about controversial issues. Mendelson argues that, in this way, midnight regulation may actually promote a more "deliberative" and therefore more democratic decision-making process.

Mendelson begins by addressing the allegedly flexible nature of the administrative state in enacting statutes and the phenomenon of "bureaucratic drift." Bureaucratic drift describes the tendency of an agency to take an action that does not exactly match the vision of the legislature. While she concedes that the flexibility of the administrative state is advantageous, as agencies deal with less technical and more "value-laden concerns" bureaucratic drift becomes problematic. She asks whether the unelected administrative state is justified in deciding questions of social value.

In addition, Mendelson considers whether presidential control is a source of democratic legitimacy for the actions of the administrative state. She rejects what she sees as Jerry Mashaw's "unduly rosy" interpretation of presidential control and claims instead that national election does not entail a more national perspective. Mendelson sees a "need to refocus on Congress" as a "vehicle for transmitting democratic views to the administrative state."

She argues that Congress represents two potential sources of democratic values for agencies. First, Congress is a more democratically representative institution than the president because it is fundamentally regional. Second, congressional views that are articulated through a constitutional process of discussion, debate, and enactment are also largely democratic in the "deliberative" sense of the term. Furthermore, deliberation in Congress is likely to be more democratic than deliberation within an agency because those involved are more representative. She calls attention to negative aspects of administrative deliberation, including the general lack of transparency and the influence of narrow and organized special-interest groups.

Mendelson believes that, in the normal course of events, Congress remains insufficiently engaged in the activities of the administrative state. She argues that oversight of agencies is "sporadic" and, when oversight does take place, "it is because the fire alarm has been pulled by well-organized interest groups." She sees in congressional reaction to midnight rulemaking a way of enhancing democratic processes.

To make her case, she analyzes two rules issued during the most recent presidential transition. The first rule exempted federal agencies from having to consult a "wildlife agency" about an action that the agency itself determined would not affect a listed endangered species, or about an action whose effects were manifested through "global processes" that would be difficult to measure. The second rule addressed the status of the polar bear as an endangered species. Prior to the midnight enactment of the rules, neither of these issues had received attention either in the media or in Congress. However, once the rules were issued they attracted immediate congressional attention, prompted substantial debate, and engaged the public. Precisely because they appear illegitimate, midnight regulations "pull the alarm" for congressional response and provide an opportunity for "constructive engagement." Legitimacy concerns in transitional moments can, Mendelson believes, have legitimacy-enhancing effects.

The next chapter shifts the focus from American presidential transitions to constitutional amendments. In "Reconstructing the Republic: The Great Transition of the 1860s," Akhil Reed Amar, Lindsey Ohlsson Worth, and Joshua Alexander Geltzer discuss the dramatic constitutional transition following the Civil War and focus particularly on the procedure by which the southern states were made to ratify the Fourteenth Amendment. They argue that the amendment process in the mid-1860s represented a "remarkable reinterpretation" of the original text.

Amar and colleagues compare the antebellum constitutional regime to the American constitution circa 1870 in order to demonstrate the extent of the post–Civil War transition. Before the war, the Constitution was essentially pro-slavery. As a result, it had no clear guarantee of racial equality. After the Civil War, southern slavocrats lost not only their extra political power, but their slaves. The Thirteenth Amendment ratified the largest re-distribution of property in American history and did so without any pro-vision for compensation. By 1870, the Constitution proclaimed the equal citizenship of black Americans and forbade race discrimination in voting. Whereas Lincoln was the first antislavery president, no president after him would again promote its practice. While the Democrats had domi-nated the presidency for more than a half century before Lincoln, the Re-publican Party controlled the office for the next half century. Furthermore, after 1870, no southern resident would serve as president until LBJ in 1963.

This chapter presents an argument about the legitimacy of the process through which the post–Civil War amendments came into being and, in particular, the controversial procedures by which the southern states were initially excluded and the Fourteenth Amendment ratified. What started as a "war for union and democracy" became a "war of emancipation." After the enactment of the Thirteenth Amendment in 1865, it became a "war for civil rights and additional national power" in order to safeguard the war's accomplishments for the Union. New federal legislation and consti-tutional amendments served this purpose.

The question remained of how to involve the ex-Confederacy in these legislative and amendment processes. In order to address this question, Amar, Worth, and Geltzer focus on the argument Representative John Bingham made in the House of Representatives. There, Bingham sought to justify Congress's refusal to seat the South and to condition southern state readmission upon ratification of the Fourteenth Amendment. Bing-ham argued that the South could be rightfully excluded from Congress because, according to the republican government clause of Article IV, they did not meet the Constitution's definition of "proper" states "in good standing."

Bingham argued that Supreme Court precedent recognized the au-thority of Congress to serve as the "proper judges" of congressional elec-tions and thus to make the "relevant determinations of republicanism." He made the case that what was true for the Article I congressional seating is-sue was also true for the Article V amendment process. Therefore, the "un-republican" southern states could also be excluded from the Article V rati-fication process.

Amar, Worth, and Geltzer argue that Bingham's speech yielded a new interpretation of the Article IV republican government clause, an inter-pretation that the Founders could not have envisioned. The enactment of the Fourteenth Amendment established a new principle of broad national control over undemocratic state franchise law. Amar and colleagues note that although not "intrinsic elements" of republican governments, the post–Civil War amendments (and therefore universal male suffrage and racial equality) were "appropriate instruments" of republican government.

They explain the reasons behind the dramatic transition of the 1860s in terms of several factors. First, American presidents, like Abraham Lincoln, can serve as "change agents" and "constitutional catalysts." Second, wars and regime failures can precipitate reform and realignment. Third, great leaps forward are generally composed of a series of smaller legal/political steps that feed off one another. And, lastly, revolutions typically end with powerful resistance. As a result, the full effects of the Civil War amendments were not felt for over a century following their controversial enactments. Because changes in a written Constitution "remain written," they can "create a long-term dynamic in which the arc of history is more apt to bend toward justice." As Amar, Worth, and Geltzer see it, even a transition whose legitimacy is not obvious can have law-improving effects. Perfecting legal institutions always requires transitions; however, those transitions need not themselves come anywhere near perfection.

David Gray's chapter moves us from the United States to take up the issue of transitional justice more generally. Here he examines the role of law and rule of law in pre- and post-transitional justice and violence. He criticizes the idea that the "law and the rule of law is a nearly unadulterated good" and challenges the assumption that the kind of targeted violence and human-rights violations characteristic of abusive regimes are only possible in lawless societies. Pre-transitional abuses express and extend a paradigm of law that justifies and often demands targeted violence. Abusive political paradigms fall, therefore, within the law. Gray offers three examples: the genocide in Rwanda, the "Dirty War" (La Guerra Sucia) in Argentina, and slavery and persistent racial injustice in the United States.

In each of those situations, perpetrators of atrocities believed they were carrying out an appropriate worldview—a view that was either supported or passively permitted by an abusive legal paradigm. Gray argues that "there is a rational social grounding for the mass, institutionalized, and targeted violence" associated with political transitions. In fact, Gray suggests that an abusive paradigm of law is the feature of abusive regimes that makes dramatic transition necessary. It follows then that successful transitional movements recognize this defining feature and attempt to reform the public norms and institutions contributing to its establishment.

As a result, transitional justice involves more than fixing law that has been "broken."

Gray's chapter highlights lessons that the study of transitions teach about the potential for "law" to maintain and achieve sustainable peace and stability. Specifically, he emphasizes that law and its complementary institutions provide a normative structure that supports the diversification of groups and group affiliation in transitional societies. Furthermore, law can construct barriers against claims of entitlement, dominance, and superiority that threaten stability. Importantly, law can also provide procedural alternatives to violence. Gray even further argues that law itself should be a field and object of contest among opposition groups. Contests over constitutional interpretation may be helpful in directing conflicts within transitional societies. In his view, apparently "messy" public debate prevents the mess of mass atrocities from overwhelming emerging dynamically stable societies.

Like Gray, our final chapter explores the significance of legal institutions and legal processes in managing transitions. Here the focus is on the emergence and significance of international law in an increasingly globalized, post–Cold War world. Ruti Teitel discusses the renewed debate over the meanings of law and legality—a debate reminiscent of the questions concerning the (non) relation between law and morality following the global transitional period at the end of World War II. She specifically emphasizes the "humanization" or "humanitarianization" of international law as it expands beyond its traditional borders.

Although Teitel recognizes the paradoxical nature of the contemporary, global situation (increased international legal interconnection without increased consensus), she believes that judicial interpretation on the international level can nonetheless be efficacious. "Judicial interpretation is well suited to making sense of diverse normative sources, under conditions of political conflict and moral disagreement." For Teitel, "Interpretation implies normative communication." She believes that this normative interpretation provides, at least in part, international law's source of legitimacy.

Teitel turns to the Hart/Fuller debate and the lessons from the first major postwar transitional period of the twentieth century. She criticizes the characterization of Hart as a "crude positivist." Hart did not adhere to the strictest definitions of positivist command theory—particularly in regard to his stance on international law. Still, Hart steered clear of any natural law emphasis on the moral categorization of an inevitably decentralized international law. Following this re-characterization, Teitel returns to a discussion of the value of interpretation in modern international law and human-rights law in its infancy. She writes, "Humanity-law, as an interpretative lens, navigates the narrow strait between the Scylla of difference and the Charybdis of the notion that these are known common values." The interpretive project has the potential to build a communicative community that protects against fragmentation. Judicial interpretation may therefore prove to be the appropriate means of managing or resolving normative conflict internationally during a period of transition to a more global legal order.

Whether offering analysis of domestic transitions within liberal regimes, or transitions from illiberal to more liberal legal orders, or transitions at the global level, the work presented in these pages charts but one small piece of a large terrain ripe for scholarly inquiry. *Transitions: Legal Change, Legal Meanings* calls on us to think about how law is implicated in moments of transition. Examining law as a cause and an effect in such moments broadens our vision and fosters inquiry about law's capacity to provide stability in turbulent times. Today, as the work presented here shows, we can no longer take for granted law's ability to manage transition. At the same time, the authors suggest that legal institutions are quite adaptive and often ingenious in devising ways to channel conflict and express normative dissent in moments of social and political change.

Notes

1. See Stanley Fish, "Law Wishes to Have a Formal Existence," in *The Fate of Law*, ed. Austin Sarat and Thomas R. Kearns (Ann Arbor: University of Michigan Press, 1991).

2. Gretchen Craft, "The Persistence of Dread in Law and Literature," *Yale Law Journal* 102 (1992): 521, 528.

3. See Sharyn L. Roach Anleu, *Law and Social Change*, 2nd ed. (London: Sage Publications, 2009).

4. For one example, see Lawrence Friedman, *A History of American Law: Revised Edition* (New York: Touchstone Books, 1986).

5. Gerald Rosenberg, *The Hollow Hope: Can Courts Bring About Social Change?* (Chicago: University of Chicago Press, 1993).

6. Social contract theories are reviewed in J. S. Gough, *The Social Contract: A Critical Study of Its Development* (Oxford: Oxford University Press, 1936).

7. See David Hume, *Political Writings*, ed. Stuart Warner and Donald Livingston (New York: Hackett Publishing, 1994), 164.

8. H. L. A. Hart, *The Concept of Law* (Oxford: Clarendon Press, 1961).

9. Ibid., 52.

10. Ibid.

11. "Roberts, Obama Jumble Presidential Oath of Office," see http://blogs .reuters.com/frontrow/2009/01/20/roberts-obama-jumble-presidential-oath- of-office/ (accessed January 20, 2009).

12. See Bruce Peabody, "Imperfect Oaths, the Primed President and an Abundance of Caution," *Northwestern University Law Review Colloquy* 104 (June 2009): 12.

13. Paul Horwitz, "Honor's Constitutional Moment: The Oath and Presidential Transitions," *Northwestern University Law Review Colloquy* 103 (2009): 1067.

14. David Hancock, "Obama Retakes Oath of Office," at http://www .cbsnews.com/8301–503544_162–4745910–503544.html (accessed January 21, 2009).

15. For an overview of that literature, see John P. Burke, *Presidential Transitions: From Politics to Practice* (New York: Lynne Rienner Publishers, 2000). Also Jack M. Beermann, "Presidential Power in Transitions," *Boston University Law Review* 83 (2003): 947, and Jack M. Beermann and William P. Marshall, "The Constitutional Law of Presidential Transitions," *North Carolina Law Review* 84 (2006): 1253.

16. Jay Cochran, "The Cinderella Constraint: Why Regulations Increase Significantly During Post-Election Quarters," Mercatus Center, George Mason University, Arlington, Virginia, October 9, 2000.

17. Ibid.

18. B. J. Sanford, "Midnight Regulations, Judicial Review, and the Formal Limits of Presidential Rulemaking," *New York University Law Review* 78 (2003): 782, and Jason Loring and Liam Roth, "After Midnight: The Durability of the 'Midnight' Regulations Passed by the Two Previous Outgoing Administrations," *Wake Forest Law Review* 40 (2005): 1441.

19. See Jack M. Beermann, "Combating Midnight Regulation," *Northwestern University Law Review Colloquy* 103 (2009): 352.

20. Ibid.

21. Ibid., 363.

22. Ibid., 366.

23. Nina Mendelson, "Quick off the Mark? In Favor of Empowering the President-Elect," *Northwestern University Law Review Colloquy* 103 (2009): 464. See also David Fontana, "The Permanent and Presidential Transition Models of Political Party Policy Leadership," *Northwestern University Law Review Colloquy* 103 (2009): 393.

24. Nina Mendelson, "Quick off the Mark?" 464.

25. On the Obama transition, see Michale Herz, "Freedom of Information: Law Lags Behind: FOIA and Affirmative Disclosure of Information," *Yeshiva University Cardozo Public Law, Policy & Ethics Journal* 7 (2009): 18.

26. See John Vile, *The Constitutional Amending Process in American Political Thought* (New York: Praeger, 1992).

27. Bruce Ackerman, *We the People, Vol 2: Transformations* (Cambridge, MA: Harvard University Press, 1998).

28. See Daniel Elazar, "The Principles and Traditions Underlying State Constitutions," *Publius* 12 (1982): 11. Donald Lutz, "Toward a Theory of Constitutional Amendment," *American Political Science Review* 88 (1994): 355.

29. See James A. Gardner, "The Failed Discourse of State Constitutionalism," *Michigan Law Review* 90 (1992): 4, and Michael Besso, "Constitutional Amendment Procedures and the Informal Political Construction of Constitutions," *Journal of Politics* 67 (2005): 69.

30. See Christopher Hammons, "Was James Madison Wrong? Rethinking the American Preference for Short, Framework-Oriented Constitutions," *American Political Science Review* 93 (1999): 837.

31. Neil Kritz, ed., *Transitional Justice: How Emerging Democracies Reckon With Former Regimes* (Washington, D.C.: U.S. Institute of Peace Press, 1995).

32. Simon Stacey, "A Lockean Approach to Transitional Justice," *The Review of Politics* 66 (2004): 55.

33. Ibid., 80.

34. Ibid., 81.

35. Ruti Teitel, "Transitional Jurisprudence: The Role of Law in Political Transformation," *Yale Law Journal* 106 (May 1997): 2009.

36. Ruti Teitel, *Transitional Justice* (New York: Oxford University Press, 2000), 216.

37. Ibid., 119.

38. Ibid., 214.

39. Ibid., 216.

40. Ibid., 220.

41. Ibid., 221. Also Paige Arthur, "How 'Transitions' Reshaped Human Rights: A Conceptual History of Transitional Justice," *Human Rights Quarterly* 31 (May 2009): 321. http://www.jstor.org/stable/20486755http://www.jstor.org/action/showPublication?journalCode=humarighquar (accessed September 8, 2010); http://www.jstor.org/stable/29734190?&Search=yes&term=justice&term=transitional&list=hide&searchUri=%2Faction%2FdoAdvancedSearch%3Fq0%3Dtransitional%2Bjustice%26f0%3Dall%26c0%3DAND%26q1%3D

%26f1%3Dall%26c1%3DAND%26q2%3D%26f2%3Dall%26c2%3DAND%26q (accessed September 8, 2010); http://www.jstor.org/stable/20069812?&Search =yes&term=justice&term=transitional&list=hide&searchUri=%2Faction %2FdoAdvancedSearch%3Fq0%3Dtransitional%2Bjustice%26f0%3Dall%26c0 %3DAND%26q1 (accessed September 8, 2010).

42. Miriam Aukerman, "Extraordinary Evil, Ordinary Crime: A Framework for Understanding Transitional Justice," *Human Rights Journal* 15 (2002): 15. Also, Jordan Paust, "Prosecuting Bush and His Entourage," *ILSA Journal of International and Comparative Law* 14 (2007–2009): 539.

1
Midnight Deregulation

Jack M. Beermann

Presidential transitions are exciting and perilous. How the president-elect will make the transition from candidate to chief executive of the world's most powerful country is unknown and essentially unknowable until it happens. Even under ordinary circumstances the transition is an emotional time, with the new president's supporters hopeful and excited and the defeated candidate's supporters disappointed and anxious. For many reasons, these emotions were magnified in 2009 when Barack Obama assumed the presidency. On the one hand, the outpouring of emotion at the inauguration of the nation's first African American president made this the most eagerly anticipated transition since the election of John F. Kennedy. On the other hand, perhaps fueled by extreme rhetoric during the campaign that questioned Obama's patriotism and status as an American citizen, Barack Obama's skeptics appeared more anxious over his ascendancy than the opposition had been to any president in living memory.

The focus of the transition is forward looking—what does the future have in store for this president and for the country that elected him? Unfortunately, in recent decades, the new president's ability to propel the country into the future has been hindered by what has become a well-known phenomenon, midnight regulation.[1] Rather than facilitate a smooth transition, outgoing administrations have attempted to push their, oft repudiated, agendas into the future, leaving messes of various shapes and sizes for their successors to clean up.

The midnight regulation phenomenon has received a great deal of scholarly and popular attention, most notably after President Bill Clinton eclipsed President Jimmy Carter's record for the greatest increase in regulatory volume at the end of the term.[2] Consider midnight regulation in normative terms, focusing on the attitude officials take during periods of transition. Imagine you are the leader of an organization facing the end of your term in office. It could be a large corporation, a large nonprofit organization, a small community service organization, or any sort of organization imaginable. What posture should you take toward the transition? Should you pave the way for your successor to have a smooth transition—for example, by resolving some thorny issues and tying up loose ends—or should you consider only your own interests and if that makes things difficult for your successor, so be it? In my view, the answer to these questions should be obvious, and it is only the inability to put politics aside for even a brief period around the transition that prevents outgoing presidents from doing right by the country rather than by their political party or personal ambitions.

The transition from George W. Bush to Barack Obama introduced a new wrinkle into the midnight regulation phenomenon: a great deal of the late-term activity of the Bush administration is best characterized as "midnight *deregulation*" because, rather than impose new regulatory burdens, it loosened them. The open scholarly question is whether midnight deregulation raises issues different from or in addition to those raised by midnight regulation. The answer to this question turns in large part on whether the law and politics underlying deregulation differ in any relevant way from the law and politics underlying regulation.

My intuition is that the Bush administration waited until late in the second term to take some of its deregulatory action because the opposition would have been great at any earlier time and because the campaign of Republican presidential nominee John McCain might have been negatively affected. This is consistent with one hypothesis underlying the midnight regulation phenomenon; namely, that presidents wait until late in the term to take potentially unpopular action when the political consequences are reduced.[3] However, there is a competing equally logical hypothesis, that at the end of the term, the president is free to rise above ordinary politics and take action that is in the public interest but which politics prevents in ordinary times when the administration is more concerned with accountability. Because these two hypotheses are each inherently plausible, a qualitative analysis and perhaps some speculation is required to offer an opinion on which better explains federal regulatory events in 2008–2009.

This chapter looks at midnight deregulation through the lens of the midnight regulation problem and asks whether the general understanding of midnight regulation should be adjusted to account for midnight deregulation. Part I describes the midnight regulation problem generally and the actions that administrations have taken to deal with the prior administration's midnight regulations. Part II is the analysis of the Bush administration's midnight regulatory action and a more general discussion of the midnight deregulation problem. Part III is the conclusion.

I. Midnight Regulation Mechanics

The midnight regulation phenomenon has become a familiar landmark on the presidential transition landscape. The volume of regulatory activity increases near the end of an outgoing president's term, especially when the incoming president is from the other political party. There are several reasons for the midnight regulation phenomenon, some of which are relatively benign and some that raise questions of the propriety of the action. The most benign reason for the increased volume of late-term regulatory activity is the natural human tendency to work to deadline. Often, regulatory actions that have been pending for a long time, even several years, finally are finished right at the end of the president's term before a new administration, with different policies or priorities, takes office. There is nothing like a firm deadline to inspire action.

The approaching deadline for completing preexisting regulatory work is not the only factor that contributes to the midnight regulation phenomenon. As the transition approaches, the incumbent administration may hurry not only to finish work that is well underway but may also try to do as much as possible to project its policy agenda into the future. If the outgoing administration knows or suspects that the new administration will have different views in important policy areas, the outgoing administration may initiate and complete regulatory action late in the term out of a conviction that its policies are superior to those of the incoming administration or to strengthen the outgoing group's future political chances. Projecting a repudiated policy agenda into the future seems less legitimate than simple hurrying to meet a deadline, because it frustrates the electorate's desire to change directions. However, continued and unending political competition creates an irresistible temptation for outgoing administrations to do whatever they can to further the agenda until the very last.

Another familiar reason for midnight regulation is what I have called "waiting." An outgoing administration may, for political reasons, wait until late in the term to take regulatory action. This includes action just before the election to maximize an anticipated positive political impact and action after the election that is anticipated to be unpopular and thus might harm the incumbent's party in the election. Waiting until just before the election seems problematic for two reasons, first because it is an abuse of the incumbency to time regulatory action to influence election results and second because, assuming earlier action would have been better for public policy, waiting to maximize positive political impacts represents placing personal political ambition ahead of the public interest.

At first blush, waiting until after the election may appear to be unambiguously problematic. We want our political leaders to be responsive to the popular will and not to time action to avoid the political consequences. From this perspective, the ability of an outgoing administration to take significant action during the transition period is an unfortunate defect in our constitutional structure. That's not to say that the lame-duck period should be eliminated. In addition to needing time to accomplish the mechanics of the presidential transition, the disputed 2000 election illustrates that the process of counting the votes and certifying the winner takes time. Although the best design of a democratic process for changing leaders may include a lame-duck period, midnight regulation may be an unfortunate side effect of a generally superior system for selecting and installing leaders.

While the negative first impression of waiting until after the election to take regulatory action is compelling, there may be circumstances when waiting is desirable or is at least a positive side effect of the constitutional structure that creates the lame-duck period. The influence of interest groups and other powerful political forces in our governmental system is often bemoaned as the reason why so much regulatory action seems counterproductive from a pure policy standpoint. During the transition period, an outgoing president is freed from immediate political concerns and may feel free to take action that may be good for the public but harmful to interest groups with disproportionate influence over the government.[4] A lame-duck president can rise above everyday politics and take public-regarding action. The lame duck's successor may benefit if the outgoing president clears the waters of political minefields and lingering problems, paving the way for a smooth transition and for the new president to hit the ground running.

It does not seem possible to predict theoretically which tendency actually dominates during the transition period. Rather, it appears to be an empirical question that can be resolved only by qualitatively examining late-term regulatory actions of the outgoing administration. One source of possible clues to whether late-term action was taken in the public interest is the reaction of the incoming administration to that action. If one takes acceptance of late-term action by the incoming administration as an indication of its consistency with the public interest or at least an indication that it is not the product of projecting a repudiated agenda into the future, then it would be helpful to look whether midnight regulation tends to be rejected or revised by the incoming administration. This is not a perfect measure because there are many reasons other than agreement for why an incoming administration might accept its predecessor's midnight regulation.[5] Although complete data are not available, the data that are available can help us get a sense of the degree to which midnight regulation is inconsistent with the preferences of the incoming administration.

Before getting to the data, it is necessary to take a step back and examine the general approach administrations take when confronted with the late-term actions of their predecessors. Incoming administrations dating back to Ronald Reagan have taken very similar approaches at the outset of their administrations to the problem of midnight regulation.[6] They have tended to take the following steps upon taking office: (1) They have instructed all agencies to stop issuing rules until they are reviewed and approved by an official appointed by the incoming president. This has amounted to a regulatory freeze because it takes some time for appointments to be made and for new appointees to conduct the reviews; (2) They have instructed the Office of Federal Register not to publish any new regulations issued by the prior administration. This results in new regulations being subjected to review by the new administration; and (3) They have instructed agencies to review regulations issued by the prior administration but not yet in effect and to delay the effective date of any such regulations if necessary to complete the review.[7]

Although the procedures put in place by the incoming administrations have been fairly uniform, the results of this action have varied. In a study of the actions of Presidents Bill Clinton and George W. Bush, the authors found that President Clinton amended or repealed a much higher percentage of the prior administration's midnight regulations than did President George W. Bush.[8] This can signify a number of differences between the two transitions. It may simply mean that Presidents Bush[9] and Clinton differed in their views on the importance of reexamining the past as opposed to embarking on the future. It may mean that more of the George H. W. Bush administration's midnight regulations were the product of "waiting" until after the election to avoid political consequences while those of the Clinton administration were simply the product of hurrying to finish work that had been delayed during the administration's eight years. It may also mean that the political differences between the George H. W. Bush and Clinton administrations were greater than the differences between the Clinton and Bush administrations so that Bush was more likely to leave the Clinton-era regulations in place. This explanation is consistent with the fact that when Bush reopened Clinton midnight regulations, it was very controversial, which may indicate that the Bush administration took office with a relatively weak mandate for change.

In light of the dubious political desirability of midnight regulatory action and the apparent institutionalization of the practice, it is not surprising that a pattern of reaction by incoming administrations to midnight regulation has developed. It is a shame that administrations cannot resist the temptation to engage in the practice even after experiencing firsthand the burdens midnight regulation imposes at a time when the new administration should be able to act on its electoral mandate as reflected in its regulatory agenda. The political gains from midnight regulation to the party of the outgoing administration must be so great that even the Bush administration, which had taken a principled stand against midnight regulation, felt compelled to engage in the practice.

The Bush administration was the first to take a stand against midnight regulation by its own agencies. President Bush's chief of staff Josh Bolten issued a memorandum that ordered all agencies to publish proposed regulations by June 1, 2008, and to finalize regulations by November 1, 2008, unless extraordinary circumstances warranted later promulgation.[10] This decision was probably born of the Bush administration's experience with the Clinton administration's record-setting volume of midnight regulation. Whether the motive behind the memorandum was to take a stand against midnight regulation or to simply immunize the Bush administration's late-term actions from reversal by the next administration,[11] the effect would have been the same—the volume of midnight regulation would have been substantially reduced and the new administration would have been relieved of the necessity of sifting through mountains of paper to ensure that its agenda was not being subverted by midnight regulation.

The Bolten memo was a partial success, regardless of whether its underlying purpose was to reduce the volume of midnight regulation or inoculate the Bush administration's midnight output from easy revision. The Bush administration issued slightly more final regulations (212) in its final year than the Clinton administration (209), but 112 of the Bush regulations were issued before November 2008, while only 63 of the Clinton regulations came out before November 1999.[12] This means that in the Bush administration there was a lower volume of true midnight rules and a higher number of final-year rules that were not subject to easy reversal or delay by the incoming Obama administration.

Further, under what has been characterized as "tremendous pressure," the Bush administration established criteria to determine when it would waive the Bolten memo's deadlines,[13] and regulatory action was taken right up to the moment of transition to the Obama administration. Most of these criteria were sensitive to common objections to midnight rulemaking.[14] Rules could be published after November 1 if they met one of the following four criteria:

1. Rules that had been submitted to the Office of Information and Regulatory Affairs (OIRA) for review before mid-October. This would relieve pressure on OIRA to rush its review.
2. Rules that the agency identified as high priority that had been publicly proposed long enough before the midnight period to allow for adequate notice and comment. This assured that midnight rules were not flying under the political radar after the election.
3. Rules that were subject to statutory or judicial deadlines. This allowed agencies to follow the law.
4. Rules that were considered presidential priorities, sometimes because of emergency situations such as rules designed to address the crises in financial and housing markets. This exception allowed for the issuance of controversial midnight rules such as the rule discussed below concerning conscience-based refusals of medical practitioners to engage in certain practices.

OMB Watch characterized as controversial 27 regulations that were published in the period from October through December 2008 with effective dates as late as January 21, 2009, the day after President Obama took office.[15] It was also reported that there was a substantial spike in significant regulations in the last quarter of the Bush administration.[16] Bush's midnight regulations are subject to the same analytical framework that has been applied to the midnight activity of prior administrations. However, there is a twist to this regulatory activity that merits separate scrutiny. While the Bush administration's late-term action included the imposition of regulatory burdens, a substantial portion of the midnight regulatory activity of the Bush administration was deregulatory, easing preexisting regulatory burdens or enforcing statutory standards leniently.[17]

The primary question explored in the remainder of this chapter is whether midnight deregulation is different from midnight regulation generally. Is there reason to believe that the politics of midnight deregulation are different from the politics of midnight regulation?

II. The Politics of (Midnight) Deregulation

Based on the number of rules in the last year and last quarter of the administration, it appears that the volume of Bush midnight regulation was fairly high. One report stated that as of November 12, 2008, there were "up to 90 proposed regulations" that might be finalized before the administration left office.[18] The report noted that the goal was to finalize them by November 22, 2008, sixty days before the Obama administration took office. Sixty days is key because under the Congressional Review Act,[19] significant regulations become final no sooner than sixty days after they are published in the *Federal Register.* Once the November 22 deadline was missed, December 19, 2008, became another key date because under the Administrative Procedure Act, rules may not go into effect less than thirty days after they are issued,[20] and that date was the last weekday more than thirty days before President Obama took office.

The Bush-era midnight regulations appear to suffer from all the defects with midnight regulation that have been previously identified. They left the Obama administration with a high volume of last-minute regulatory activity to sift through, which can be a distraction for a new administration trying to take the reins of government. The new administration was also put in the uncomfortable position of having to expend political capital cleaning up the mess that it might have better used on pursuing its own agenda. Many of the midnight regulations had been rushed through the regulatory process much faster than usual, raising the specter of ill-considered regulations that had not gone through the normal vetting process. Finally, the Bush midnight regulations, as should be expected, reflected the political agenda of the outgoing administration, which the electorate had arguably rejected in the November election.

The midnight regulations issued by the Bush administration can be sorted into three categories. The first category involves the imposition of new regulatory burdens in areas in which it would be expected based on the policy views of the administration. For example, on January 21, 2009, the Department of Labor published a rule increasing annual reporting requirements for small labor unions,[21] and on December 19, 2008, the Department of Health and Human Services (HHS) issued a rule requiring health care providers to certify, on penalty of losing federal funds, that they will allow their employees to withhold services based on the employees' religious or moral beliefs.[22] These rules increased regulatory burdens on the regulated parties although the rule regarding health care providers increased the liberty of the employees of the regulated entities.

These may be good rules, but their timing should raise suspicions—if they are such good ideas, why did the administration wait until its last month in office to issue them? This question is especially relevant with regard to these rules because they involve reporting to government agencies. By issuing these rules, the two departments are basically saying that we operated under an inadequate reporting regime for eight years and we happened to get around to fixing it just as we are about to transfer power to a new regime that might not share our view that the preexisting reporting was inadequate. The Obama administration took steps to reverse both rules, and the labor union reporting requirement was successfully withdrawn based on substantive disagreements with the Bush rule.[23] Comments were accepted on a proposal to withdraw the health care rule, but although the comment period ended in April 2009, it has apparently not yet been acted upon.[24]

The second category of Bush-era midnight regulations includes rules that imposed regulatory burdens but were attacked as too lenient. When Congress requires an agency to adopt regulations and the agency adopts lenient rules, the agency's action is best understood as deregulatory in spirit when measured against congressional intent in favor of more stringent regulation. A prime example is a rule issued on January 15, 2009, by the Department of Agriculture imposing revised country-of-origin labeling rules.[25] Although this rule may have imposed new regulatory burdens, it is best understood as a deregulatory action. The rule was a statutorily required element of enforcing a 2008 statute that increased country-of-origin reporting requirements.[26] The statute imposed a September 2008 deadline for new rules, which the administration met with interim rules imposed on August 1, 2008. The final rules were attacked as allowing exemptions for a high percentage of pork, frozen vegetables, nuts, fruit salads, and salad mixes.[27]

The third category of Bush midnight rules includes several controversial rules that are indisputably deregulatory. Prime examples are two rules adopted by the Environmental Protection Agency, emissions measuring provisions adopted on January 15, 2009,[28] and hazardous waste burning rules adopted on December 19, 2008.[29] Both of these rules were very controversial and were viewed by some as potentially harmful to the environment. Both eased preexisting environmental regulations and are classic examples of waiting until after the November election to issue rules that might have had political consequences for the election. Environmental issues were important to the 2008 election, and there was no apparent reason why these rules could not have been issued before the election, given that they had been proposed in 2006 and 2007, respectively. They were not driven by new legislative developments and they were not delayed by any external force such as an appropriations rider.

These and several additional examples of Bush-era midnight deregulation[30] raise the question of whether midnight deregulation is special. Is midnight deregulation more likely to reflect waiting to avoid political consequences, less likely to reflect such waiting, or basically the same as midnight regulation generally in this regard? While this question may be impossible to answer definitively, it may be possible to form an impression of the phenomenon of deregulation during the midnight period.

Consider the politics of deregulation outside the midnight period. The politics of deregulation are indeterminate. In some circumstances, deregulation can result from a rebellion against protectionist regulation that raises prices and reduces quality and variety by suppressing competition. In the 1970s, for example, Stephen Breyer, then a staffer for Massachusetts senator Edward Kennedy, advocated for airline and trucking deregulation and Senator Kennedy took up the cause.[31] The politics of deregulation at that time aligned established regulated industries against the general public as consumers and potential competitors who would benefit from deregulation. Greater competition and price deregulation would reduce prices and increase consumer choice. In this situation, continuing regulation would have involved bowing to powerful and narrow special interests that enjoyed significant benefits at the expense of the general public, which is the least desirable situation for regulation. The deregulation movement of the 1970s was a reform in favor of broad interests against narrow opposition.

The deregulatory movement of the 1970s may to some seem aberrant, reflecting a unique set of circumstances. Those who are generally supportive of environmental and health and safety regulation, for example, may suspect that most instances of deregulation reflect the triumph of narrow special interests over the general public good. Environmental regulation imposes costs on industry for the benefit of people who benefit from clean air, water, and soil—in other words, everyone. The wide dispersion of benefits and the concentration of costs mean that such regulation is unlikely to occur in the first place, and when it does, there will be constant pressure from regulated industry for reform and repeal.

The problem with this analysis is that it is always possible that the initial regulation was not in the public interest but rather reflected narrow powerful interests such as regulatory entrepreneurs and businesses seeking to raise the costs of their competitors. The realities of national politics may make any government action impossible without some powerful interest pushing behind the scenes even if regulation on its face appears to be motivated by the public interest. Even if regulators are well intentioned, they are likely to make mistakes or be forced by political realities to settle for regulation that is worse than the status quo. This leads some regulatory skeptics to adopt a libertarian position, being convinced that regulation always ends up benefiting the few at the expense of the many.

The indeterminacy of the politics of deregulation makes generalizing concerning midnight deregulation impossible. Despite the uncertainty, it seems safe to say that some of the Bush-era midnight deregulation suffers from the worst tendencies of midnight regulation and that those tendencies may be exacerbated in the case of deregulation. Agencies waited until after the November election because they feared the political consequences if they had acted earlier. The public may have viewed action such as easing restrictions on burning hazardous wastes and deregulating runoff from factory farms into waterways as benefiting narrow interests at the expense of the health and welfare of the general public. Had these actions and others like them been in the public interest, it is unclear why the administration waited until after the election to reveal them.

The differences between the deregulatory movement of the 1970s and the midnight deregulation of 2008–2009 also support the possibility that the Bush-era action was not an instance of rising above politics to take public-regarding action that could not have been accomplished in ordinary times. These actions may have been motivated by intense lobbying by regulated industries who wanted out from under what they viewed as excessive regulation. Reports are that there was constant zealous lobbying for deregulation during the Bush administration. The opponents of deregulation appear to have been general public-interest advocates rather than representatives of regulated industries pushing to maintain the regulatory status quo against a public-spirited deregulatory movement. When regulated parties are anxious to be relieved of regulatory burdens, and constituency for change in favor of the general public interest is absent, deregulation during the midnight period seems more likely to reflect narrow interests than the broad public interest.

A look at a few of the deregulatory actions taken during the midnight period of 2008–2009 illustrates that these do not look like the sort of public interested deregulatory actions that we would want an outgoing president to take. For example, on December 16, 2008, the Fish and Wildlife Service (Department of Commerce) and the National Oceanic and Atmospheric Administration (Department of the Interior) published a final rule implementing the Endangered Species Act (ESA) that allowed federal officials to approve some projects without, as had been previously required, consulting government habitat managers and biological experts.[32] This rule also provided that in cases in which consultation over species protection is required, global warming cannot be a consideration. What public interest could possibly support excluding global warming from consideration in the protection of species?

The ESA consultation rule discussed above was the product of a rushed regulatory process, and there was no apparent need to change preexisting consultation requirements that required quick, end-of-term, action. The rule was proposed on August 15, 2008, which means that the entire rule-making process took four months, a relatively short period for rulemaking. It was so controversial that the initial thirty-day comment period was extended and ultimately 235,000 comments were received by the end of the comment period in mid-October. One of the primary arguments made against the proposal was that the preexisting regulations that had been in effect for more than twenty years were working fine and there was no need for change. Others who commented complained that the process was rushed with inadequate time for analysis and comment. This rule appears to be a paradigm case of midnight deregulation.

The most damning element of the ESA consultation rulemaking is inherent in the type of rule involved. The ESA consultation rule does not regulate conduct in the private sector. Rather, it addresses only internal government operations. The outgoing Bush administration operated for eight years less thirty-four days under the broader 1986 consultation requirements. Suddenly, in its last few months in office, it found it necessary to change an internal government procedure that would be implemented only by its successors. It would seem especially appropriate to leave internal government operations to the next administration once it is so late in the administration that the change would not affect operations in the outgoing administration.[33] Given that this change was inconsistent with the general political views of the incoming administration and the Democratic Congress, it is not surprising that Congress legislatively allowed the agencies to withdraw this rule without going through normal notice and comment procedures[34] and that the administration did so shortly thereafter.[35]

Another example of Bush midnight deregulation is a rule promulgated by the Environmental Protection Agency under the Comprehensive Environmental Response, Compensation, and Liability Act of 1980, exempting certain categories of farms from reporting airborne emissions of hazardous substances from animal waste.[36] This rule was proposed on December 28, 2007, and was published as final nearly a year later on December 18, 2008, with an effective date of January 20, 2009, the day that President Obama was inaugurated. The *Wall Street Journal* reported that agribusiness lobbied hard for this change, arguing that existing reporting requirements imposed unnecessary burdens.[37] The subject matter of this rule, emergency reporting of the release of air hazardous pollutants from animal waste, is a small element of a substantial controversy over emissions from animal wastes. Farm animals generally, and cows, in particular, emit significant amounts of methane, which is a greenhouse gas, and efforts to monitor and regulate these emissions have provoked substantial political fighting.[38] In a related matter, the House of Representatives voted to bar the EPA from monitoring greenhouse gas emissions from farms. OMB Watch reports that environmental groups have filed suit to block the effectiveness of this rule.[39]

The animal waste pollution reporting rule appears to be another example of waiting to take politically sensitive action for the wrong reason, that is, to avoid political heat for something that is not in the public interest. The timing of the rule's adoption and the effective date of Inauguration Day strongly support this impression. However, it is not as clear cut a case as the ESA consultation rule for a variety of reasons. First, the regulatory process was not so rushed this time. The proposal was exposed to the light of day for nearly a year before the election, allowing plenty of time for the proposal to be relevant in the November election. By contrast, when a rule is proposed after or shortly before the November election, it seems more likely that the process was timed to avoid accountability. Second, the House vote on the subject shows that there is substantial political support for lenient regulation of farm animal waste emissions. The constituency behind this rule may not be as narrow as some midnight rules. Third, the agency's explanation for the change makes sense, that the reason for reporting emissions under this rule is to allow for emergency responses, and such responses are never forthcoming in notifications regarding farm animal emissions. Finally, the fact that the Obama administration has not reversed the rule indicates that the rule may not be all bad.

Despite the impossibility of determining whether midnight deregulation is generally less desirable than midnight regulation, a look at some of the Clinton administration's midnight actions might help get a handle on the differences. Few if any of the midnight regulations promulgated by the Clinton administration were deregulatory. Two of the most widely known Clinton-era midnight regulations were OSHA's ergonomics rule,[40] which contained wide-ranging provisions concerning repetitive stress workplace injuries, and an EPA rule regarding arsenic levels in drinking water.[41] The ergonomics rule does not fit the paradigm very well because OSHA had been working on the issue even before President Clinton took office, and the final rulemaking was delayed by appropriations riders until the last year of the Clinton presidency. After a veto threat resulted in an OSHA appropriation free of the rider, OSHA proposed a rule on November 23, 1999, and a final rule was issued on November 14, 2000, just after the election of George W. Bush. This rule was very controversial for imposing potentially massive costs on business, and the final rule ultimately was rejected by Congress under the Congressional Review Act, the only time a rule has been rejected under that act.[42]

The arsenic in drinking water rule is a more classic example of midnight regulation, although it, too, has a wrinkle in that action on arsenic in drinking water was legislatively compelled. In 1996, Congress directed the EPA to propose an arsenic standard in early 2000 and to finalize that standard before January 1, 2001. Despite four years notice that it had to act, the EPA did not propose a rule until June 2000, and the rule it promulgated was not actually published in the *Federal Register* until January 22, 2001, after George W. Bush had been president for two days. Acting under directives from the president, the EPA administrator suspended the effectiveness of the rule, but after an extended delay, when further study supported the necessity of the rule, it was allowed to go into effect as written.

There was at least one example of midnight deregulation in the Clinton era as well, in the abortion area. In the first week of his presidency, President Clinton ordered the Department of Health and Human Services to suspend what had been known as the abortion gag rule and promulgate a substitute, presumably one that would be more permissive. The subject of the abortion gag rule is funding for family planning clinics. Federal law prohibits federally funded clinics from using abortion as a "method of family planning." The interpretation of this prohibition, which by law must be announced via legislative rulemaking, has wavered from permissive in mainly Democratic administrations to restrictive mainly in Republican administrations. HHS under President Clinton operated without a regulation in effect between February 3, 1993, and July 3, 2000, when a permissive regulation, similar to the rule that governed during the Carter administration, was put in place.[43] This regulation would govern HHS funding decisions for the last six months of the Clinton administration and then Clinton's successor. This is also not a classic midnight regulation because it was adopted months before the November election, perhaps timed to attempt to influence the election but certainly to be applied (or revised) mainly by President Clinton's successor.

President Clinton's rule on abortion funding presents a prime example of undesirable waiting to promulgate midnight (de)regulation. Like President Bush's rule on ESA consultation, it governed internal government processes and owing to its timing, it would mainly bind the administration's successors. Also like the ESA consultation rule, there was no apparent reason why the rule could not have been issued earlier in the administration. In the abortion case, the agency essentially operated illegally for more than seven years with no guidelines for determining whether federally funded clinics were acting within permissible statutory bounds related to abortion. The two examples also have another element in common— they may have been designed in part to force the incoming administration to expend political capital to reverse them. This raises one of the most nefarious aspects of midnight regulation, that it distracts incoming administrations from their forward-looking agendas and forces them to spend time, energy, and political capital cleaning up the leftovers. This may be good politics but it is unlikely to be good government.

More generally, these examples suggest that midnight deregulation is more likely than midnight regulation to reflect favors to special interests that would not be palatable absent timing that reduces the political consequences. The passage of broad, public-interest-oriented programs such as environmental regulation and consumer protection is often difficult to explain given public choice predictions that narrow interests are likely to dominate politically. Programs with widely dispersed benefits and concentrated costs are the least likely to be adopted because the beneficiaries are at an economic disadvantage in lobbying. They come about from public interest that is so intense that the general population is able to overcome barriers to organizing and push regulation over the objections of organized narrow interests. When such programs are attacked during the midnight period, deregulation is likely to reflect the narrow interests that were defeated in the public-regarding initial regulatory push. This is how the Bush midnight deregulation was portrayed by some, although it is not certain that the portrayal is accurate. Conversely, when an administration increases regulatory burdens after the election, this may be an instance of taking advantage of the opportunity to rise above normal politics and act in the public interest when the administration is more likely to be able to ignore interest-group naysayers.

There are obvious challenges to my argument that midnight deregulation is more likely to be contrary to the public interest than midnight regulation. Critics would dispute the premise that regulation is often in the public interest. They would argue that behind every apparently public-interested instance of regulation is a narrow interest that is the primary beneficiary. Doesn't it make proponents of health care reform nervous when the American Medical Association endorses the plan? Fred McChesney argued that Federal Trade Commission (FTC) regulation of the funeral industry benefited competitors who offered cremation and other less-expensive funeral options.[44] Because McChesney found dubious public-interest support for the FTC funeral rules, his study strongly suggests that the influence of competitors of traditional funeral providers combined with misguided public concern resulted in unwise regulation. His hypothesis was that "the Rule exists to improve the position of specialized cremators and other sellers not subject to the Rule."[45]

Accepting the argument that behind every supposedly publicly oriented regulatory program is a private, narrow beneficiary likely to have secretly financed the lobbying campaign necessary to establish the program would lead inexorably to an extreme libertarian position under which all regulation is suspect and the only good regulatory action is complete deregulation.[46] The only acceptable reason for federal government regulatory action would be to protect the public from unwise state law, although it is theoretically difficult to explain why the federal system, in light of public-choice problems, would be able to produce better regulatory decisions than the states.[47] This analysis circles back to the indeterminacy of midnight regulation in the first place. In line with the pessimistic public-choice model, midnight deregulation would be more likely to reflect the public interest than midnight regulation, and the midnight period would be a welcome escape from the political pressures that lead to unwise regulation. Under a neutral model, the contrary appears more plausible, that midnight deregulation is more likely to reflect the triumph of narrow interests than midnight regulation. This may be a case in which beauty is in the eye of the beholder, and people with different views on the general wisdom of regulation will have irreconcilably different views on the desirability of midnight deregulation.

III. Conclusion

Midnight regulation has become a common element of presidential transitions in the United States. The volume of deregulatory activity at the end of the presidency of George W. Bush raised the question whether midnight deregulation should be understood differently from midnight regulation generally or whether it is simply a manifestation of the same general tendency to work to deadline and wait to take unpopular action until after the presidential election. While it is impossible to answer this question definitively, it appears that when an administration waits until the midnight period to take deregulatory action, it is more likely to be contrary to the public interest than when an administration waits to increase regulatory burdens. There are many reasons to be skeptical of midnight regulation, and the ability of an outgoing administration to slip deregulation beneath the political radar adds to the reasons why reform aimed at midnight regulation may be in order.

Notes

1. For a general analysis of the midnight regulation phenomenon, see Jack M. Beermann, "Presidential Power in Transitions," *Boston University Law Review* 83 (2003): 947.

2. The most widely noted quantification of the volume of midnight regulation is Jay Cochran, "The Cinderella Constraint: Why Regulations Increase Significantly during Post-Election Quarters" (Working paper, Mercatus Center at George Mason University, 2001). http://mercatus.org/publication/cinderella -constraint-why-regulations-increase-significantly-during-post-election-quarte (last accessed June 25, 2011). See also Veronique de Rugy and Antony Davies, "Midnight Regulations and the Cinderella Effect," *Journal of Socio-economics* 38 (2009): 886; Susan E. Dudley, "Midnight Regulations at All-Time High," *Intellectual Ammunition*, Heartland Institute, 2001. http://www.heartland.org/ policybot/results/99/Midnight_Regulations_a t_AllTime_High.html (last accessed June 25, 2011). William G. Howell and Kenneth R. Mayer, "The Last One Hundred Days," *Presidential Studies Quarterly* 35 (2005): 533.

3. See Beermann, "Presidential Power in Transitions," 955–960.

4. Term limits can have a similar effect. Presidents in their second term may be somewhat less beholden to interest groups because they don't have to worry about reelection. For a study of the effects of term limits on the behavior of state governors, see Timothy Besley and Anne Case, "Does Electoral Accountability Affect Economic Policy Choice? Evidence from Gubernatorial Term Limits," *Quarterly Journal of Economics* 110 (1995): 769.

5. The new administration may have different priorities, it might not want to expend its political capital on reversing controversial regulations, or it might have a long-term or comprehensive plan for new regulations in an area under which the prior administration's midnight action would endure for some time after the transition.

6. See Christopher Carlberg, "Early to Bed for Federal Regulations: A New Attempt to Avoid 'Midnight Regulations' and Its Effect on Political Accountability," Essay, *George Washington Law Review* 77 (2009): 995, 996 (detailing actions by incoming presidents since Ronald Reagan).

7. For discussion of steps incoming administrations can take against midnight regulation, see Beermann, "Presidential Power in Transitions," 992–998; Jack M. Beermann, "Combating Midnight Regulation," *Northwestern University Law Review Colloquy* 103 (2009): 352; Nina Mendelson, "Quick off the Mark? In Favor of Empowering the President-Elect," *Northwestern University Law Review Colloquy* 103 (2009): 464.

8. Jason M. Loring and Liam R. Roth, "After Midnight: The Durability of the 'Midnight' Regulations Passed by the Two Previous Outgoing Administrations," *Wake Forest Law Review* 40 (2005): 1441.

9. For simplicity, the administration of George W. Bush is referred in this chapter as the "Bush administration." The administration of his father is referred to as the administration of George H. W. Bush.

10. Joshua B. Bolten, "Issuance of Agency Regulations at the End of the Administration," Memorandum, 2008. http://www.ombwatch.org/files/regs/PDFs/BoltenMemo050908.pdf (last accessed June 25, 2011).

11. For an argument that the Bolten memo was designed to immunize the administration's midnight actions from reversal, see Carlberg, "Early to Bed for Federal Regulations," 997. This raises a definitional question: are actions taken before the November election properly called "midnight regulation"? There are arguments both ways. On the one hand, if an administration completes its work before the election of its successor, then it has not used the lame-duck period to avoid the political consequences of its actions and it has not loaded last-minute work on its successor. On the other hand, if the vol-

ume of regulatory activity increases substantially just before the earlier deadline and if new proposals are rushed through during this period, then it seems like midnight regulation with the clocks turned back a few hours.

12. See Susan Dudley, "Regulatory Activity in the Bush Administration at the Stroke of Midnight," *Engage* 10 (2009): 27, 28. The measurement of the final "year" actually includes all regulations issued from January 1 of the election year through the end of the administration on January 20 of the following year.

13. Dudley, "Regulatory Activity in the Bush Administration," 28. Dudley was the director of OIRA for the last two years of the Bush administration. She provides the following data comparing Clinton administration midnight rulemaking to Bush administration midnight rulemaking: in the postelection quarter in 2008–2009, there were 100 final regulations issued, as opposed to 143 in the same quarter in 2000–2001. The Bush administration issued 20 final regulations in its last three weeks, as compared with 72 in the last three weeks of the Clinton administration. The number of economically significant regulations issued by each administration in its final quarter was similar, 27 by the Bush administration and 31 by the Clinton administration. The number of *Federal Register* pages was 21,000 in the postelection quarter of the Bush administration as compared with 27,000 (the record) in the Clinton administration.

14. This description is drawn from Dudley, "Regulatory Activity in the Bush Administration," 28.

15. OMB Watch, "Turning Back the Clock: The Obama Administration and the Legacy of Bush-era Midnight Regulations," http://www.ombwatch.org/files/regs/PDFs/turning_back_the_clock.pdf (last accessed June 25, 2011).

16. See Veronique de Rugy, "Bush's Midnight Regulations: The 43rd president may set yet another dubious record," *Reason Magazine,* January 2009, 24 ("George W. Bush is set to out-regulate even his father, with a projected 70 significant rules during his midnight period.").

17. Some of the Bush-era midnight regulations were indisputably deregulatory in that they removed or eased preexisting regulatory burdens or paved the way for privatization. Others might be characterized as deregulatory because they provoked charges that the regulated industries got off easy in the regulatory process. Some Bush-era midnight regulations imposed new, increased regulatory burdens on groups such as labor unions, women seeking reproductive services including abortion, and charities suspected of raising money for terrorist activities.

18. Matthew Blake, "The Midnight De-Regulation Express," 2008, http://

washingtonindependent.com/17813/11-hour-regulations (last accessed June 25, 2011).

19. Congressional Review Act, 5 U.S.C. § 801 et seq.

20. 5 U.S.C. § 553(d).

21. Labor Organization Annual Financial Reports, 74 *Federal Register* 3678-01 (January 21, 2009).

22. Ensuring That Department of Health and Human Services Funds Do Not Support Coercive or Discriminatory Policies or Practices in Violation of Federal Law, 73 *Federal Register* 78072–78101 (December 19, 2008).

23. Labor Organization Annual Financial Reports, 74 *Federal Register* 52401–52413 (October 13, 2009).

24. Rescission of the regulation entitled "Ensuring That Department of Health and Human Services Funds Do Not Support Coercive or Discriminatory Policies or Practices in Violation of Federal Law"; Proposal, 74 *Federal Register* 10207 (March 10, 2009).

25. See http://www.federalregister.gov/articles/2009/03/10/E9-5067/rescission-of-the-regulation-entitled-ensuring-that-department-of-health-and-human-services-funds-do (last accessed June 25, 2011). Mandatory Country of Origin Labeling of Beef, Pork, Lamb, Chicken, Goat Meat, Wild and Farm-Raised Fish and Shellfish, Perishable Agricultural Commodities, Peanuts, Pecans, Ginseng, and Macadamia Nuts 74 *Federal Register* 2657–2707 (January 15, 2009).

26. The *Federal Register* states: "This final rule is issued pursuant to the 2002 Farm Bill, the 2002 Appropriations, and the 2008 Farm Bill, which amended the Act to require retailers to notify their customers of the origin of covered commodities." Ibid., 2658.

27. See Letter from Wenonah Hauter, Executive Director of Food and Water Watch, to the Department of Agriculture, September 20, 2009, available at http://documents.foodand waterwatch.org/COOL-letter.pdf (last accessed June 25, 2011).

28. Prevention of Significant Deterioration (PSD) and Nonattainment New Source Review (NSR): Aggregation and Project Netting, 74 *Federal Register* 2376-2383 (January 15, 2009). This rule was proposed in 2006.

29. Expansion of RCRA Comparable Fuel Exclusion, 73 *Federal Register* 77953-78017 (December 19, 2008). This rule was proposed in 2007. Expansion of RCRA Comparable Fuel Exclusion, Proposal, 72 *Federal Register* 33284 (June 15, 2007).

30. Examples include the following: Exemption of reporting for federal contractors, 12/19/08; Privatization of Public Toll Roads, 12/19/08; Certifica-

tion for the Employment of H-2B Aliens, 12/19/08; Revisions to H-2A Guest Worker program, 12/18/08; Air Pollution Reporting from Farms, 12/19/08; Endangered Species Consultation, 12/16/08; Mountaintop Mining, 12/12/08; Gun Safety in National Parks, 12/10/08; Vertical Tandem Lifts, 12/10/08; Emergency Land Withdrawals, 12/5/08; Rerouting Hazmat Rail Shipments, 11/26/08; Rail Transportation Security, 11/26/09; Runoff from Factory Farms, 11/26/09; Truck Driver Hours of Service, 11/09/08; Family and Medical Leave, 11/17/08; Definition of Solid Waste, 10/30/08. This list is drawn from the OMB Watch report "Turning Back the Clock."

31. See Martha Dethick and Pauk J. Quirk, *The Politics of Deregulation* (Washington, D.C.: Brookings Institution Press, 1985).

32. Interagency Cooperation Under the Endangered Species Act, 73 *Federal Register* 76272–76287 (December 16, 2008).

33. The Bush administration apparently considered a major change in OSHA risk assessment procedures in the waning days of its administration, after completing "only one major health rule for a chemical in the workplace, and it did so under a court order." Carol D. Leonnig, "U.S. Rushes to Change Workplace Toxin Rules," *Washington Post*, July 23, 2008. This proposal surfaced in July 2008 after the administration's own June deadline for new regulatory proposals. As a procedural change that would be applied, if at all, to the Bush administration's successor, it raises the same sort of questions as the ESA consultation rule, namely if the procedural change was so important to accomplish in the final months of the administration, why wasn't it worth doing in the previous seven plus years?

34. Section 429(a)(1) and (2) of the 2009 Omnibus Appropriations Act, Public Law 111-8.

35. Interagency Cooperation Under the Endangered Species Act, 74 *Federal Register* 20421–20423 (May 4, 2009). The State of California had previously filed suit to overturn the rule. See Samantha Young, "California Sues Bush to Block Midnight Deregulation of Endangered-Species Rules," Associated Press, December 30, 2008.

36. CERCLA/EPCRA Administrative Reporting Exemption for Air Releases of Hazardous Substances from Animal Waste at Farms, 73 *Federal Register* 76948–76960 (December 18, 2008).

37. See Stephen Power, "EPA Exempts Factory Farms From Emissions Reporting Rule," *Wall Street Journal*, December 12, 2008, http://online.wsj.com/article/SB122911925393902761.html (last accessed June 25, 2011).

38. See Mike Markarian, "A Free Pass for Factory Farms?" http://hslf.typepad.com/political_animal/2009/10/free-pass-for-factory-farms.html

(last accessed June 25, 2011), October 28, 2009 (reporting House vote to include provision in appropriations legislation that would prevent the EPA from monitoring greenhouse gas emissions from farms).

39. OMB Watch, "Turning Back the Clock."

40. Ergonomics Program, 64 *Federal Register* 65,768 (proposed November 23, 1999) (to be codified at 29 C.F.R. pt. 1910).

41. National Primary Drinking Water Regulations; Arsenic and Clarifications to Compliance and New Source Contaminants Monitoring, 66 *Federal Register* 6976 (January 22, 2001) (codified at 40 C.F.R. pts. 9, 141, 142).

42. Ergonomics Rule Disapproval, Public Law No. 107-408, 115 Stat. 7 (2001). Rejection by Congress was facilitated by the fact that the rule was promulgated late enough in the Clinton administration that President Bush was in office by the time Congress's resolution rejecting the rule was presented to the president. President Bush signed it, while President Clinton, had he still been in office, might have vetoed it.

43. Standards of Compliance for Abortion-Related Services in Family Planning Service Projects, 65 *Federal Register* 41,270, 41,278 (July 3, 2000) (to be codified at 42 C.F.R. pt. 59).

44. Fred McChesney, "Consumer Ignorance and Consumer Protection Law: Empirical Evidence from the FTC Funeral Rule," *Journal of Law and Politics* 7 (1990): 66. State regulation of the funeral industry is portrayed as likely to be contrary to the public interest in David E. Harrington and Kathy J. Krynski, "The Effect of State Funeral Regulations on Cremation Rates: Testing for Demand Inducement in Funeral Markets," *Journal of Law and Economics* 45 (2002): 199. The authors conclude that state regulation of the funeral business increases costs and allows traditional funeral homes to steer clients toward more expensive services.

45. McChesney, "Consumer Ignorance and Consumer Protection Law," 67.

46. See Cynthia R. Farina, "Faith, Hope, and Rationality or Public Choice and the Perils of Occam's Razor," *Florida State University Law Review* 28 (2000): 111. This view cannot be true; that is, it cannot be true that regulation is never in the public interest. For a detailed account of how industry defends itself against regulation, see David Michaels, *Doubt Is Their Product: How Industry's Assault on Science Threatens Your Health* (New York: Oxford University Press, 2008). In thinking, for example, about the current controversy over global warming recall that companies like DuPont fought tooth and nail against regulation of the substances scientists claimed had caused ozone depletion in the upper atmosphere. The skeptics did whatever they could to cast

doubt on the scientific basis for concern over ozone depletion and they also predicted dire economic consequences of the proposed ban on the substances that were allegedly behind the problem. See Jeffrey Masters, "The Skeptics vs. the Ozone Hole," http://www.wunderground.com/education/ozone_skeptics .asp. The fight against ozone depletion is now regarded as a success, although it is unclear whether the ozone hole is actually shrinking and whether factors other than chemicals, such as weather patterns, may contribute to the size of the hole. See News Staff, "Ozone Layer—An Environmental Regulation Success Story," http://www.scientificblogging.com/news_articles/ozone_layer _environmental_regulation_success_story (reporting on research indicating that atmospheric ozone levels have increased over the last fourteen years at a rate of 1 percent per decade); Ozone Hole in 2008 Is Larger Than Last Year (ANI: October 8, 2008), http://www.thaindian.com/newsportal/india-news/ozone -hole-in-2008-is-larger-than-last-year_100104758.html (last accessed June 25, 2011).

47. This is why I am suspicious of advocates of federal regulatory preemption of state tort law. The advocates of preemption find public choice problems with federal regulation except when it matches one of their policy preferences, such as a distaste for state products liability litigation.

Commentary on Chapter 1
Judicial Review of Midnight Deregulation
Heather Elliott

When an outgoing president is a lame duck (he's lost the election but holds office until the new president takes office the next January 20), he need not fear political punishment; after all, the election is past. Thus the lame duck may take regulatory action, unconstrained by electoral worries. Action to *increase* regulatory burdens in this "midnight" period—midnight regulation—has received ample attention in the academic literature.[1]

But a lame duck may also act to *lessen* regulatory burdens in the midnight period—midnight *de*regulation. Professor Beermann convincingly demonstrates that George W. Bush engaged in midnight deregulation, and finds that midnight deregulation "is more likely to be contrary to the public interest" than midnight regulation.[2] Such deregulatory actions may be more likely to "benefit[] narrow interests at the expense of the health and welfare of the general public"[3] and may "reflect favors to special interests that would not be palatable absent timing that reduces the political consequences."[4]

As a result, Beermann argues, reforms aimed at preventing or mitigating last-minute regulatory actions are more important than previously thought.[5] Such reforms, as he has argued elsewhere, might include legislation that makes it harder for outgoing presidents to take midnight actions, legislation that makes it easier for incoming presidents to reverse midnight actions, and doctrinal changes by the Supreme Court that reflect the special problems raised by midnight action.[6]

I agree with Beermann's assessment. In this chapter, I present another reason that midnight deregulation is more problematic than midnight regulation: deregulation is harder to challenge in the federal courts because of the Supreme Court's constitutional standing doctrine. Thus, in an area where political controls are ineffective—where the outgoing president has acted precisely at the time that he cannot suffer electoral punishment—the federal courts are also less available to provide judicial review and thus an alternative form of accountability.

After an overview of the Supreme Court's constitutional standing doctrine, I discuss the doctrine in the context of midnight actions. I conclude that the obstacles to judicial review of midnight deregulation make it even more imperative that Congress act to restrict an outgoing president's ability to take such midnight action.

I. Standing to Sue

Courts have traditionally limited the cases they will hear by applying a variety of tests to assure that a suit is susceptible of judicial resolution. For example, a case must be ripe: the factual context of the legal claim must have developed sufficiently that the court has a concrete dispute to resolve, rather than a mere battle of ideas. A case must also not be moot: the situation sued over must not have been resolved (by, for example, settlement between the parties), for that would leave the court with nothing to do.

Standing to sue is similarly a doctrine that ensures the presence of a dispute susceptible of judicial resolution. The plaintiff must answer the question, "what's it to you?"[7] Under current doctrine, that requires a plaintiff to demonstrate three things: (1) she must have suffered, or face an imminent threat of, "injury-in-fact"; (2) the plaintiff's injury must be "fairly traceable" to the actions of the defendant; and (3) the relief requested in the suit must redress (at least in part) the plaintiff's injury.[8] Stated in this form, it is easy to see the relation between ripeness, mootness, and standing: all require that a concrete dispute be presented to the court, one that is a proper subject of judicial action.

The doctrine emerges from a brief phrase in the Constitution: Article III's assignment to the federal courts the responsibility of deciding "Cases" and "Controversies."[9] Traditionally the standing doctrine has been used to assure that the plaintiff "allege[s] such a personal stake in the outcome of the controversy as to assure that concrete adverseness which sharpens the presentation of issues upon which the court so largely depends."[10]

But standing doctrine now asks many more questions than merely, "what's it to you?" Instead, because standing "is built on a single basic idea—the idea of separation of powers,"[11] standing doctrine is used to ask plaintiffs "why are you here, rather than in the political branches?" and "are you here because Congress has impermissibly given you a right to enforce the law, when that's the president's job?" Put less colloquially, standing doctrine has been used by the federal courts to avoid cases because they are more properly resolved by the political branches (for example, because many people share the same injury and thus should be able to lobby effectively) and to resist being pulled into disputes between Congress and the president (as when Congress empowers citizen suitors to privately enforce the laws, for fear that the president will not take sufficient enforcement action).[12]

Standing thus is forced to perform many functions, and many of those functions it performs very poorly.[13] As a result, and by the Court's own admission, the standing doctrine "incorporates concepts concededly not susceptible of precise definition."[14] The doctrine is widely criticized for its incoherence and manipulability.[15]

Most relevant here, recent standing cases have established an asymmetry in access to the federal courts: it is far easier for regulated entities—for example, companies that must comply with federal environmental laws—to show standing to sue, than it is for regulatory beneficiaries—for example, those who would breathe cleaner air if the environmental laws are followed. According to the Supreme Court, the standing of a regulated entity is typically self-evident: when "the plaintiff is himself an object of the action (or forgone action) at issue . . . there is ordinarily little question that the action or inaction has caused him injury, and that a judgment preventing or requiring the action will redress it."[16] Thus regulated entities seeking to ease their regulatory burdens easily satisfy the tripartite standing test and find ready access to judicial review in the federal courts.

In contrast, regulatory beneficiaries find it much more difficult to satisfy the Court's standing doctrine: "When . . . a plaintiff's asserted injury arises from the government's allegedly unlawful regulation (or lack of regulation) of someone else, much more is needed."[17] So, for example, a man who had once suffered from a police officer's use of a dangerous chokehold was found to lack standing to challenge the police department's failure to properly regulate those chokeholds, because he could not show that he had any likelihood of suffering from another chokehold.[18] Parents who sought an integrated education for their children were found to lack standing to challenge the IRS's granting of tax-exempt status to whites-only private schools, because they could not show that action of the IRS would result in integration of the private schools.[19] And plaintiffs who studied endangered species in the wild were found to lack standing to challenge U.S. actions that might cause the extinction of those species in other parts of the world, because those plaintiffs could not show they had any concrete plans to visit those parts of the world.[20]

The Supreme Court's standing doctrine thus makes it highly likely that regulated entities will have standing, but makes it less likely that any particular beneficiary of a regulation will have standing. Regulated entities usually seek to strike down regulatory action, while regulatory beneficiaries usually seek to force an agency to initiate regulatory action, strengthen existing regulations, or enforce existing regulations. If regulated entities have easier access to the courts, courts will more often hear cases seeking to challenge regulations, and will less often hear cases seeking more regulation. Standing's asymmetry produces a one-way ratchet *against* regulation.[21]

Now, just because regulated entities have standing to sue does not mean their arguments will succeed; the courts can certainly uphold regulations in those lawsuits despite the attacks from the regulated entity. But if a regulation is not strict enough, or if government chooses not to enforce existing regulations or not to regulate at all, the likely challengers are those who would have benefited from the stronger regulation; those regulatory beneficiaries have a hard time satisfying the threshold standing requirements. In general, the asymmetry imposed by standing is anti-regulatory. This asymmetry in access has received wide attention among critics.[22]

What's more, Richard J. Pierce has shown that this asymmetry affects more than the courts. Once it becomes clear that regulated entities are the ones who can seek court review most easily, the agencies will work to appease the regulated industry.[23] As a result, standing doctrine makes it easier for regulated entities to "capture" the agencies that regulate them.[24] As Pierce puts it, such capture "is a version of the phenomenon the Framers called 'factionalism.' [Standing doctrine thus may] maximiz[e] the potential growth of the political pathology the Framers most feared and strived to minimize."[25]

II. Judicial Review of Midnight Actions

How, then, does standing doctrine play out in the context of midnight regulatory action? I first have to clarify the nature of midnight regulation and deregulation; I will then show that the relative difficulty of seeking judicial review of midnight deregulation gives us another reason to fear such midnight actions.

A. Midnight Actions

Midnight actions arise when "[t]he volume of regulatory activity increases near the end of an outgoing president's term, especially when the incoming president is from the other political party."[26] Extensive attention has been paid to midnight actions that involve *increasing* regulatory burdens—midnight regulation.[27] Beermann's valuable contribution turns our focus to midnight deregulation, those actions that *relieve* regulatory burdens.

Midnight regulation may arise for innocuous reasons: it is the rare human being who can finish all projects ahead of deadline. As Professor Beermann puts it, "there is nothing like a firm deadline to inspire action."[28] A president may also use midnight regulation "to project [his] policy agenda into the future."[29] Such action is "less legitimate than simple hurrying to meet a deadline, because it frustrates the electorate's desire to change directions," but the midnight action may be "an irresistible temptation."[30]

Finally, a president may time midnight regulation to his political advantage, a process Professor Beermann calls "waiting." Waiting may take two forms. First, the president may release popular regulations right before the election to "maximize an anticipated positive political impact." Such "waiting" creates at least two problems. The president abuses his power when he times regulations to affect election results; and, assuming the regulation provides public benefits, the president sacrifices the benefits that would have accrued to the public by an earlier release in favor of his political goals.[31]

Second, the president may hold the release of unpopular regulations until after the election, to prevent "harm [to] the incumbent's party in the election."[32] In this form of waiting, the president takes advantage of the lame-duck period to take action that he is unwilling to subject to electoral accountability. Such waiting can, of course, arise for nefarious reasons: a president might, for example, wait to do favors for special-interest groups until the election has passed. But Beermann points out that "there may be circumstances when waiting is desirable."[33] He goes on: "During the transition period, an outgoing president is freed from immediate political concerns and may feel free to take action that may be good for the public but harmful to interest groups with disproportionate influence over the government. A lame-duck president can rise above everyday politics and take public-regarding action."[34] As a consequence, we cannot deem midnight regulation a generally bad thing: such midnight action may be the only way to overcome the gridlock of normal politics.

Midnight deregulation, by contrast, "eas[es] preexisting regulatory bur-dens or enforce[es] statutory standards leniently."[35] Beermann notes that deregulation outside the midnight period is politically "indeterminate."[36] Sometimes deregulation works in the public interest and against special-interest groups, as when the deregulation of the trucking and airline in-dustries in the early 1980s "reduce[d] prices and increase[d] consumer choice" at the expense of the formerly protected industries.[37] By contrast, relieving industry of environmental regulatory burdens may seem to "reflect the triumph of narrow special interests over the general public good"[38]— "[p]rograms with widely dispersed benefits and concentrated costs are the least likely to be adopted because the beneficiaries are at an economic dis-advantage in lobbying. They come about from public interest that is so in-tense that the general population is able to . . . push regulation over the objections of organized narrow interests."[39] Of course, Beermann notes, regulations that seem to be in the public interest may actually be pushed by narrow interests for their private benefit. The overall point, however, is that "the politics of deregulation are indeterminate."[40]

Is deregulation *at midnight* a different animal? According to Beermann, "some of the [George W.] Bush-era midnight deregulation suffers from the worst tendencies of midnight regulation and . . . those tendencies may be exacerbated in the case of deregulation."[41] After reviewing a number of George W. Bush's midnight actions, Beermann concludes that "mid-night deregulation is more likely than midnight regulation to reflect favors to special interests that would not be palatable absent timing that reduces the political consequences."[42] Thus midnight deregulation "is more likely to be contrary to the public interest" than midnight regulation.[43]

B. Judicial Review of Midnight Actions

As the above discussion makes clear, midnight actions raise our suspicions because they look like efforts to avoid electoral accountability. While some such actions may represent a president's welcome efforts to rise above poli-tics and take action truly in the public interest, other midnight actions re-flect the president's desire to do favors for special interests without being held accountable to the public. And, in particular, as Beermann has argued, midnight *deregulation* raises such concerns.

Of course, it has long been feared that special interests will "capture" ad-ministrative agencies,[44] whether through midnight action or not. Agency personnel are insulated from politics: they are not elected, most are not even appointed by elected officials, and most have civil service job protection. The concern is thus that agency personnel will not be responsive to public concerns, but will instead (on the cynical view) be easy prey for industry lobbying or (on a less cynical view) come to know and pay more attention to the arguments of those with whom they most regularly interact—the regulated industry.

A variety of mechanisms have been adopted to ameliorate the risks of capture. Congress has, for example, used procedures (imposed generally by the Administrative Procedure Act [APA] and specifically by the statutes that give agencies their substantive mandates) to constrain agency officials; for example, agencies must give notice of proposed regulations, receive public comment on those regulations, adjust the regulation to reflect consideration of those comments, and so on.[45] And judicial review is widely available to ensure that those procedures are followed.[46]

Judicial review thus makes agencies accountable in the absence of electoral safeguards. Judicial review should provide a fallback when a lame-duck president wishes to take politically unpalatable action in the midnight period; courts will be there at least to ensure that proper procedures have been followed. If, however, judicial review is unavailable, little exists to constrain the lame-duck president, even if he cuts procedural corners in completing his midnight actions.

What judicial review is available of midnight action? If the midnight action imposes additional regulatory burdens, those who bear that burden—the regulated entities—will almost certainly have standing to challenge the action. As I described above, the Supreme Court has held that the standing of regulated entities is essentially self-evident. This means that, even if the incoming president takes no steps to reverse the midnight action, plaintiffs should be readily available to challenge the midnight regulation in the courts. Even though the political system had a loophole—the lame-duck period that permitted the midnight action—the judicial system provides a backstop to ensure that the midnight action was not arbitrary, capricious, or not in accordance with law under the Administrative Procedure Act.[47]

Note that judicial review will be available even if the midnight action represents the laudable effort of the outgoing president to rise above politics and take action in the public interest despite special-interest opposition. As Beermann describes it, "A lame-duck president can rise above everyday politics and take public-regarding action. The lame duck's successor may benefit if the outgoing president clears the waters of political minefields and lingering problems, paving the way for a smooth transition."[48] The outgoing president may promulgate public-regarding regulations, the incoming president may view such regulations with gratitude, and nonetheless regulated entities—the very entities who lost the debate in the legislative branch (which passed the enabling statute) and the executive branch (which implemented the statute through regulation)—will be able to seek relief in the courts.

Judicial review of midnight *deregulation* raises quite different issues. Regulated entities are likely to be quite happy with midnight actions that lessen regulatory burdens; they will not bring suit. Those harmed by the deregulatory action—those who would have benefited from the higher regulatory burdens—face a much tougher test to gain access to the federal courts. As I discussed above in part I, the Supreme Court has made clear that standing doctrine requires much more of regulatory beneficiaries. This is not to say that judicial review is unavailable; there may be plaintiffs with standing. The issue is one of likelihood: a midnight deregulation is more likely to avoid court oversight than a midnight regulation.

Moreover, the courts are less available precisely when they are most needed: midnight deregulation, Beermann demonstrates, is more likely to represent a gift to special interests. Like midnight regulation, it occurs during the lame-duck period when the electorate is powerless to act; unlike midnight regulation, however, midnight *deregulation* is less likely to be public spirited.[49] Under George W. Bush, at least, midnight deregulation "may have been motivated by intense lobbying by regulated industries . . . . The opponents of deregulation appear to have been general public-interest advocates."[50]

In addition, an incoming president may not take action to overturn a midnight deregulation, even if it is a gift to special interests. As Beermann describes it, "one [might] take[] acceptance of late-term action by the incoming administration as an indication of its consistency with the public interest."[51] But the new administration "may have different priorities [or] might not want to expend its political capital on reversing controversial regulations."[52] Court review may be the only realistic option for overturning a midnight deregulatory action that is contrary to the public interest. Yet precisely when political controls are at their weakest, and judicial oversight is most needed, the standing doctrine works to prevent court challenges.

III. Consequences

As I have mentioned, the Supreme Court's Article III standing doctrine may obstruct judicial review of midnight deregulation. Exactly when we lack electoral accountability—after all, midnight action is always timed to avoid electoral constraints—and exactly when we have reason to fear that the president's actions are against the public interest—after all, as Beermann demonstrates, midnight deregulation "is more likely to be contrary to the public interest" than midnight regulation[53]—we also may be unable to obtain the accountability provided by judicial review. What solutions are available?

This analysis shows, first of all, that Congress cannot safely rely on expanded judicial review to solve the midnight deregulation problem. Because standing is a constitutional doctrine, rooted in Article III, Congress's ability to alter the boundaries of standing is limited by the Constitution. If no plaintiff can be found to satisfy the constitutional standing requirements, the federal court will lack jurisdiction no matter how desirable judicial review might be for holding the agency accountable, and no matter how many laws Congress might pass trying to authorize judicial review. As I have argued elsewhere, Congress's power to deal with this problem is quite limited.[54]

Second, the standing problem gives a (somewhat complicated) supporting argument for at least one of Beermann's suggestions for reform of midnight action. In offering solutions for the problem of midnight *regulation*, Beermann suggests that the Supreme Court change its doctrine regarding rescission or revision of existing rules.[55] Since the *Seatbelts* case, the Supreme Court has essentially required a complete new rulemaking if an agency seeks to revise or rescind an existing rule.[56] Professor Beermann notes that this doctrine greatly diminishes the freedom of an incoming administration to deal with midnight regulations; he suggests that the court could adopt a more relaxed doctrine allowing revision or rescission of the rule, so long as the new approach is supported by the *original* rulemaking record. In other words, if the administration who first adopted a rule had a menu of regulatory options, all supported by the original rulemaking record, subsequent administrations should be able to make a different choice from that menu in later years, without undertaking a new rulemaking.[57]

As Beermann makes clear, this suggestion would be extremely helpful for the new president in addressing midnight action—it relaxes the standard by which revision or rescission is evaluated. It has no obvious relevance, however, to midnight action that is left as is by the new president. Indeed, one might argue that the *Seatbelts* doctrine provides some help in preventing abusive midnight *deregulation*, at least in situations where the midnight action attempts to revise an existing, stricter regulation. If would-be regulatory beneficiaries can gain access to the courts to challenge the midnight deregulation, they can use the strict *Seatbelts* doctrine to show that the midnight action was shoddy or otherwise not in conformity with general administrative procedure.

But that tool is also available to regulated entities who challenge the public-regarding actions that may be undertaken by a lame-duck president. *Seatbelts* would help those regulated entities reverse *good* midnight actions. And, as shown above, regulated entities will have an easier time gaining access to the courts than regulatory beneficiaries. Since a strong *Seatbelts* is helpful to the public only if regulatory beneficiaries can get into court to use it, and since a strong *Seatbelts* is also helpful to the regulated entities who would seek to strike down public-regarding midnight actions, the asymmetry of access created by the Supreme Court's standing doctrine makes *Seatbelts* a tool for narrow special interests at the expense of the public. Standing's asymmetry thus gives support to Beermann's argument for weakening *Seatbelts*.

The standing problem most straightforwardly gives support to congressional action to prevent midnight action altogether. As Beermann notes, Congress could simply "ban outright the adoption of final rules by executive agencies for a specified period of time prior to inauguration day . . . with exceptions for rules required by emergency, statutory deadline, or court order."[58] The asymmetry in access created by the standing doctrine makes it hard to challenge those midnight actions that are most problematic—midnight deregulations—and that suggests that an outright ban on midnight action would be beneficial.

Conclusion

Professor Beermann's exploration of midnight deregulation provides a valuable contribution to our understanding of midnight action. He correctly points out that midnight deregulation "is more likely to be contrary to the public interest" than midnight regulation. And, as I have shown above, midnight deregulation is also less likely to be subject to court scrutiny than other midnight actions. The potential harm that midnight deregulation poses, and the absence of the courts as a corrective to that harm, demand congressional action to rein in presidential power in the midnight period.

Notes

1. Jack M. Beermann, "The Constitutional Law of Presidential Transitions," *North Carolina Law Review* 84 (2006): 1253; Jack M. Beermann, "Presidential Power in Transitions," *Boston University Law Review* 83 (2003): 947.

See also Christopher Carlberg, "Early to Bed for Federal Regulations: A New Attempt to Avoid 'Midnight Regulations' and Its Effect on Political Accountability," *George Washington Law Review* 77 (2009): 992; Jerry Brito and Veronique de Rugy, "Midnight Regulations and Regulatory Review," *Administrative Law Review* 61 (2009): 163; Jacob E. Gersen and Anne Joseph O'Connell, "Hiding in Plain Sight? Timing and Transparency in the Administrative State," *University of Chicago Law Review* 76 (2009): 1157; Heidi Kitrosser, "The Accountable Executive," *Minnesota Law Review* 93 (2009): 1741; Anne Joseph O'Connell, "Political Cycles of Rulemaking: An Empirical Portrait of the Modern Administrative State," *Virginia Law Review* 94 (2008): 889; Jason M. Loring and Liam R. Roth, "After Midnight: The Durability of the 'Midnight' Regulations Passed by the Two Previous Outgoing Administrations," *Wake Forest Law Review* 40 (2005): 1441; Nina A. Mendelson, "Agency Burrowing: Entrenching Policies and Personnel Before a New President Arrives," *New York University Law Review* 78 (2003): 557; Andrew P. Morriss et al., "Between a Hard Rock and a Hard Place: Politics, Midnight Regulations and Mining," *Administrative Law Review* 55 (2003): 551; John P. Burke, *Presidential Transitions: From Politics to Practice* (Boulder, CO: Lynne Rienner Publishers, 2000); Jay Cochran, "The Cinderella Constraint: Why Regulations Increase Significantly During Post-Election Quarters" (Arlington, VA: Mercatus Center, 2001).

2. Jack M. Beermann, "Midnight Deregulation," in this volume, 32. Professor Beermann has contributed other thoughtful pieces on the subject of midnight regulatory action. Beermann, "The Constitutional Law of Presidential Transitions," and Beermann, "Presidential Power in Transitions."

3. Beermann, this volume, 27.

4. Ibid. at 31.

5. Ibid. at 33.

6. Jack M. Beermann, "Combating Midnight Regulation," *Northwestern University Law Review Colloquy* 103 (2009): 361–369.

7. Antonin Scalia, "The Doctrine of Standing as an Essential Element of the Separation of Powers," *Suffolk University Law Review* 17 (1983): 882.

8. *Lujan v. Defenders of Wildlife*, 504 U.S. 555 (1992).

9. United States Constitution, Article III, section 2.

10. *Baker v. Carr*, 369 U.S. 186 (1962); see also *Massachusetts v. EPA*, 549 U.S. 497, 517 (2007) (quoting same language from Baker).

11. *Allen v. Wright*, 468 U.S. 737 (1984).

12. Heather Elliott, "The Functions of Standing," *Stanford Law Review* 61 (2008): 459.

13. Ibid.

14. *Allen v. Wright*, 468 U.S. 737 (1984).

15. Elliott, "The Functions of Standing," 459; Jonathan R. Siegel, "A Theory of Justiciability," *Texas Law Review* 86 (2007): 73; William A. Fletcher, "The Structure of Standing," *Yale Law Journal* 98 (1988): 221; Cass R. Sunstein, "Standing and the Privatization of Public Law," *Columbia Law Review* 88 (1988): 1432; Steven L. Winter, "The Metaphor of Standing and the Problem of Self-Governance," *Stanford Law Review* 40 (1988): 1371.

16. *Lujan v. Defenders of Wildlife*, 504 U.S. 555, 561–562 (1992).

17. Ibid.

18. *City of Los Angeles v. Lyons*, 461 U.S. 95 (1983).

19. *Allen v. Wright*, 468 U.S. 737 (1984).

20. *Lujan v. Defenders of Wildlife*, 504 U.S. 555 (1992).

21. Cass R. Sunstein, "Reviewing Agency Inaction After *Heckler v. Chaney*," *University of Chicago Law Review* 52 (1985): 653.

22. Elliott, "The Functions of Standing"; Richard J. Pierce, "*Lujan v. Defenders of Wildlife*: Standing as a Judicially Imposed Limit on Legislative Power," *Duke Law Journal* 42 (1993): 1170; Cass R. Sunstein, "What's Standing After *Lujan*? Of Citizen Suits, 'Injuries,' and Article III," *Michigan Law Review* 91 (1992): 163.

23. Pierce, "*Lujan v. Defenders of Wildlife*: Standing as a Judicially Imposed Limit on Legislative Power," 1194–1195. See also Philip Weinberg, "Unbarring the Bar of Justice: Standing in Environmental Suits and the Constitution," *Pace Environmental Law Review* 21 (2003): 27.

24. George J. Stigler, "The Theory of Economic Regulation," *Bell Journal of Economics and Management Science* 2 (1971): 3. A good example of such capture exists in environmental enforcement: "Cooperative enforcement makes the risks especially acute; by putting regulator and regulatee in close and frequent cooperation, it provides many of the prerequisites for collusion. This risk of capture means that agencies may not use the optimal blend of cooperation and deterrence in enforcement." Matthew D. Zinn, "Policing Environmental Regulatory Enforcement: Cooperation, Capture, and Citizen Suits," *Stanford Environmental Law Journal* 21 (2002): 83–84, 107–111.

25. Pierce, "*Lujan v. Defenders of Wildlife*: Standing as a Judicially Imposed Limit on Legislative Power," 1195.

26. Beermann, this volume, 19.

27. See note 1.

28. Beermann, this volume, 19.

29. Ibid.

30. Ibid., 19.

31. Ibid., 19–20.

32. Ibid., 19.

33. Ibid., 20.

34. Ibid.

35. Ibid., 23.

36. Ibid., 26.

37. Ibid.

38. Ibid.

39. Ibid., 31–32.

40. Ibid., 26.

41. Ibid., 27.

42. Ibid., 31.

43. Ibid., 32.

44. Thomas W. Merrill, "Capture Theory and the Courts: 1967–1983," *Chicago-Kent Law Review* 72 (1997): 1039.

45. 5 U.S.C. §§ 554–555.

46. 5 U.S.C. § 702.

47. 5 U.S.C. § 706.

48. Beermann, this volume, 20.

49. Ibid., 25–26, 27–28.

50. Ibid., 27.

51. Ibid., 20–21.

52. Ibid., 34n5.

53. Ibid., 33.

54. Heather Elliott, "Congress's Inability to Solve Standing Problems," *Boston University Law Review* 91 (2011): 159. Congress may, of course, tinker at the margins, but "[i]t is settled that Congress cannot erase Article III's standing requirements by statutorily granting the right to sue to a plaintiff who would not otherwise have standing." *Raines v. Byrd,* 521 U.S. 811, 820 n. 3 (1997).

55. Beermann, "Combating Midnight Regulation," 361–365.

56. *Motor Vehicles Manufacturers Association v. State Farm Mutual Automobile Insurance Company,* 463 U.S. 29 (1983). In this case, the Reagan administration attempted to relax a rule promulgated under President Carter that imposed stringent requirements on automakers to provide seatbelts and air bags. The Supreme Court held that the new rule could survive only if supported by evidence of changed circumstances; it was not enough that the Reagan ad-

ministration would have decided the matter differently, had it conducted the original rulemaking.

57. In the *Seatbelts* case, then, the Reagan administration could have rescinded the seatbelts rule only if the rulemaking record from the Carter administration would have permitted the agency to take no action. Beermann, "Combating Midnight Regulation," 362.

58. Ibid., 368.

2
Midnight Rulemaking and Congress

Nina Mendelson

I. Introduction

The 2008 presidential transition was accompanied by a familiar pattern of midnight rulemaking. Shortly before leaving office, executive branch agencies in the administration of President George W. Bush issued a host of final rules, many on controversial subjects. In late November and December 2008 alone, the following rules, among others, were issued: The Transportation Department, over criticism from safety advocates, lengthened the number of hours long-haul truck drivers could drive daily.[1] The Department of Health and Human Services issued its "conscience rule" in late December, stating that a condition of federal funding for governments, hospitals, and other entities would be that those organizations accommodate an individual employee who refuses to participate in a health service program or research activity contrary to his religious beliefs or moral convictions.[2] The rule was controversial not only because it could limit access to abortion, but also to birth control and infertility treatment, particularly in rural areas with few medical facilities. And the Interior Department issued two Endangered Species Act (ESA) rules: one limiting an agency's obligation to consult with the Interior Department prior to taking an action that could affect an endangered species or its habitat and the other limiting the protections available for the polar bear, despite the department's earlier declaration of the polar bear's status as a "threatened" species under the act.

This issuance by administrative agencies of significant, controversial rules[3] late in a presidential administration has become utterly typical of presidential transitions. Such rules were issued by the outgoing Carter,

Reagan, George H. W. Bush, and Clinton administrations.[4] Owing to broad delegations of authority from Congress, the administrative state is now a primary—perhaps *the* primary—engine of federal policy making, and it operates under the significant influence and even the direction of the president.[5] In the transition from one presidential administration to another, an outgoing president can use the administrative state to entrench his preferred policy positions through actions that I have collectively termed "agency burrowing."[6] Administrative agencies might act in a way that is relatively cumbersome for a new administration to reverse. The highest-impact, most-difficult-to-reverse actions are probably notice-and-comment rules, which are typically broad, prospective, and have the force of law. Once issued, these notice-and-comment rules may be revised or repealed only if the new administration conducts a new time– and resource-consuming notice-and-comment proceeding and explains its reasons for selecting a new position.[7] Agencies also might hire or promote individuals who are likely to share the president's policy positions.[8] Finally, these sorts of actions may be undertaken despite—or perhaps *because*—the incoming president would choose a different path. On occasion, an outgoing president's actions have resulted in an incoming president bearing significant political costs. For example, for his proposal to reverse the Clinton administration rule setting standards for arsenic in drinking water, President George W. Bush was tarred in his first year as an "antienvironmentalist" president.[9]

In a striking acknowledgment of the commonplace nature of this practice, the George W. Bush administration Office of Management and Budget director Joshua Bolten wrote agencies in May 2008, stating that "regulations to be finalized in this Administration should be proposed no later than June 1, 2008, and final regulations should be issued no later than November 1, 2008."[10] That memorandum could be understood either as an attempt to reduce late-term, lame-duck rulemaking or, more cynically, especially in view of the president's poor poll numbers at the time,[11] as a message to agencies to get their controversial decisions finalized early.

Actions such as these have been widely criticized as an outgoing president's last-chance grasp at power.[12] The electorate has selected someone new—very often of a different political party—to run the country. The new president can appoint new members of the cabinet and new top agency officials. The prospect of those changes has been associated with significant midnight rulemaking by the outgoing president's administration. Indeed, one commentator has reported that the higher the level of turnover among top executive branch officials, the more "midnight regulations" are likely to be issued.[13]

No one would, of course, want the government to effectively shut down after the election. The sitting president continues to have the obligation to execute the laws until the term ends on January 20. Nonetheless, an outgoing president's use of the mechanisms of the administrative state to entrench particular policies or viewpoints that diverge from those preferred by the newly elected president seems problematic at best. At worst, it could be seen as a distasteful and antidemocratic power grab—an attempt to distribute rents, for example, or to set rights and obligations in the face of a rare and important concerted expression of will from the electorate.

The point of this chapter, however, is to discuss the extent to which these sorts of actions represent not just a potential cost to democracy, but also an opportunity, in some cases, for our system of representative democracy to function better. In previous work, I have discussed the extent to which midnight rulemaking can prompt greater attention to particular presidential activities by the public. Greater public engagement, if it happens, can in turn prompt a decision by the new president that is better informed and more responsive to public preferences.

This chapter focuses on Congress, our most democratic federal institution. Congress is generally responsible for defining the authorities possessed by the administrative state, and congressional oversight is key to holding agencies accountable for their actions. Midnight rulemaking also has the potential to increase congressional engagement. Two commentators have recently argued that relative inattention from Congress can facilitate midnight rulemaking, because Congress may meet less frequently during the lame duck period and there is no "repeat player" relationship between the outgoing president and the Congress.[14] To the contrary, however, Congress retains considerable formal power to respond to and override presidential decisions, whether during the transition period or later on.[15] To the extent there is a problem with congressional control over the administrative state, it is a more general one—whether Congress is sufficiently engaged to react to agency actions that veer too far from public concerns or preferences.

I want to suggest that midnight rulemaking can present a special opportunity to create an interbranch dialogue about the appropriate direction of the administrative state. Midnight rulemaking actions have been relatively high profile and controversial. As a consequence, they have prompted heightened public discussion. This in turn can generate greater attention in Congress and an interbranch dialogue regarding agency actions. In short, midnight rulemaking may on occasion ironically prompt a more deliberative, and ultimately a more democratic, decision-making process.

II. The Administrative State, the President, and Congress

In the setting of federal statutes ranging from environmental and banking regulation to housing subsidies, the administrative state possesses substantial power to make binding standards, resolve disputes, and implement programs. In so doing, agencies decide important questions of policy. Those policy questions can implicate technical issues: how much wearing a seatbelt would reduce risk to an automobile or airplane passenger, for example. But agencies also may resolve critical value questions: for example, how much government should protect people from their own bad decisions; how much risk society should tolerate; or which risks government should first seek to address. That agencies must often resolve these issues raises a question: how can we best assure that agencies are properly accountable and that their decisions appropriately respond to public views?

It is no longer plausible—if it ever was—to say that agencies are merely the "transmission belt" for critical policy decisions made, in statutes, by Congress.[16] A bureaucracy that implements a fairly vague statutory delegation may well take an action different from that envisioned by the legislative coalition enacting the statute.[17] This sort of "bureaucratic drift" alone may not be entirely problematic. One might interpret broad statutory language as incorporating an *expectation* by the enacting coalition that administrative implementers will flexibly apply the statute to meet the country's changing needs. Indeed, one of the claimed benefits of the administrative state over Congress is that the administrative state is more flexible and able to adapt to changing circumstances. For example, Congress's 1938 delegation to the Food and Drug Administration (FDA), in the Federal Food, Drug, and Cosmetic Act, to regulate substances qualifying as "drugs," together with a long list of medications Congress itself identified at the time, reflects Congress's recognition of ongoing active scientific research into new medications and its wish that the FDA be able to flexibly respond to regulate new substances that Congress was unaware of in 1938.[18] Similarly, Congress's direction to the Environmental Protection Agency (EPA) to regulate polluting discharges to the water by reference to the "best available technology" is meant to allow the agency to continue to increase the stringency of effluent limits as technology improves.[19]

As agencies address less technical and more value-laden concerns, however, "bureaucratic drift" may become more problematic. If the EPA is supposed to regulate pollutants to "protect the environment," just how much protection is appropriate? Do we protect the environment with no regard to cost or to other social priorities? Again, Congress may not resolve these questions in authorizing legislation and instead may leave the issues up to the agency. This presents a dilemma, since deciding how much risk or benefit is appropriate implicates not only available technology and scientific understanding of risk, but also social notions of the role of government, the proper allocation of social resources, and our collective tolerance of certain sorts of risks.

Nonetheless, built into statutory delegations to agencies is often the power—even the responsibility—to resolve these sorts of questions. How can the extensive power to decide questions of value that is exercised by the (unelected) administrative state be justified as legitimate governmental authority?

A central part of the legitimacy assessment depends on the extent to which an agency decision—a decision rendered by unelected officials—can be characterized not only as compliant with the law and nonarbitrary, but as democratically responsive. It is worth a moment to more clearly specify the term "democratic." Under a pluralist notion of democracy, government decisions may be considered democratic to the extent they aggregate and reflect preferences held by the public at large. Assuming that the public possesses coherent, formed preferences, the critical question for evaluating the "democratic" quality of an institution is the effectiveness of the means for communicating public preferences and the institution's incentives to pay heed to those preferences. In the case of Congress and the presidency, the elections and related processes (such as polling) might serve both functions. In the setting of agency decision making, agencies, as institutions accountable to the president and to Congress, also have an incentive to learn and to respond appropriately to public preferences. Beyond this, agencies may be able to collect information on public preferences directly, through the notice-and-comment process for rulemaking. Political supervision of the agencies, as well as judicial review, may provide agencies with an incentive to respond appropriately to those preferences.

Alternatively, we might adopt a deliberative notion of democracy, where a democratic dialogue helps establish the proper direction for society. A particular institution's decision might be viewed as democratic to the extent the institution facilitates deliberation and reasoned, public justifications are offered for its proposed decisions. Not only can the process of deliberation offer an opportunity for people to change one another's preferences and reach a socially regarding outcome through reasoning, but it can also develop civic virtue in the participants.[20] Effective representation of an appropriate array of viewpoints is key to such a dialogue.[21] A national electoral process might be conceived of as deliberative, for example. With respect to agencies, again, they might be deemed democratic under a deliberative view because they are accountable to and responsive to democratically deliberative institutions. Even without these mechanisms, agencies engaging in rulemaking may qualify as democratically deliberative because they are required to collect public comment and give reasons (subject to judicial review) for rejecting significant comments.[22]

Currently, in view of the relatively unconstrained statutory delegations to agencies, administrative law scholarship places a great deal of emphasis on presidential control as a source of democratic legitimacy for the actions of the administrative state.[23] The president can convey the electorate's views on such matters as the role of government and the most significant health and safety concerns. He or she possesses the power to appoint and remove the heads of executive agencies at will, and it is generally accepted that statutes delegating authority to agencies contemplate at least some presidential supervision.[24] Since the Reagan administration, executive branch agencies have been required by executive order to submit significant draft proposed and final rules to the White House Office of Management and Budget for prepublication approval. The president thus is in a position to oversee the activities of the entire executive branch and to coordinate agency actions.

Jerry Mashaw has argued that presidential control over an executive branch agency may better assure democratic responsiveness than the agency's close accountability to Congress. Beyond the coordination function, the claim is that the president may be a better conduit for public preferences than Congress because he or she is chosen through a national election. This will prompt that president to take a more national viewpoint; he or she will not be in thrall to either narrowly regional interests or the demands of small constituent groups.[25] Members of Congress focused on re-election, by comparison, may concentrate too heavily on distributing pork to narrow interest groups or home state or home community constituents.[26]

As recent scholarship has explored, however, this is an unduly rosy picture of the president's electoral incentives. For a number of reasons, the presidential election may not effectively communicate voter preferences. Voters pay little attention to electoral issues. Voter turnout in presidential elections, though far higher than other elections, is low. It has not exceeded 60 percent of registered voters since the 1960s. Even if voters pay attention to electoral issues and participate in the presidential election, they have highly limited choices by the time of the general election. A voter generally must choose between two candidates, each of whom represents a package of policy views that probably does not correspond very well to the voter's own preferences. Further, as Cynthia Farina has argued, a voter may often cast a vote incorrectly in the sense of misunderstanding, in a basic way, the chosen candidate's stance on an issue important to the voter.[27] Meanwhile, although the president must win reelection in a national election, the structure of the electoral college results in presidential priorities being focused particularly on swing states and even on particular communities in swing states.[28] Finally, voter preferences are very often not well formed. On a wide array of issues, voter views may be inchoate at the time of an election, leaving the president with no possibility of a mandate or even a clear sense of national preferences on a given issue.[29] In short, the presidential election may only imperfectly transmit the views of the national electorate, and the president may have strong incentives to respond to small subgroups within that electorate. That will in turn impair the president's ability to transmit public preferences to the administrative state. Accordingly, as Anne O'Connell has suggested, "administrative law needs to attend more to Congress."[30]

Congress can, of course, define or redefine the terms of an agency's delegation by modifying an agency's authorizing statute by new legislation. Further, Congress has other well-established means of influencing the administrative state short of passing or modifying authorizing legislation. Congress can define the size of an agency's budget or pass specific legislation, such as through appropriations riders, that directs the agency to take (or not take) particular actions. With respect to agency decisions in particular, Congress has created the special tool of the Congressional Review Act, a tool for expedited passage of legislation that overrides particular agency actions. Admittedly, the potential of that act has not been fully realized, as it has been used only once and its use seriously threatened only one other time.[31] Less formally, Congress can conduct oversight, seeking an agency official's explanation of reasons for a particular decision,[32] or send less formal messages to an agency, such as through discussion at a confirmation hearing, in language contained in a committee report or conference committee report, or through floor statements.

Through these activities, Congress can communicate policy preferences to the agencies, and Congress may be able to transmit and engage a wider and more representative set of public views than the president. First, Congress is, of course, a regional institution, the members of which are elected by state or by district. By dint of the electoral process, five hundred thirty-five members of Congress are more likely than the president to represent a wide range of public views and to capture regionally distinctive views.[33] While Mashaw may be correct to accept the assumption that the ability to "bring home the bacon" to local constituents plays more of a role in congressional elections than it does in presidential elections, so that "the congressperson's position on various issues of national interest is of modest" importance,[34] a growing number of legislators have been elected from "ideologically homogenous constituencies," leaving them more "discretion to pursue their own preferred policy goals," rather than bacon-bringing.[35] Variation in local interests and values is less likely to be overlooked in congressional elections than in the presidential election. And the presidential election is not free from the pressures to deliver special benefits either— it is just that the pressures primarily relate to areas in which the vote may swing.[36] In sum, views held by a significant portion of the population are likely to receive at least *some* active representation through the congressional election process, and possibly greater representation than through the presidential election process.

As with the presidential election process, there are limits here, too. Because many members of Congress are elected from so-called safe districts, a change in voter views or values may not always correspond to a change in the identity of any particular representative or senator. Even in a district that is not a "safe" one, a voter's choice among congressional candidates, as with presidential candidates, represents a choice among two bundles of preferences, neither of which is likely to perfectly correspond to the voter's preferences. Nonetheless, the congressional election process seems likely to result in a range of views, particularly district and state views, being expressed among the collection of individuals that compose the House and Senate.

Consider, in addition, that voter views on particular topics may be ill-formed at the time of an election. Assuming this is the case, looking simply at electoral incentives to detect and transmit public views seems an unsatisfactory way to assess an institution's democratic responsiveness or to assess whether an institution has a "sense of the popular will." More critically, we should consider the institution's ability to conduct meaningful deliberation and to engage a wide range of views. On this deliberative view of democracy, an institution has a claim to democratic legitimacy when its process is participatory and deliberative, and proposed decisions are justified with publicly articulated reasons.[37]

Here, Congressional deliberation may have the advantage over presidential deliberation because it is likely to engage a wider range of views and preferences. The president may well deliberate with his or her staff and with groups with whom he or she meets—and members of Congress can do this too—but the president, not the voters, selects the administration's cabinet and staff members. The president can choose whether to attempt to make those individuals representative of a wide range of public views or whether to have advisors whose views, for the most part, mirror his or her own. Moreover, the president can decide whether to make that debate public. For the most part, internal White House debates on regulatory policy have remained opaque to the public eye.[38] By contrast, congressional deliberation often takes place through public statements, as members of Congress articulate the reasons for their positions.[39]

Finally, compared with an agency, congressional deliberation also is likely to be more "democratic" because the discussants are more representative. Even though agencies must respond to significant comments they receive in rulemaking, it is unclear that groups participating in a rulemaking process are likely to be any more representative than those transmitting information to Congress or to the president. Second, agencies may be biased toward well-organized and more narrowly focused interest groups, particularly those groups representing regulated entities.[40] Such groups are likely to more effectively transmit their views in the rulemaking process. Wholly apart from the question of whether agencies might be captured by those they regulate, they are acquainted with those groups, have a long-term incentive to understand the information transmitted by regulated entities, and seek to obtain their compliance. All this can prompt agencies to pay particular attention to the views of regulated entities.[41] Third, comments submitted may well focus more on technical questions than on value-laden questions. Finally, even if values-focused comments are submitted, the incentives for the agency decision maker to decide value-laden questions in a democratically responsive way are limited.[42] Presidential supervision may prompt an agency official to choose a policy that is responsive to the president's views—and if the president is electorally responsive, ultimately to public views. Congressional supervision, if it is present, may create similar incentives. Otherwise, if the agency official is a well-intentioned, public-interested official,[43] the president may independently seek to implement a policy that is democratically responsive, in the sense of responding thoughtfully and fairly to value-laden views expressed in the administrative process. In short, though, the incentives for an agency decision to be "democratic" in nature largely collapse down to those faced by the president and Congress, except that the agency may have a more formalized means for collecting information from the public at large. Apart from supervision by the president or Congress or a sense of personal obligation, there is no particular *direct* incentive for the agency official to be democratically responsive.[44]

Moreover, compared with agency deliberation, a congressional debate potentially can be more visible and more transparent. Even certain submajority debates within Congress, such as the committee hearing and the floor debate in one house, may still amount to a more public deliberative discussion than that available within the executive branch. While some deliberative discussion likely does take place within the executive branch, its benefits are undermined by a general lack of transparency.[45] Citizens hearing reports of a congressional debate on a topic of interest are more likely to perceive that their viewpoints are receiving actual representation and view the outcome as more legitimate.[46]

Needless to say, congressional deliberation may not always be public or necessarily superior to presidential deliberation or agency deliberation. Nor, if only one "best" institution could be selected to oversee agency decision, is it a foregone conclusion that Congress would be the institution. And at the time of this writing, the level of public confidence in Congress—as with the government at large—was at a quarter-century low.[47] Nonetheless, because Congress is a valuable forum for the airing of public views, congressional debate, even by a submajority, clearly is—and ought to be—an important source of information and guidance for agencies as they implement their statutes.

These arguments are, of course, strongest when the entire Congress is involved—or has the opportunity to be involved—in the passage of legislation. Constitutional bicameralism and presentment requirements and Senate and House rules make it likely that legislation, a concerted expression of congressional will, will be passed only after significant deliberation or opportunity for deliberation. Beyond this, however, even some views articulated by a *submajority* of Congress—and not even in the process of enacting legislation—can be valuable for agencies. While deliberation by a submajority is inferior to deliberation by the entire Congress, such statements could contribute importantly to an agency decision-making process on public preferences or policy matters. Again, I mean to focus upon the less formal discussions and articulations of views within Congress, whether or not legislation results. For example, House or Senate committee members may discuss an agency action with a cabinet official at an oversight hearing, or individual members of Congress may make floor statements.

Information transmitted by even a few members of Congress can be highly valuable to a decision-making agency. As elected officials, members of Congress do have an incentive to understand and engage public views, and they generally are likely to engage a wider range of policy issues than agency officials. For a very basic example, the vast majority of congressional committees have jurisdiction over more than one federal agency. Committee service alone, then, can provide a member of Congress with a comparatively broad perspective.

Concern might be expressed that congressional statements, particularly informal ones, might be unreliable. Gersen and Posner have suggested, for example, that informal statements—anything less than a one-house or concurrent resolution—may not fairly indicate a member of Congress's preferences for legislation.[48] Member statements of use to agencies, however, include those that convey information regarding the workability or consequences of a particular regulatory approach or on public preferences with respect to a particular topic.[49] Despite Gersen and Posner's arguments that speeches are "cheap talk" consuming few resources,[50] these congressional statements are likely to be reliable. First, an elected official typically has a substantial investment in his or her reputation. For example, a reputation for fairness and commitment to a policy stance can be connected not only to electoral success, but to a legislator's success in advancing socially desirable policies.[51] Similarly, a reputation for reliability and consistency generally will enhance a legislator's ability to obtain campaign contributions.[52] The value of a reputation for reliable statements obviously increases with the chances of "repeat play." Legislators will have repeat play with other legislators with whom they wish to collaborate or whose support they wish to obtain for legislative measures, with voters in their district or state, with agencies, and with interest groups who are deciding whether to make campaign contributions. Not only do legislators already function in institutions with substantial repeat play opportunities, recent political science scholarship suggests that the committee system may in part be explained by the fact that it keeps the opportunities for repeated play high, so that an individual legislator can obtain confirmation of a reputation for reliability and "collect" on the benefits of that reliability.[53] Finally, a congressional statement that is public, particularly one made in an active debate, will be more costly if unreliable because the statement can be more easily monitored by interest groups, voters, and colleagues.

Congress cannot, of course, encourage agencies to violate existing law, both because agencies are bound by the law and because Congress is constrained to follow only constitutionally prescribed means of enacting legislation.[54] And any formal action vetoing an agency's decision or limiting its options must, of course, be done through the constitutionally prescribed mechanisms.[55] Further, Congress and its members are barred from executing the laws.[56] But these statements are made in the context of broad and constitutional delegations of administrative authority.[57] Broad statutes are widely perceived to evince an expectation on the part of the enacting Congress that the agency's application of particular laws will evolve with time. Application may evolve to take account of changed scientific circumstances, but also changed social circumstances, including views of the role of government. If an agency's application of a statute is to evolve in accordance with changed social circumstances, then information from congressional discussion must—along with information gathered from the public and from executive officials—be seen as a useful source to an agency seeking to detect those changed social circumstances.

The biggest difficulty with Congress supplying public values information to the agencies is simply that Congress is insufficiently engaged. As is widely recognized, its attention to the work of agencies is at best sporadic.[58] As Matt McCubbins and Thomas Schwartz have famously observed with respect to oversight of the administrative state, Congress may function less like a police patrol and more like a fire department triggered by an individual or interest group's pulling of an alarm.[59] One implication is that Congress will try to redirect an administrative agency heading down the wrong path only if (presumably well-organized) individuals and interest groups ask it to do so.[60] Congress may thus inadequately police an agency when the agency misapprehends democratic values that are held more widely and more diffusely.

Further, congressional deliberation, even at its most active, could also be criticized. For example, the committee structure, set up to develop expertise in a wide variety of specialized subjects,[61] may end up instead disproportionately rewarding well-organized interest groups.[62] Richard Lazarus has noted the extent to which changes in congressional structure have reduced effective deliberation on environmental issues.[63] The incentives created by the Budget Act to refocus congressional deliberations on appropriations, rather than authorizing legislation, have prompted a decline in the specialized, knowledgeable authorizing committees and an increase in oversight being conducted by appropriations committees, often smaller, less well-staffed, less-specialized committees.[64] Even where authorizing committees exercise oversight, the committee may not be representative of Congress as a whole. Such oversight may represent another bite at the apple for interest groups who lost in the administrative process.[65]

In short, as it currently stands, congressional oversight of agencies can offer important information to agencies, but oversight is generally sporadic and when it does take place, it can be at the behest of well-organized interest groups.

III. Midnight Rulemaking and Congress: Two Examples

So what about midnight rulemaking and democracy? Midnight rulemaking is primarily criticized as antidemocratic because it takes place post-election—and thus in the face of the electorate's expressed preferences. As Jack Beermann and I have both discussed, midnight rulemaking may be motivated by the need to keep the government going, the desire to finish longtime projects before a deadline, and the goal of avoiding the delays that can come from bringing a new team up to speed. Less attractively, some midnight rules and other actions can be motivated by the desire to entrench policies that a new president would not otherwise select or even to impose political costs on a new president, should that new president wish to choose a different option.[66]

In some instances, however, midnight rulemaking may have the potential to enhance democratic processes by prompting greater congressional engagement. Take a pair of examples from the most recent presidential transition. In mid-December 2008, the Department of the Interior's Fish and Wildlife Service finalized a new rule regarding the obligations of federal agencies to consult with the Service prior to taking an action that might affect endangered species.[67] Section 7 of the Endangered Species Act requires federal agencies considering permit or license applications or authorizing or funding some other sort of action to consult first with a so-called wildlife agency—the National Marine Fisheries Services (NMFS) or the Fish and Wildlife Service (FWS)—if the action could "jeopardize the continued existence of any endangered species or threatened species or result in the destruction or adverse modification of [critical] habitat of such species."[68] Under regulations in effect prior to December 2008, if the permitting agency determined that the proposed action is not likely to adversely affect a listed species or habitat and the NMFS or FWS concurred, the statutory obligation to protect the species would be met. The new regulations exempted agencies from having to consult if the agency *itself* determined the action would not affect a listed species and the effects of the action would be manifested through "global processes" or would be difficult to measure.

The practical effect was that in many cases the permitting agency—often an agency with no particular expertise in endangered species or habitat—could unilaterally determine the appropriateness of its action under the Endangered Species Act. Most controversially, perhaps, was the exception for "global processes," which was targeted at project-related climate change impacts and represented a judgment that the Endangered Species Act should not be a means of dealing with climate change. Again, for potential effects evinced through global processes, the permitting agency could be the final authority on whether its action was appropriate under the Endangered Species Act. The rule received significant public attention, and the agency received many comments; a high percentage of those comments consisted of form letters submitted by the public at large.[69]

At around the same time, the administration finalized a special rule addressing the polar bear's status as a listed threatened species. The earlier listing of the polar bear as "threatened" triggered statutory requirements that agencies consult with the Interior Department regarding any federal action, including permitting or licensing, that could jeopardize the species or negatively affect its habitat. Typically, designation of a species as "threatened" would also be associated with a regulatory decision prohibiting at least some "takes" of the species, including indirect harm through habitat destruction.[70] The special rule, however, specified that any activity occurring outside of the current range of the species, even if it would have a significant effect on polar bears or bear habitat, such as through emission of greenhouse gases connected with the melting of arctic ice, would *not* be deemed a prohibited act under the Endangered Species Act.[71]

Prior to this time, neither of these issues had received sustained attention either in the media or in Congress. References in the popular media to the Endangered Species Act or to the issues raised by these rules in the year previous to the rules' issuance were occasional at best, and mentions in Congress were almost nonexistent. Members of Congress did occasionally refer to the polar bear, but generally with respect to other issues, such as the status of the Arctic National Wildlife Refuge. Similarly, the relationship of endangered species protections to global climate change policy received no focused public attention during the 2008 presidential campaign.

Once the rules were issued, however, they attracted immediate congressional attention. Shortly after they were issued, Congressman Markey mentioned both the consultation and polar bear rules at a hearing on "midnight" regulations.[72] When it was introduced in February 2009, the House Omnibus Appropriations Act of 2009 (with appropriations for the Interior Department, the EPA, and a large number of other agencies) contained a rider relating to these two rules. Section 429 of the introduced bill gave the Interior and Commerce Departments sixty days to summarily withdraw the two ESA rules and reinstate the rules previously in effect.

In the Senate, however, Senator Murkowski and three colleagues offered an amendment to delete the rider, so that any repeal of the ESA rules would be subject to the usual notice-and-comment rulemaking requirements. This prompted debate among several members of the Senate on the substantive merits of the rules. With respect to the polar bear rule, Murkowski and others argued in favor of maintaining administrative procedures for repeal of the rules, since without the special rule for the polar bear, there could be "lawsuits to stop any action that would increase carbon dioxide or any greenhouse gas emissions anywhere in the country . . . if the project had not first consulted with U.S. Fish and Wildlife on potential impacts." Murkowski further suggested that using the endangered species listing as a way to "regulate greenhouse gas emissions" would be "overreaching," potentially triggering "such a backlash that it harms support for the Endangered Species Act."[73]

Senator Feinstein and others called the consultation rule "wrongheaded" because it would leave species-related decision making up to the acting agency "without any input from scientists or biologists."[74] Senator Boxer noted that the rules were "midnight regulations" and "capricious."[75] The Murkowski amendment failed and the rider remained in the bill.

After the presidential transition, eight senators, including Senators Durbin, Boxer, and Kerry, wrote Interior Secretary Salazar in April 2009 urging Salazar to use the authority granted in the appropriations bill to summarily reverse the polar bear and consultation rules so that the Interior Department would continue to retain the ability to "consider[] and address[] the very factors that are causing the ice to melt [and the decline of the polar bear], including climate change."[76] Forty-four members of the House wrote a similar letter regarding the consultation rule, though not the polar bear rule.[77] The possibility of reversal of the midnight rules also energized twenty conservation and environmental groups, who wrote the Interior Department separately to encourage it to use its authority to reverse both ESA rules. (The Center for Biological Diversity sent a petition with nearly 50,000 signatures as well.)[78] The transition period was marked by significant news coverage, both of the late-term Bush administration rules,[79] of congressional debate,[80] and of the Obama administration's reactions.

The Obama administration reversed the consultation rule shortly after the passage of the appropriations legislation. Rather than simply reinstating the status quo ante, however, the agency said this: "We believe that it is appropriate to withdraw the new regulations and return to the *status quo ante* pending a comprehensive review of the ESA section 7 consultation regulations. Recognizing the widespread public concern about the process in the promulgation of the new regulations, the Departments agree that a thoughtful, in-depth, and measured review would be beneficial before a determination is made regarding potential changes to the section 7 consultation regulations. The section 7 consultation process is important for the conservation of species and critical habitat and involves complex and highly technical issues; the input from career conservation biologists who have experience with the section 7 consultations and who can provide scientific and technical expertise should, of course, be a key part of the process. In addition, any rulemaking process should be accorded a sufficient period of time to provide for careful, meaningful involvement of the affected public and to ensure consistency with the purposes of the ESA. This thorough review will allow the Departments to identify a range of options and implement improvements, if appropriate."[81] The formal statement from the agencies—their publication in the *Federal Register* of the decision to revoke the rule—is opaque regarding potential political influences on the decision. Indeed, the agencies describe the decision as solely their own, although evidence elsewhere suggests that the White House Office of Management and Budget obtained some changes in the rule before its final publication.[82]

The polar bear rule ended up on a different track, however. Initial indications were that the Obama administration sought an easy reversal of this rule as well. Federal law requires the president to submit a comprehensive federal budget on or before the first Monday in February, and that submission typically begins the congressional budget process.[83] It accordingly could have been the Obama administration that suggested the rider in the first place. Moreover, the same interest groups hopeful of reinstating the earlier version of the consultation rule also lobbied heavily on the polar bear rule.[84]

Despite its likely initial position, however, the Obama administration ultimately decided to retain the polar bear rule. The Interior Department published no statement in the *Federal Register*, as it was leaving the Bush administration rule in place. However, Secretary Salazar did make a statement that the rule would be retained. Salazar acknowledged that greenhouse gases threaten the polar bear, but stated that "the global risk from greenhouse gases . . . requires comprehensive policies, not a patchwork of agency actions carried out for particular species. 'It would be very difficult for our scientists to be doing evaluations of a cement plant in Georgia or Florida and the impact it's going to have on the polar bear habitat.'"[85]

Based solely on the written record, it is very difficult to know conclusively which influences led the Interior and Commerce Departments to take different paths on the consultation and polar bear rules. Nonetheless, the change in approach to the polar bear rule, together with the fact that the agencies took nearly all the time Congress allotted them to act, is very suggestive that the agencies were reconsidering their original positions in light of the public and congressional views expressed on the issue in early 2009.

In particular, the agency decisions appeared to be consistent with some of the reasons offered in the congressional debate. With respect to the consultation rule, senators participating in the debate on the Murkowski amendment appeared neither to raise any specific objection to abandoning the consultation rule nor to dispute Senator Feinstein's point that consideration of the status of threatened or endangered species ought to be done by trained scientists residing in the Interior and Commerce Departments.

By contrast, Murkowski and her colleagues supporting the amendment to strike the rider nearly all focused on the virtues of the Bush administration's polar bear rule and the difficulties of abandoning it. Namely, it would be challenging to make an individual regulatory decision based on the small incremental effect a project would have on greenhouse gases, arctic ice, and in turn the polar bear. Meanwhile, Endangered Species Act litigation could become a significant forum in which climate change policy would be developed. This is not a scientific argument about whether greenhouse gases affect the polar bears. Instead, it is an argument about the best way to make policy decisions. Even though reducing greenhouse gases and addressing climate change are clearly important goals, creating a veto on nationwide greenhouse-gas creating projects—or subjecting them to an Endangered Species Act permit to be issued by the Interior Department—would not only be impracticable but would not be an appropriate means to develop global warming policy. Instead, as Secretary Salazar stated, a more comprehensive approach would be preferable to a simple focus on a small project's effect on polar bear habitat. Salazar's statement ended up picking up some of the most thoroughly argued points in the congressional debate. While it is unclear exactly how many senators supported one view or another on the polar bear rule, the agency decision should be seen as more democratically responsive to the extent it was informed by the well-developed views expressed in the Senate and the open debate on the question.[86]

Ultimately, the polar bear decision was met with approval from mainstream newspapers as well. For example, the *Washington Post* praised the decision: "Interior Secretary Ken Salazar ruffled more than a few feathers this month when he let stand a Bush administration decision to prohibit the use of the Endangered Species Act to regulate greenhouse gas emissions. It was the right call when it was made in 2008, and it is the right call now."[87] Despite declining to require any agency activity that might increase greenhouse gases to obtain a "take permit" prior to proceeding, the Obama administration instead has increased the size of the polar bear's critical habitat.[88] Agency activities within that habitat will remain subject to consultation with the wildlife agencies.

In short, the Endangered Species Act example suggests an administration decision that changed over time, in light of public and congressional engagement. The Obama administration decisions on both the consultation and the polar bear rule were likely better informed and more democratically deliberative than either the Bush administration's rules of December 2008, or the position, implicit in the adopted appropriations rider, that the two rules should be reconsidered with an option for summary reversal.

The Bush administration "midnight rules" on endangered species and the Obama administration's desire to reverse them ultimately had the effect of engaging Congress and heightening public interest in the issues. As I have written elsewhere, the identity of the president and his or her agency heads, together with the content of a "midnight rule," can not only generate public interest in the rule, but also can supply important information about the range of regulatory options. For example, in its outgoing months, the Clinton administration issued a rule known as the "roadless rule," restricting road building in national forests. The Clinton rule provided the public with a benchmark with which to evaluate other regulatory options, such as those proposed by the George W. Bush administration.

Here, the endangered species rulemakings of the Bush administration similarly provided the public and Congress with an additional benchmark against which to evaluate a range of policy options. The midnight rules represented the outgoing administration's analysis and preferred policy regarding how to administer the Endangered Species Act and what protections to afford the threatened polar bear. The timing of the rule prompted debate in Congress, but it also provided a concrete proposal which members of Congress could react to and discuss. That process of congressional debate prompted better informed and more democratically deliberative final decisions than if the Bush administration had done nothing on these issues and left it all up to the Obama administration.

Not only might the midnight rulemaking have had benefits for the ultimate agency decision, but we might also see it as encouraging better congressional functioning. As McCubbins and Schwartz have suggested, Congress usually acts in a "fire-alarm" mode. The primary criticism of fire-alarm functioning is that the congressional agenda is limited and that fire alarms are pulled by organized interest groups.[89] By contrast, in the midnight rulemaking setting, members of Congress may already be attuned to the activities of the outgoing president, and the fire alarm is effectively pulled by the fact that the outgoing president has placed the issue on the agenda.

Again, consider the endangered species rules. These issues did not receive significant congressional attention during the year prior to the issuance of the rules, apart from scattered statements in the *Congressional Record* on other issues.[90] The *Congressional Record* contains no discussion of any sort regarding whether acting agencies should be required to consult with the Interior and Commerce Departments prior to taking action that could negatively impact endangered species. The issuance of the rules, however, caused a number of senators to join issue and debate the relevant policy questions.

This is an improvement to the usual fire alarm pulling. The rule has been placed on the agenda by an outgoing president rather than, say, an organized interest group. A midnight rule can highlight the space between the outgoing and incoming president's views. That space, once identified by the outgoing president's concrete action, provides an opportunity for constructive engagement. Especially because issue may not have been joined during the presidential election, these sorts of issues can be particularly valuable ones for congressional debate.

A significant concern might be that it is a lame-duck president who is selecting these topics to engage the attention of the public and of Congress, arguably displacing the new president's political agenda and sometimes yielding to a temptation to distribute rents as well as to make policy serving the outgoing president's view of the public interest.[91] Further, a deluge of midnight regulations could overwhelm both Congress and the incoming president, and many such rules might stay in place simply because too many resources, both fiscal and political, would be required to revise or repeal them. But rules that make good policy in the eye of the departing president may prompt genuine political discussion, because they also likely possess support from a significant portion of the political community. In the setting of the Endangered Species Act midnight rules, the result was a debate that otherwise would not have taken place. Even if it might be characterized as an outgoing president's late-term power grab, then, teeing up an issue for public debate through a midnight rule may ultimately be more democracy enhancing than no action at all.

IV. Conclusion

None of this is to say that midnight rulemaking is always a good thing—or even that it is, overall, the best way to prompt congressional debate or renewed congressional attention to the actions of the administrative state. Nonetheless, we can learn something from the productive and valuable debate midnight rules sometimes engender. Public views on particular issues may not be fully crystallized at the time an incoming president is elected. Congress may not have focused—or have been made to focus—upon particular policy issues. A silver lining of the midnight rule may be that it prompts more direct and concentrated congressional engagement on particular policy issues. That has the potential to improve both the agency decision ultimately made by the new president and congressional deliberation itself. A critical lesson we should take away is the value of congressional discussion for agency action and the need for innovative ways to better engage Congress in difficult, value-laden issues handled by the administrative state. It revised the rule at the end of 2011.

Notes

1. See Federal Motor Carrier Safety Administration, Department of Transportation, Hours of Service of Drivers, 73 *Federal Register* 69,567 (November 19, 2008). The Obama administration agreed to reconsider the rule. See Federal Motor Carrier Safety Administration, Motor Carrier Safety Advisory Committee Public Meeting, 74 *Federal Register* 62,882 (December 1, 2009).

2. Department of Health and Human Services, Ensuring that Department of Health and Human Services Funds Do Not Support Coercive or Discriminatory Policies or Practices in Violation of Federal Law, 73 *Federal Register* 78,072 (December 19, 2008). Under the Obama administration, the agency issued a proposed rule to rescind that regulation in March 2009. See Department of Health and Human Services, Proposed Rules: Rescission of the Regulation Entitled "Ensuring that Department of Health and Human Services Funds Do Not Support Coercive or Discriminatory Policies or Practices in Violation of Federal Law," 74 *Federal Register* 10,207 (March 10, 2009). As of December 2011, no final rule had been issued.

3. This chapter focuses only on so-called notice-and-comment rulemaking conducted by agencies. Other actions, such as adjudication, funding of grants, and other such decisions, are beyond the scope of this chapter.

4. Although the activities themselves have characterized presidential transitions for decades, so-called midnight rulemaking and other entrenchment activities within the administrative state just before the arrival of a new president first received significant analysis in the legal literature around the time of the Clinton/Bush transition. See, e.g., Jack M. Beermann, "Presidential Power in Transitions," *Boston University Law Review* 83 (December 2003): 947; Jay Cochran, "The Cinderella Constraint: Why Regulations Increase Significantly During Post-Election Quarters" (unpublished, March 8, 2001); Nina Mendelson, "Agency Burrowing: Entrenching Policies and Personnel Before a New President Arrives," *New York University Law Review* 78 (May 2003): 557.

5. E.g., Peter Strauss, "Foreword: Overseer, or 'The Decider'? The President in Administrative Law," *George Washington Law Review* 75 (June 2007): 696.

6. Nina Mendelson, "Agency Burrowing," 557.

7. *Federal Communications Commission v. Fox Television Stations, Inc.,* 129 S. Ct. 1800, 1810–1811 (2009).

8. David Barron, "From Takeover to Merger: Reforming Administrative Law in an Age of Agency Politicization," *George Washington Law Review* 76 (2008): 1095, 1097 (noting "politicization of the national bureaucracy itself").

9. Nina Mendelson, "Agency Burrowing," 557, 602.

10. Memorandum from Joshua B. Bolten, White House Chief of Staff, to Heads of Executive Departments & Agencies (May 9, 2008), available at http://www.ombwatch.org/files/regs/PDFs/BoltenMemo050908.pdf (last accessed July 8, 2011).

11. See Fox News/Opinion Dynamics poll data regarding favorability rating of George W. Bush (showing 2007 and 2008 favorability ratings con-

sistently at or below 40 percent), available at http://www.pollingreport.com/ BushFav.htm (accessed December 7, 2009).

12. See generally Beermann, "Presidential Power in Transitions," 947; Jerry Brito and Veronique de Rugy, "Midnight Regulations and Regulatory Review," *Administrative Law Review* 61 (2009): 163; Cochran, "The Cinderella Constraint"; Susan E. Dudley, "Reversing Midnight Regulations," Cato Review of Business & Government 24 (2001): 9; Nina Mendelson, "Agency Burrowing: Entrenching Policies and Personnel Before a New President Arrives," 557.

13. See Antony Davies and Veronique de Rugy, "Midnight Regulations: An Update 4" (Mercatus Center, George Mason University, 2008), available at www.mercatus.org/uploadedFiles/Mercatus/Publications/WP0806_RSP _Midnight%20Regulations.pdf (Last accessed July 8, 2011).

14. Brito and de Rugy, "Midnight Regulations and Regulatory Review," 163, 174 ("If there are no such future interactions [with Congress and the electorate], an administration will be more likely to 'defect' and pursue a regulatory course that might have otherwise invited retaliation."); ibid. at 174–175 ("The accountability provided by the threat of congressional retaliation is also weakened once a president knows that there is no 'next period' in which he will need Congress's cooperation on legislative, budgetary, and other matters").

15. Beermann, "Presidential Power in Transitions," 947.

16. Richard B. Stewart, "The Reformation of American Administrative Law," *Harvard Law Review* 88 (1975): 1667, 1675–1676; Jerry L. Mashaw, "Should Administrators Make Political Decisions," in *Greed, Chaos, and Governance* (New Haven, CT: Yale University Press 1997).

17. But see, e.g., Kenneth A. Shepsle, "Congress is a 'They,' not an 'It': Legislative Intent as Oxymoron," *International Review of Law and Economics* 12 (1992): 239.

18. See, e.g., *Food & Drug Administration v. Brown & Williamson Tobacco Corp.,* 529 U.S. 120, 164 (2000) (discussing the view that the federal Food Drug and Cosmetic Act was a purposely broad delegation of discretionary powers to the FDA) (Breyer, J., dissenting).

19. Clean Water Act sec. 301(b)(2)(A), codified at 33 U.S.C. 1311(b)(2)(A).

20. Amy Gutmann and Dennis Thompson, *Democracy and Disagreement* (Cambridge, MA: Harvard University Press, 1996).

21. Ibid.

22. Mark A. Seidenfeld, "A Civic Republican Justification for the Bureaucratic State," *Harvard Law Review* 105 (1992): 1511, 1515 (describing rulemak-

ing as "best hope of implementing civic republicanism's call for deliberative decisionmaking informed by the values of the entire polity"); *United States v. Nova Scotia Food Products Corp.*, 568 F.2d 240 (2d Cir. 1977) (overturning agency rule for failure to "discuss [or] answer[]" relevant comment).

23. A prominent example is found in Jerry L. Mashaw, "Should Administrators Make Political Decisions?" in *Greed, Chaos, and Governance* (New Haven, CT: Yale University Press 1997).

24. See Elena Kagan, "Presidential Administration," *Harvard Law Review* 114 (2001): 2245; Kevin Stack, *Columbia Law Review* 100 (2006): 263; Nina Mendelson, "Another Word on the President's Statutory Authority Over Agency Action," *Fordham Law Review* 79 (2011): 2455.

25. See Mashaw, "Should Administrators Make Political Decisions?"; Steve Calabresi, "Some Normative Arguments for the Unitary Executive," *Arkansas Law Review* 48 (1995): 23; Nina Mendelson, "Agency Burrowing," 557, 583 ("[S]he will be better able to counteract narrowly regional interests and the demands of small groups of constituents.").

26. See Calabresi, "Some Normative Arguments for the Unitary Executive," 23.

27. Cynthia Farina, "False Comfort and Impossible Promises: Uncertainty, Information Overload, and the Unitary Executive," *University of Pennsylvania Journal of Constitutional Law* 12 (February 2010): 357.

28. See Jide Nzelibe, "The Fable of the Nationalist President and the Parochial Congress," *University of California at Los Angeles Law Review* 53 (2006): 1231–1246. See also Wallace Mendelson, "Separation, Politics, and Judicial Activism," *Indiana Law Review* 52 (1977): 313, 316 ("a presidential candidate who has substantial support in some fifteen or twenty major metropolitan areas is virtually assured of victory"); Nelson Polsby, *Congress and the Presidency* (Englewood Cliffs, NJ: Prentice-Hall, 1986 (presidential candidates tend both to be chosen from populous states with large electoral college impact and to have made alliances with urban interest groups).

29. See Evan Criddle, "Fiduciary Administration," *Texas Law Review* 88 (2010): 441; Farina, "False Comfort and Impossible Promises," 357.

30. See Anne O'Connell, "Political Cycles of Rulemaking: An Empirical Portrait of the Modern Administrative State," *Virginia Law Review* 94 (2007): 889, 969.

31. The Congressional Review Act was used to override the Clinton "ergonomics" rule, and its use was threatened seriously on only one other occasion.

32. Mark Seidenfeld, "The Psychology of Accountability and Political Review of Agency Rules," *Duke Law Journal* 51 (2001): 1059.

33. George A. Bermann, "Regulatory Federalism: European Union and the United States," *Recueil des Cours* 263 (1997): 48, 53; Herbert Wechsler, "The Political Safeguards of Federalism," *Columbia Law Review* 54 (1954): 543; Ernest Young, "Two Cheers for Process Federalism," *Villanova Law Review* 46 (2001): 1349.

34. Jerry L. Mashaw, *Greed, Chaos, and Governance: Using Public Choice to Improve Public Law* (New Haven: Yale University Press, 1999), 152.

35. See Lawrence R. Jacobs and Robert Y. Shapiro, *Politicians Don't Pander* (Chicago: University of Chicago Press, 2000), 33, 36–37.

36. Farina, "False Comfort and Impossible Promises," 291–292 ("what cannot be disputed is [the electoral college's] success in focusing the attention of would-be Presidents on geography").

37. See Gutmann and Thompson, *Democracy and Disagreement*, 12, 16, 40–41.

38. See Nina Mendelson, "Disclosing 'Political' Oversight of Agency Decision Making," 108 Michigan Law Review (2010), 1127.

39. Of course, whether accompanied by published reasoned debate or not, legislation has its own legitimacy because it is the product of a constitutionally prescribed process, and it may have a particularly strong claim if it is indeed the product of reasoned debate.

40. See generally Jason Webb Yackee and Susan Webb Yackee, "A Bias Toward Business? Assessing Interest Group Influence on the U.S. Bureaucracy," *Journal of Politics* 68 (2006): 128, 133; Wendy Wagner, "Administrative Law, Filter Failure, and Information Capture," *Duke Law Journal* 59 (2010): 1324, 1367; Cornelius M. Kerwin, *Rulemaking: How Government Agencies Write Law and Make Policy* (Washington, D.C.: CQ Press, 2003), 182–183.

41. Nina Mendelson, "Regulatory Beneficiaries and Informal Agency Policymaking," *Cornell Law Review* 92 (2007): 397, 428–430.

42. See Mariano Florentino-Cuellar, "Rethinking Regulatory Democracy," *Administrative Law Review* 57 (2005): 411, 414; see also Nina Mendelson, "Foreword: Rulemaking, Democracy, and Torrents of E-Mail," *George Washington Law Review* 79 (2011).

43. This is Seidenfeld's assumption. See Seidenfeld, "A Civic Republican Justification for the Bureaucratic State," 1511, 1555 ("Staff bureaucrats focus on what they believe the public interest is and whether the suggested policy furthers it.").

44. Judicial review requiring that an agency answer significant comments is no guarantee of democratic responsiveness, though it may help assure rationality.

45. Nina Mendelson, "Disclosing 'Political' Oversight of Agency Decision Making."

46. Private efforts by members of Congress to pressure agencies accordingly would not have this same benefit to citizens.

47. See Pew Research Center for the People and the Press, "Distrust, Discontent, Anger and Partisan Rancor," available at http://people-press.org/report/606/trust-in-government (accessed April 28, 2010) (noting that discontent with Congress and elected officials is "epic" and that favorable opinions of Congress have declined from 50 percent of those polled in 2009 to 25 percent in 2010).

48. See Jacob Gersen and Eric Posner, "Soft Law: Lessons from Congressional Practice," *Stanford Law Review* 61 (2008): 573; see also Guy Hafteck, "Legislative Threats," *Stanford Law Review* 61 (2008): 629. With respect to the intent of an individual member of Congress or of some sort of collective intent, statements may be subject to some of the same criticisms as those leveled against legislative history. For example, statements can be strategic, may not be representative, and so forth. Compare Antonin Scalia, "Common-Law Courts in a Civil Law System: The Role of United States Federal Courts in Interpreting the Constitution and Laws," in Antonin Scalia, *A Matter of Interpretation: Federal Courts and the Law*, ed. Amy Gutmann (Princeton, NJ: Princeton University Press, 1997) with Stephen Breyer, "On the Uses of Legislative History in Interpreting Statutes," *Southern California Law Review* 65 (1992): 845. This is particularly an issue for statements from congressional committees. While the idealistic notion of committees is a smaller body representative of the whole that has an opportunity to develop expertise, committees have been criticized as composed of "preference outliers," who seek committee membership in order to distribute benefits to their constituents or to well-organized interest groups. Keith Krehbiel has compiled statistical evidence tending to suggest that committees are not, in fact, composed of preference outliers. Keith Krehbiel, "Are Congressional Committees Composed of Preference Outliers," *American Political Science Review* 84 (1990): 149. My suggestion, however, is not that congressional statements should be used to rewrite a statute *de facto*, or as a form of soft law, but instead as valuable information—particularly on broader questions of policy or value—to an agency implementing a broad statutory delegation.

49. The "intention"/"technical" dichotomy comes from the work of David Austen-Smith. David Austen-Smith, "Strategic Models of Talk in Political Decision Making," *International Political Science Review* 13 (1992): 45–58.

50. Gersen and Posner, "Soft Law: Lessons from Congressional Practice," 573, 589.

51. Hafteck, "Legislative Threats," 629, 668.

52. See Randall Kroszner and Thomas Stratmann, "Corporate Campaign Contributions, Repeat Giving, and the Rewards to Legislator Reputation," *Journal of Law and Economics* 48 (2005): 41, discussed in Hafteck, "Legislative Threats."

53. Randall Kroszner and Thomas Stratmann, "Congressional Committees as Reputation-building Mechanisms," *Business and Politics* 2:1 (2000): 35–52.

54. Cf. Scalia, *A Matter of Interpretation*, (critiquing reliance on legislative history as de facto revision of legislation without following constitutional procedures).

55. *Immigration and Naturalization Service v. Chadha*, 462 U.S. 919 (1983).

56. E.g., *Metropolitan Washington Airports Authority v. Citizens for Abatement of Aircraft Noise*, 501 U.S. 252, 276 (1991).

57. See *Whitman v. American Trucking Associations*, 531 U.S. 457 (2001) (describing current nondelegation standards).

58. E.g., Thomas McGarity, "Some Thoughts on 'Deossifying' the Rulemaking Process," *Duke Law Journal* 41 (1992): 1385, 1450 (noting the sporadic nature of congressional review of agency rules); Seidenfeld, "A Civic Republican Justification for the Bureaucratic State," 1511, 1551 (noting high transactions costs of congressional overrides); Jerry L. Mashaw, "Prodelegation: Why Administrators Should Make Political Decisions," *Journal of Law, Economics and Organization* 1 (1985): 81, 85 (same).

59. See Mathew D. McCubbins and Thomas Schwartz, "Congressional Oversight Overlooked: Police Patrols versus Fire Alarms," *American Journal of Political Science* 28 (1984): 165.

60. Ibid. at 172 ("To be sure, fire-alarm oversight tends to be *particularistic* . . . emphasiz[ing] the interests of individuals and interest groups more than those of the public at large. . . . [W]hether [the lack of emphasis on some public interest concerns] is a shortcoming of fire-alarm oversight depends on one's ideological point of view.")

61. Keith Krehbiel, *Information and Legislative Organization* (Ann Arbor: Michigan Studies in Political Analysis, 1991), 105 (Committees "as agents of their parent chambers, exist to investigate, deliberate, apply specialized knowledge, and recommend action.").

62. E.g., William Eskridge, "Politics without Romance: Implications of Public Choice Theory for Statutory Interpretation," *Virginia Law Review* 74 (1988): 275.

63. Richard Lazarus, "Congressional Descent: The Demise of Deliberative Democracy in Environmental Law," *Georgetown Law Journal* 94 (2005–2006): 619.

64. One result may be less far-seeing environmental legislation. Ibid.

65. J. R. DeShazo and Jody Freeman, "The Congressional Competition to Control Delegated Power," *Texas Law Review* 81 (2009): 1443.

66. See page 55, this volume (discussing political costs suffered by President George W. Bush from attempting to reopen EPA drinking water arsenic rule). More recently, the Obama HHS's announcement that it would revisit the Bush administration's "conscience rule" was described as "trigger[ing] an immediate political firestorm" by the *Washington Post.* See Rob Stein, "Health Workers' 'Conscience' Rule Set to Be Voided," *Washington Post,* February 28, 2009.

67. Department of the Interior Fish & Wildlife Service, Interagency Cooperation under the Endangered Species Act, 73 *Federal Register* 76,272 (December 16, 2008).

68. See 16 U.S.C. sec. 1536.

69. See Department of the Interior Fish & Wildlife Service, Interagency Cooperation under the Endangered Species Act, 73 *Federal Register* 76,272 (December 16, 2008) ("Approximately 235,000 comments were received; of these, approximately 215,000 were largely similar 'form' letters.").

70. See Endangered Species Act, sec. 4(d); e.g., NOAA's National Marine Fisheries Service, Northwestern Regional Office, ESA 4(d) Rules (Protective Regulations), available at http://www.nwr.noaa.gov/ESA-Salmon-Regulations-Permits/4d-Rules/ (accessed December 18, 2009) ("The ESA prohibits ANY take of species listed as endangered, but some take of threatened species that does not interfere with salmon survival and recovery can be allowed. Before 2000, NOAA Fisheries Service had simply adopted 4(d) rules that prohibited take of threatened species").

71. See Department of the Interior, Endangered and Threatened Wildlife and Plants; Special Rule for the Polar Bear, 73 *Federal Register* 76,249 (December 16, 2008) ("In addition, this special rule provides that any incidental take of polar bears that results from activities that occur outside of the current range of the species is not a prohibited act under the ESA.").

72. See Allison Winter, "Interior cleared to finalize controversial rule revisions," *Land Letter,* December 11, 2008, available at http://www.eenews.net/Landletter/2008/12/11/archive/2?terms'polar+bear. The December 11, 2008, hearing of the House Select Committee on Energy Independence and Global Warming was entitled, "Approaching Midnight: Oversight of the Bush Administration's Last-Minute Rulemakings." For Congressman Markey's opening statement, see http://www.globalwarming.house.gov/tools/3q08materials/files/0076.pdf ("Meanwhile, the Department of the Interior is seeking to gut the Endangered Species Act by removing scientific input, weakening protec-

tions for iconic species like the polar bear and preventing consideration of the impacts of global warming.").

73. See 155 *Congressional Record* S 2677-78, daily ed. March 5, 2009 (statement of Senator Murkowski); 155 *Congressional Record* S 2679, daily ed. March 5, 2009 (statement of Senator Inhofe) ("Any permit for a powerplant, refinery, or road project that increases the volume of traffic anywhere in the United States could be subject to litigation, if it contributes to local carbon emissions"); 155 *Congressional Record* S2598, daily ed. March 2, 2009 (statement of Senator Kyl) ("The practical effect of this rule withdrawal is that any acts that increase carbon dioxide or greenhouse gas emissions, which means almost anything we do, since, of course, we breathe carbon dioxide, would be subject to a lawsuit if it did not first consult the U.S. Fish and Wildlife Service on mitigation against potential impacts of climate change and harm to polar bears.").

74. See *Congressional Record* daily ed. March 5, 2009, at S 2800 (statement of Senator Feinstein); see also 155 *Congressional Record* S2782, daily ed. March 5, 2009 (statement of Senator Cardin) ("Professional scientific organizations argued, came out and said, quite frankly, this is unacceptable.")

75. See *Congressional Record* daily ed. March 5, 2009, at S 2810 (statement of Senator Boxer). She also inserted several news articles and editorials into the Record.

76. See Patrick Reis, "Senators Urge Reversal of Bush-era ESA regs," *E&E News PM,* April 23, 2009, available at http://www.eenews.net/eenewspm/2009/04/23/archive/12?terms'polar+bear (last visited December 18, 2009); letter available at http://www.biologicaldiversity.org/campaigns/save_the_act_save_species_from_the_climate_crisis/pdfs/DF-to-Salazar-ESA-Approps-Authority-04–23–2009.pdf (last visited December 18, 2009).

77. The letter is available at http://www.biologicaldiversity.org/campaigns/save_the_act_save_species_from_the_climate_ crisis/pdfs/040309_ESA_Letter_to_Salazar_Locke.pdf (last visited December 18, 2009).

78. See Allison Winter, "Groups press Obama to quickly toss Bush's ESA rules," *E&E News PM,* April 9, 2009, available at http://www.eenews.net/eenewspm/2009/04/09/archive/4?terms'polar+bear (last visited December 18, 2009).

79. E.g., Juliet Eilperin, "New Rule Would Discount Warming as Risk Factor for Species," *Washington Post,* November 21, 2008, at A3; Editorial, "Protections in Peril," *Washington Post,* December 27, 2008, at A14.

80. Cornelia Dean, "Bid to Undo Bush Memo on Threats to Species," *New York Times,* March 4, 2009, at A14 ("A rider undoing the Bush change has been attached to the budget bill, and if it passes, the change would be undone.").

81. See Departments of the Interior and Commerce, Interagency Cooperation Under the Endangered Species Act, 74 *Federal Register* 20,421 (May 4, 2009).

82. Www.reginfo.gov, which reports data on White House review of rules, shows that the rule was published "consistent with change," referring to a change made during the regulatory review process. The Web site does not indicate the content of the change or whether it was made at the behest of the White House or on the agencies' own initiative. See www.reginfo.gov (archival search for RIN 1018-AW73 performed December 21, 2009).

83. See 31 U.S.C. 1105(a); Bill Heniff Jr., "The Congressional Budget Process Timetable" 2, Congressional Research Service Order Code 98-472 GOV, March 20, 2008, available at http://budget.house.gov/crs-reports/98-472.pdf.

84. E.g., Allison Winter, "As deadline looms, Interior mulls Bush's polar bear rule," *New York Times* online, May 4, 2009 (quoting Bill Snape of Center for Biological Diversity: "The [consultation rule] repeal was a huge victory in favor of sound science and common sense, but it's only half the pie . . . we need to get rid of that bad Bush rule on polar bears and global warming").

85. Andrew Revkin, "U.S. Curbs Use of Species Act in Protecting Polar Bear," *New York Times,* May 9, 2009, at A13.

86. As noted, several senators had written the agency supporting reversal of the polar bear as well as the consultation rule. See Patrick Reis, "Senators Urge Reversal of Bush-era ESA regs," *E&E News P.M,* April 23, 2009, available at http://www.eenews.net/eenewspm/2009/04/23/archive/12?terms'polar+bear (last visited December 18, 2009).

87. Editorial, "Cold Reality: Addressing climate change is a job for Congress, not the Endangered Species Act," *Washington Post,* May 18, 2009, at A18. William N. Andreen's excellent comment points out that a number of these views were also enunciated by senior Bush administration officials, so they were not new to the agencies. Even if, as Andreen suggests, congressional debate might not have helped an agency learn the potential policy implications, it might have helped the agency weigh them.

88. Fish and Wildlife Service, Department of the Interior, Proposed Rule: Designation of Critical Habitat for the Polar Bear in the United States, 74 *Federal Register* 56,058 (October 29, 2009); Fish and Wildlife Service, Department of the Interior, Rules and Regulations: Endangered and Threatened Wildlife and Plants; Designation of Critical Habitat for the Polar Bear *(Ursus maritimus)* in the United States, 75 *Federal Register* 76,086 (December 7, 2010).

89. See McCubbins and Schwartz, "Congressional Oversight Overlooked,"

165; Jacob Gersen and Anne Joseph O'Connell, "Hiding in Plain Sight? Timing and Transparency in the Administrative State," *University of Chicago Law Review* 76 (2009): 1157.

90. E.g.: 154 *Congressional Record* S6886-01 (July 17, 2008) (Senator Stevens) (with respect to ANWR); 154 *Congressional Record* 6554-01 (July 10, 2008) (Senator Crapo) (related to energy prices).

91. In "Agency Burrowing," I wrote that an outgoing president had a defensible claim to put an issue on the nation's policy agenda. See Nina Mendelson, "Agency Burrowing," 557, 640–641 (arguing that the outgoing president possesses expertise and resources to identify issues of concern to substantial minority of public and that agenda contributions should be seen as legitimate if public support for them is substantial).

Commentary on Chapter 2
Is There a Silver Lining to Midnight Mischief?
William L. Andreen

I. Introduction

Even the dullest of publications can make good reading during the last few months of a presidential administration. This is especially true when the incoming president is from the opposing political party. Those months typically witness, at least since the 1970s, a rush to publish many new regulations in the *Federal Register* as the incumbent administration scrambles to leave its mark on national policy.[1]

Such midnight rulemaking often produces "an instinctively negative reaction."[2] The reasons why this kind of last-minute activity is so roundly condemned are not altogether clear, but the reaction is likely linked to three factors identified by Nina Mendelson. First, it appears antidemocratic "because it seems aimed at undermining the control and authority of the newly elected President."[3] Second, since these rulemakings often occur after an election, the "voters potentially lose an important tool for holding agencies accountable."[4] Perhaps the most important reason for this often-visceral reaction is the perception by many that the lame-duck president is simply thumbing his nose at the president-elect and those who voted for him.[5] In short, the outgoing administration is not acting in an honorable, sportsmanlike fashion because it is trying to tie the hands of the duly elected, incoming administration, a figure of speech that is especially apt in the case of rulemaking since rescinding or otherwise altering a final administrative rule can consume a great deal of time and effort.

Despite the fact that late-term rulemakings are often considered unsporting and a form of policy mischief, Nina Mendelson has identified in her chapter an instance where such rulemakings appear to facilitate greater democratic participation in the rulemaking process. The example involves two rulemakings involving the Endangered Species Act that were finalized during the waning days of the administration of President George W. Bush.[6] The rules were controversial, and widely opposed,[7] and the new administration indicated, at least initially, that it would seek to reverse both.[8] All of this attracted the attention of Congress, and a debate ensued that otherwise might not have occurred.[9] That debate, Mendelson suggests, may have prompted the new Obama administration to reevaluate its initial position on one of the rules and eventually embrace it rather than rejecting it.[10] Thus, Mendelson concludes that midnight rulemakings can lead to better-informed and more democratically responsive decisions than might otherwise be the case.[11]

Mendelson, therefore, has identified a possible silver lining in midnight mischief. The controversy surrounding these rules, undoubtedly heightened by their eleventh-hour timing, did generate attention and debate in Congress. And the content of that debate may have influenced the administration, at least to some extent, to change its position and accept one of the rules rather than reject it out of hand. Mendelson, as a result, has made an important contribution to a richer, more accurate understanding of this phenomenon. Midnight rules are not necessarily always a negative factor, even when an outgoing administration promulgates a rule knowing that it will create difficulties for the new president.

Did this congressional involvement, however, actually change the Obama administration's mind? Even if it had some influence in doing so, is it an odd case? Is it just an interesting anecdote that proves little about the overall costs and benefits of late-term rulemaking? In short, are the problems posed by midnight mischief offset by the occasional salutary effect? This chapter is an attempt to place Mendelson's valuable observation into the overall context of late-term administrative actions.

II. Distinguishing between Midnight Mischief and Legitimate Last-Minute Administrative Action

Not all administrative work done during the waning days of a presidential administration is objectionable as a form of midnight mischief. As long as the Constitution provides for an approximately eleven-week transition period,[12] the normal processes of government must continue while the new president-elect waits off-stage. Most of this work is routine.[13] Permits must be processed; grants made; enforcement actions instituted; projects overseen; and civil servants hired. None of that is problematic. In addition, it is not truly objectionable that administrative activity tends to rise during the last weeks of an administration. As Jack Beermann has pointed out, there are perfectively natural aspects of human life—such as working to a deadline and hurrying to do as much as possible at the last minute—that also animate or reflect the life of administrative bodies.[14]

Nonetheless, a number of late-term actions certainly appear "unseemly."[15] One obvious example is when an outgoing administration attempts to embed its ideological bent into the administrative state by placing political appointees, who serve at the will of the president, into key civil service positions or even the Senior Executive Service where they can only be removed from office for cause.[16] While some such moves may at least occasionally be well motivated, placing well-qualified and not overtly political individuals into career positions, such appointments appear, overall, to be an effort to insert some loyal retainers into agencies in order to undercut new policy directions the next administration may wish to pursue.[17] Last-minute rulemakings may also appear particularly political in nature. They may be hurried and as a result poorly considered.[18] Even more troubling is the fact that many late-term rulemakings appear to involve policy decisions on which the incoming administration will likely disagree. Such actions will, of course, divert a new administration from pursuing its policy initiatives as it attempts to repair the damage that it perceives has just been done.

The distraction caused by such rulemakings is not insignificant. Agencies are bound to follow their own regulations until the rules are validly amended or rescinded.[19] Thus, agencies must promulgate a new rule to undo eleventh-hour regulations, and that involves a lengthy and complicated process. Not only must agencies give notice and take comment on proposed rules,[20] but they must also respond in writing to every significant comment made in the final rulemaking.[21] In addition, although an agency may have good reason for abrogating all or part of a recently promulgated rule, the existence of an administrative record supporting or tending to support a contrary position may add substantially to the litigation difficulties the agency will face on judicial review.[22]

Finally, an agency may well have to contend with a myriad of add-on analyses that Congress and various presidents have appended to the rulemaking process for certain kinds of rules such as the Regulatory Flexibility Act,[23] the Unfunded Mandates Reform Act,[24] the Paperwork Reduction Act,[25] the Congressional Review of Agency Rulemaking Act,[26] the Data Quality Act,[27] and Executive Order 12,866, which provides for cost-benefit assessments and review by the Office of Regulatory Affairs located within the Office of Management and Budget.[28] These congressional- and presidential-level analytical requirements have slowed down the rulemaking process and have imposed even greater administrative costs.[29]

So, outgoing administrations that hurry through last-minute rulemakings knowing that they will be anathema to an incoming administration are clearly acting in a cynical and wasteful fashion, knowing that their action will not likely survive long, but also knowing that the process of rescission or amendment will chew up precious time and resources. That is bad enough for a substantive rule that is aimed at regulating the conduct of the private sector. It is, however, perhaps even worse when a procedural rule, pertaining to internal governmental processes, is promulgated, such as the last-minute Bush rule that dealt with federal agency consultation under section 7 of the Endangered Species Act. In such cases, the only entity the new rule is going to govern is the incoming administration, at least until such time as the new process is altered by rulemaking. Such an attempt to procedurally hamstring a new administration seems especially pernicious to me since it is so invasive of the internal decision-making process within the next administration.

On the one hand, one can argue that the outgoing administration should pursue its policy agenda until the last possible moment. That is certainly within its authority, and it might even feel entitled to do so since it may have been treated in similar fashion when it initially took office. On the other hand, the more problematic actions of an outgoing administration do not contribute to an easy or efficient transition, which is a serious problem since smooth transitions of power could advance the public interest by encouraging the healing of some of the raw nerves exposed during the preceding electoral cycle. By setting a good example and exhibiting more civility, the outgoing administration would set a more constructive tone that could promote the kind of bipartisan discussion and compromise necessary on Capitol Hill to more effectively govern our nation.

III. A Closer Look at Mischief's Silver Lining

Midnight mischief, due to its timing and often due to its ideological content, often precipitates controversy and produces ill will. This reaction is most notable among those stakeholders who are especially concerned with the subject matter of the mischief. However, the alarm bells may also be set off in Congress. This was the case with the two Endangered Species Act rules examined by Mendelson, both of which were finalized in mid-

December 2008—approximately one month before the inauguration of the new president.

The Endangered Species Act requires that all federal agencies "in consultation with and with the assistance of" the Fish and Wildlife Service or National Marine Fisheries Service must "insure" that their actions are "not likely to jeopardize the continued existence" of any endangered or threatened species.[30] To facilitate compliance with that prohibition, the statute requires these agencies to inquire of the Services about the presence of listed species within areas to be affected by their actions.[31] If such species may be present, the action agency must complete a biological assessment to identify any endangered or threatened species.[32] The rule, which was altered by the first midnight rule Mendelson examined, required the action agency to submit its biological assessment to the appropriate wildlife service for review and to initiate formal consultation unless the service concurred in writing that the action was not likely to adversely affect any listed species.[33] Instead, the midnight rule would permit the action agency to avoid consultation, without seeking concurrence from either service, if the action agency on its own determined that the action would not cause a take of a listed species[34] and (1) would not have an effect on a listed species; (2) would have effects that would be manifested through a global process such as climate change; or (3) would have effects that are difficult to measure or detect.[35] The new rule, therefore, would have eliminated consultation under the Endangered Species Act for a wide number of actions and permit action agencies to "unilaterally determine the appropriateness of its action" under the act.[36]

The second rule was a direct response to the May 2008 listing of the polar bear as a threatened species and reflected concern that any project located anywhere in the country might be affected if it could be linked to an enhancement of anthropogenic climate change and thus harm the polar bear. This rule, consequently, eliminated the prohibition on incidental takes of the polar bear for activities outside the bear's range. It also declared that the act's prohibition on take would not apply to any activity that is conducted in compliance with the Marine Mammal Protection Act or the Convention on International Trade in Endangered Species of Wild Fauna and Flora.[37]

The two rules created quite a stir. Over 265,000 comments were submitted on the proposed rules, most in opposition, and lawsuits were filed immediately to overturn the final consultation rule. The controversy reached Congress as well where a rider to an appropriations bill was passed giving the relevant agencies the authority to summarily withdraw both rules and reinstate the prior consultation rule.[38] According to Mendelson, it appeared at the time that this course of action was in line with the desires of the Obama administration.[39] However, the administration only withdrew the consultation rule, reinstating the older one,[40] while leaving in place the polar bear rule,[41] a move that may have been presaged by the president's memorandum of March 3, 2009, which called upon the relevant agencies to review only the consultation rule.[42]

Mendelson suggests that the apparent change in the administration's approach may have resulted from a debate that occurred in the Senate on an amendment offered by Senator Murkowski of Alaska[43] and three colleagues to delete the appropriations rider.[44] During this debate, which occurred on March 5, 2009, a number of senators attacked the Bush administration's consultation rule, while those supporting the amendment focused upon the polar bear rule.[45] Those supporting the amendment argued that, without the polar bear rule, the Endangered Species Act would be transformed into a forum where climate change policy would be developed case by case on the basis of projects involving small incremental increases in total greenhouse gases and the impacts projects would have upon Arctic ice and the polar bear.[46] The amendment failed to pass, however, and the rider was enacted into law.[47]

Following enactment of the rider, a great deal of pressure was applied to overturn both rules. Forty-one members of the House, eight senators, over 13,000 scientists, and more than 200,000 citizens asked the agencies to rescind both rules.[48] However, there were indications that the polar bear rule was not as controversial, as broadly damaging, or perhaps as easily understood as the consultation rule. While 235,000 comments had been submitted on the proposed consultation rule, not quite 30,000 were filed on the proposed polar bear rule.[49] Some groups, moreover, concentrated their efforts in the spring of 2008 upon overturning the consultation rule.[50] There may have been good reason for the differential levels of intensity in the public's response to the two rules.

During the prior year, the polar bear rule had been widely discussed within the executive branch. The U.S. Geological Service (USGS), for example, had concluded in May 2008 that it was "currently beyond the scope of existing science to identify a specific source of CO_2 emissions and designate it as the cause of specific climate impacts at an exact location."[51] In addition, the EPA observed in early October 2008 that "[t]he climate change research community has not yet developed tools specifically intended for evaluating or quantifying end-point impacts attributable to the emissions of [greenhouse gases] GHGs from a single source, and we are not aware of any scientific literature to draw from regarding the climate effects of individual, facility-level GHG emissions."[52] The solicitor of the Department of the Interior, therefore, concluded in the fall of 2008 that "any observed climate change effect on a member of a particular listed species or its critical habitat cannot be attributed to the emissions from any particular source."[53] In short, the Endangered Species Act is not well designed to address the problem of climate change; it is too narrow and reactive.[54] So, even though these memoranda were signed by political appointees, the professional staff in both services were likely well aware of the administrative difficulties that would follow a rescission of the polar bear rule. Many members of the public might also have realized this problem. It should have been no surprise, therefore, that the new secretary of the interior, Ken Salazar, mirrored these concerns when he announced in May 2009 that the polar bear rule would be retained. While recognizing the impact of climate change upon the polar bear, he said that the control of greenhouse gases "requires comprehensive policies, not a patchwork of agency actions carried out for particular species. It would be very difficult for our scientists to be doing evaluations of a cement plant in Georgia or Florida and the impact it's going to have on the polar bear habitat."[55] He added that "I just don't think the Endangered Species Act was ever set up with that contemplation in mind."

IV. Evaluating the Value of the Silver Lining

It appears that the Senate debate that occurred on March 5, 2009, may have had little to do with the eventual decision by Secretary Salazar to keep the polar bear rule in place. The difficulty of predicting the impact of individual projects around the country upon the polar bear and its habitat was well known within the relevant portions of the government and some segments of the public.[56] The specter of a morass of litigation, if the polar bear rule was not retained, was also likely well understood.[57] Furthermore, the president's memorandum of March 3 gave a strong signal that the administration was already considering retention of the polar bear rule.[58] Nevertheless, one cannot rule out the possibility that the debate might have had some impact on the administration's decision. In any case, discussion of issues like this on Capitol Hill always has value. Such discussions shed light on the views of the members and their constituents; such discussions can also cast certain issues in a new way, with new facts and new arguments. Finally, congressional discussions tend to receive more attention than most discussions in our society. They are, if you will, amplified in such a way that much of what is said on Capitol Hill is heard at least by the relevant stakeholders.

Regardless of the impact of this particular debate, it is not difficult to envision situations where congressional consideration of midnight rules would make a significant difference.[59] Certainly, the passage of the appropriations rider made it easier for the Obama administration to rescind the Bush administration's consultation rule and reinstate the prior rule. Congress can also enact legislation overturning a midnight rule.[60] Congressional consideration can also, as Mendelson argues, prompt heightened public discussion and interbranch dialogue and, in doing so, encourage a more deliberative and more democratic decision-making process.[61] Whether the cost of midnight rulemaking is outweighed by the value of this kind of additional dialogue depends, in part, upon how often it occurs. Certainly, Congress's ability to respond would be swamped if a deluge of last-minute rulemaking were to take place.[62] Even in the absence of a deluge, however, it may well be that Congress only has the time or inclination to respond to the most controversial of rules. After all, Congress is a political institution, not an expert agency that is charged with executing thousands of tasks, many of them highly technical in nature and others that, while more value-oriented in nature, are nevertheless constrained to one extent or another by statutory standards and technical considerations.

V. Conclusion

The legitimacy of policymaking performed by unelected administrators depends in no small measure upon the accessibility of those officials to the ideas and arguments presented by the public from whom their authority derives.[63] Congress, in turn, can serve as a vehicle for distilling and communicating these views to the administrative state. On occasion, midnight rules can spark the kind of controversy that ignites additional public debate, including discussions on Capitol Hill, all of which may lead to more thoughtful and democratic decision making at the administrative level. Determining whether a particular debate in Congress actually affected an administrative decision is a difficult undertaking as illustrated by the two rulemakings that Mendelson and I address. One cannot, however, gainsay the value of additional dialogue in a democratic society. The ultimate question, however, is whether it occurs often enough and in significant enough fashion to outweigh all of the negatives produced by midnight mischief. Chief among those negatives, perhaps, is the fact that the outgoing administration has abjured an opportunity to set a more constructive tone during the transition, a tone that could reduce the level of partisan rancor and lead to more bi-partisan cooperation in the next administration. One might hope that future administrations would demonstrate more civility in pursuit of smoother and more productive transitions. Unfortunately, that is most likely a vain hope.

Notes

1. As Susan E. Dudley has noted, "sudden bursts of regulatory activity at the end of a presidential administration are systematic, significant, and cut across party lines." Susan E. Dudley, "Reversing Midnight Regulations," *Regulation* (Spring 2001): at 9.

2. Jack M. Beermann, "Combating Midnight Regulation," *Northwestern University Law Review* 103 (2009): 352.

3. Nina Mendelson, "Agency Burrowing: Entrenching Policies and Personnel Before a New President Arrives," *New York University Law Review* 78 (2003): 557, 566.

4. Ibid., 566–567.

5. Ibid., 565.

6. Nina Mendelson, "Midnight Rulemaking and Congress," this volume, 54.

7. The Department of the Interior, for example, received nearly 30,000 comments on the proposed polar bear rule (73 *Federal Register* 76,249, 76,263 [December 16, 2008] and a whopping 235,000 comments on the consultation rule (73 Federal Register 76,272 [December 16, 2008]), most of them opposed to it. 39 Envt. Rep. (BNA) 2371, 2372 (2008). Four lawsuits were immediately filed to challenge the consultation rule. *Ctr. for Biological Diversity v. Kempthorne,* No. 08-5546 (N.D. Cal., filed December 11, 2008); *Natural Resources Defense Council v. Dep't of Interior,* No. 08-5605 (N.D. Cal., filed December 16, 2008); *Nat'l Wildlife Fed'n v. Kempthorne,* No. 08-5654 (N.D. Cal., filed December 18, 2008); *State of Cal. v. Kempthorne,* No. 08-5775 (N.D. Cal., filed December 29, 2008). An earlier version of the polar bear rule had already been challenged in *Ctr. for Biological Diversity v. Kempthorne,* No. 08-1339 (N.D. Cal.) (Second Amended Complaint).

8. Mendelson, "Midnight Rulemaking and Congress," 69.

9. Ibid., 70.

10. Ibid., 71.

11. Ibid., 71, 72–73.

12. A fairly lengthy transition period appears to be absolutely necessary given our system of government. Absent a parliamentary approach to government, where a shadow government with likely cabinet members already exists in the legislative branch, a nearly three-month period within which to organize a government is not unreasonable.

13. Mendelson, "Agency Burrowing," 564.

14. See Jack M. Beermann, "Presidential Power in Transition," *Boston University Law Review* 83 (2003): 950–951.

15. Mendelson, "Agency Burrowing," 564.

16. See Juliet Eilperin and Carol D. Leonnig, "Administration Moves to Protect Key Appointees," *Washington Post*, November 18, 2008, http://www.washingtonpost.com/wp-dyn/content/article/2008/11/17/AR2008111703537.html (last visited June 26, 2011) (recounting the Bush administration's move of fourteen political appointees into career jobs and six others into the Senior Executive Service [SES]). This is not unusual. The Clinton administration shifted forty-seven political appointees into the SES or other career positions during its last year in office. Ibid.

17. Agency reorganizations can also play havoc in some instances with the policy aims of an incoming administration. See Mendelson, "Agency Burrowing," 607–608.

18. The consultation rule discussed by Mendelson appears to have been particularly rushed. According to the Associated Press, the Fish and Wildlife Service set a deadline and assembled a special team in Washington to review over 200,000 public comments in a four-day period. See "Feds Rush to Ease Endangered Species Rules," msnbc.com, October 21, 2008, http://www.msnbc.msn.com/id/27312289/ (last visited June 26, 2011).

19. *United States v. Nixon*, 418 U.S. 683 (1974); *Accardi v. Shaughnessy*, 347 U.S. 260 (1954).

20. 5 U.S.C. § 553(b), (c).

21. *Portland Cement Ass'n v. Ruckelshaus*, 486 F.2d 375, 393–394 (D.C. Cir. 1973), cert. denied, 403 U.S. 921 (1974) (construing 5 U.S.C. § 553(c)).

22. See *Motor Vehicle Manufacturers Ass'n v. State Farm Mutual Automobile Ins. Co.*, 463 U.S. 29 (1983).

23. 5 U.S.C. §§ 601 et seq.

24. 2 U.S.C. §§ 658, 1501–1503, 1531–1536, 1571.

25. 44 U.S.C. §§ 3501 et seq.

26. 5 U.S.C. §§ 801–808.

27. Treasury and General Government Appropriations Act for Fiscal Year 2001, Pub. L. No. 106–554, § 515 (2001).

28. 58 *Federal Register* 51,735 (September 30, 1993), as amended by Exec. Order 13,258, 67 *Federal Register* 9,385 (February 26, 2002), and by Exec. Order 13,422, 72 *Federal Register* 2,763 (January 23, 2007).

29. While more stringent judicial review and the judicial elaboration upon the bare procedural bones of informal rulemaking under the Administrative Procedure Act may have slowed the rulemaking process, those developments certainly improved the overall quality of agency deliberation without ossifying the process itself. See William L. Andreen, "Administrative Rulemaking in the United States: An Examination of the Values that Have Shaped the Process," *Canberra Bulletin of Public Administration* 66 (October 1991): 112, 116. I am afraid that I cannot say the same for the cumulative efforts of Congress and a series of presidents to try to control the direction of agency rulemaking. When the total impact of the requirements imposed by the three branches is considered, however, it is relatively easy to conclude that the process has become ossified. See Thomas O. McGarity, "Some Thoughts on 'Deossifying' the Rulemaking Process," *Duke Law Journal* 41 (1992): 1385.

30. Endangered Species Act (ESA) § 7(a)(2), 16 U.S.C. § 1536(a)(2). The Fish and Wildlife Service is an office located within the Department of the Interior and the National Marine Fisheries Service is a division in the Commerce Department.

31. ESA § 7(c)(1), 16 U.S.C. § 1536(c)(1). The rule was promulgated in 1986.

32. Ibid.

33. 50 C.F.R. §§ 402.12(j); 402.13(a); 402(b)(1) (2009).

34. A take is broadly defined to include "harm, . . . kill, [or] capture" (ESA § 3(19), 16 U.S.C. § 1532(19)), and "harm" has been administratively defined as "significant habitat modification or degradation where it actually kills or injures wildlife by significantly impairing essential behavioral patterns, including breeding, feeding, or sheltering." 50 C.F.R. § 17.3 (2009).

35. 73 *Federal Register* 76,272, 76,287 (December 16, 2008).

36. Mendelson, "Midnight Rulemaking and Congress," 67.

37. See 73 *Federal Register* 76,249 (December 16, 2008). The rule basically restated, with some modifications, an interim final rule, which was promulgated, without prior notice and comment, on the same day as the polar bear was listed as a threatened species. See 73 *Federal Register* 28,306 (May 15, 2008).

38. Mendelson, "Midnight Rulemaking and Congress," 68.

39. Ibid. A presidential memorandum, issued on March 3, 2009, however,

requested only the secretaries of the Interior and Commerce review the consultation rule. Memorandum from Barack Obama, President, to Heads of Executive Departments and Agencies: The Endangered Species Act (March 3, 2009) (requesting, moreover, the heads of all agencies to exercise their discretion and continue following the prior, long-standing practices involving consultation and concurrence), http://www.whitehouse.gov/the_press_office/Memorandum-for-the-Heads-of-Executive-Departments-and-Agencies/ (last visited June 26, 2011).

40. 74 *Federal Register* 20,421 (May 4, 2009).

41. Mendelson, "Midnight Rulemaking and Congress," 69–70.

42. See n. 39.

43. Senator Murkowski had previously criticized the listing of the polar bear as a threatened species calling the decision "grossly premature" due to uncertainties about climate change. She also expressed concern that the listing decision had opened "a Pandora's Box that the [Bush] administration" would not be able to close. Tom Kizzia, "Listing Disappoints State Political, Industry Leaders," *Anchorage Daily News,* May 14, 2008, http://www.adn.com/2008/05/14/406461/listing-disappoints-state-political.html (last visited June 26, 2011). Then-Senator Stevens of Alaska was even more strident in his denunciation, calling the decision "an unequivocal victory for extreme environmentalists" (ibid.), while Representative Don Young of Alaska deemed it "an assault on common sense." Erika Balstad, "Senators Blast Polar Bear's 'Threatened' Status," *Anchorage Daily News,* May 14, 2008, http://www.adn.com/2008/05/14/405693/senators-blast-polar-bears-threatened.html (last visited June 26, 2011). The State of Alaska, at the behest of then-governor Palin, later filed suit challenging the listing decision. See Mary Gilbert, "Palin Sued to Push Polar Bears Off Endangered List," *National Journal* Online, September 1, 2008, http://www.nationaljournal.com/conventions/co_20080901_2202.php (last visited June 26, 2011).

44. Mendelson, "Midnight Rulemaking and Congress," 68.

45. Ibid.

46. Ibid.

47. Ibid.

48. See "Save the Act, Save Species from the Climate Crisis," Center for Biological Diversity, http://www.biologicaldiversity.ort/campaigns/save_the_act_save_species_from_the_climate_crisis/index.html (last visited June 26, 2011).

49. See n. 7.

50. See Letter from the Center for Progressive Reform, to Ken Salazar, Secretary of the Interior, and Gary Locke, Secretary of Commerce (April 1, 2009) (on file with author).

51. See Memorandum from David Longly Bernhardt, Solicitor, U.S. Dept. of the Interior, to the Secretary of the Interior, Guidance on the Applicability of the Endangered Species Act's Consultation Requirements to Proposed Actions Involving the Emission of Greenhouse Gases at 1 (March 3, 2008) (referring to a May 14, 2008, memorandum from the USGS entitled "The Challenges of Linking Carbon Emissions, Atmospheric Greenhouse Gas Concentrations, Global Warming, and Consequential Impacts"), http://www.doi.gov/solicitor/opinions/M-37017 (last visited June 26, 2011).

52. Ibid., 5 (referring to a Letter from Robert J. Meyers, Principal Deputy Assistant Administrator, Office of Air and Radiation, EPA, to H. Dale Hall, Director, U.S. Fish and Wildlife Service, and James Lecky, Director of Protected Resources, National Marine Fisheries Service, "Endangered Species Act and GHG Emitting Activities" (October 3, 2008).

53. Ibid., 6.

54. See Holly Doremus, "Polar Bears in Limbo: How a Legal Morass Could Save the Environment," *Slate,* May 20, 2008, http://www.slate.com/id/2191707 (last visited June 26, 2011). Doremus, however, added that the litigation that would ensue, in the absence of the polar bear rule, might not be an altogether bad thing because it "would force us to confront the need for national greenhouse-gas legislation sooner rather than later." Ibid.

55. Andrew C. Revkin, "U.S. Curbs Use of Species Act in Protecting Polar Bear," *New York Times,* May 8, 2009, http://www.nytimes.com/2009/05/09/science/earth/09bear.html (last visited June 26, 2011).

56. See nn. 51–54 and accompanying text.

57. See Doremus, "Polar Bears in Limbo." The possibility of a massive amount of litigation may well have been the inspiration for Senator's Murkowski's Pandora's Box reference in May 2008. See n. 43.

58. See n. 42 and accompanying text.

59. See Mendelson, "Agency Burrowing," 620–627 (recounting the effect of congressional discussions, as well as public outcry, on the Bush administration's original plan to reverse the Clinton administration's last-minute rule restricting road building in national forests).

60. See Congressional Review of Agency Rulemaking Act, 5 U.S.C. §§ 801–808. Of some 50,000 final rules that have been submitted to Congress since the enactment of this legislation in 1996, the act has been used only once to disapprove of a rule. The rule that was overturned was the Occupational

Safety and Health Administration's November 2000 rule on ergonomics. See Curtis W. Copeland, Congressional Research Service, *Midnight Rulemaking: Considerations for Congress and a New Administration* 13 (2008).

61. Mendelson, "Midnight Rulemaking and Congress," 72; see also n. 59 (referring to the roadless area rule illustration).

62. Mendelson, "Midnight Rulemaking and Congress," 73.

63. *Sierra Club v. Costle,* 657 F.2d 298, 400–401 (D.C. Cir. 1981).

3
Reconstructing the Republic

The Great Transition of the 1860s

Akhil Reed Amar, Lindsey Ohlsson Worth,
and Joshua Alexander Geltzer

America's postbellum Constitution sharply departed from America's antebellum Constitution, yet legal reformers managed to maintain formal continuity with the prior legal and institutional order. Seen in this light, the decade of the 1860s was the proverbial mother of all transitions.

I. New Rules

Consider first the American constitutional regime as it existed prior to the Civil War. Both on paper and in practice, America's antebellum Constitution was painfully pro-slavery where it counted most—on the question of political power. Thanks to the three-fifths clause, southern slavery translated into extra southern seats in the House of Representatives and extra southern votes in the electoral college—and thus extra southern clout over the presidency, which in turn predictably meant extra southern power in a judiciary whose members were picked by presidents.[1] The more human beings the South held in cruel bondage, the more political power southern slavocrats would wield in or over every branch of the federal government. Prior to 1860, no sitting president had ever called for slavery's ultimate extinction, nor had any sitting cabinet officer. The rules of the game as of 1860 effectively guaranteed the slaveholding South a majority of seats on the Supreme Court even though by then this region represented less than a third of the nation's free population.

Also, no clear guarantee of racial equality existed under the antebellum Constitution. Thus, free blacks were subjected to widespread denigration by both state and federal governments and disfranchisement in both state and federal elections. While the antebellum Bill of Rights declared a wide range of abuses off limits to federal officials, the bill had no explicit language to rein in comparably abusive states. The first words of the First Amendment said it all: "Congress" could "make no law" abridging free expression and free exercise, but no similarly specific text limited states on these issues or on many other matters of civil right and civil liberty. In the years leading up to the Civil War, many southern states made criticism of slavery a criminal (and in some places a capital) offense, and the Republican Party was in effect outlawed in the Deep South. Lincoln received not a single popular vote south of Virginia in the 1860 election.

Now flash forward to the American Constitution circa 1870. Thanks to the Civil War amendments, slavocrats were stripped not only of their extra political clout over all three branches, but also of their slaves. Unlike previous emancipation schemes in various antebellum states, the Thirteenth Amendment abolished slavery immediately, everywhere, on a massive scale, and without a dime of compensation to slaveholders. The old Constitution had insulated property holders from confiscatory takings, but the new one ratified and extended the largest redistribution of property in American history.[2] Slaves were worth more than any other capital asset in the nation except land. In 1860, human chattel represented about three times as much wealth as the entire nation's manufacturing and railroad stock,[3] yet the Thirteenth made no provision for compensation, even of loyal masters in true-blue states. (Section 4 of the Fourteenth went even further, prohibiting any federal or state compensation of slave masters.) A structurally pro-slavery Constitution became, in a flash, stunningly anti-slavery. Now *that's* a transition!

By 1870, the Constitution officially proclaimed the equal birthright citizenship of black Americans, flamboyantly repudiating high-profile antebellum case law—specifically, Chief Justice Roger Taney's execrable *Dred Scott* decision—that said the exact opposite. (Another transition.) The Reconstructed Constitution further proclaimed in plain English that no state should be allowed to abridge free speech, free exercise, or any other truly fundamental civil right, freedom, privilege, or immunity, thus reversing the federalism spin of the Founders' Bill of Rights and its subsequent elaboration in Chief Justice John Marshall's landmark ruling in *Barron v. Baltimore*. (Yet another large transition.) Instead of imposing special limits on federal power, as had the antebellum Constitution's first eleven amendments, three new amendments explicitly empowered the feds. Thus the Anti-Federalistic words of the First Amendment—"Congress shall make no law . . ."—met their Nationalistic opposites in a repeated Reconstruction amendment refrain: "Congress shall have power." (Still more transition.)

Whereas the old order had allowed states to disfranchise blacks openly and without penalty, the new order forbade race discrimination in voting and penalized a wide range of other forms of disfranchisement. In 1860, only about 2 percent of America's blacks had been eligible to vote on equal terms; a decade later, the Constitution declared that all black men should enjoy voting equality. Whereas no president before Lincoln ever said that slavery should eventually be abolished, no president thereafter has ever said that it should be restored. Although Democrats had dominated the presidency for more than a half century before Lincoln, the Republican Party ordinarily controlled the office for the next half century and more. A majority of presidents before Lincoln had come from south of the Mason-Dixon Line, but after 1870 no southern resident would occupy the White House until Texas's Lyndon Johnson became president in 1963.[4] In short: transition, transition, transition.

II. Controversial Procedures

How and why did these massive constitutional transitions occur? This chapter centers on one key piece of this puzzle, a piece implicating the role of the southern states in the process of framing and ratifying the Fourteenth Amendment.

First, a few general reminders about the political and legal context of Reconstruction. After Appomattox made clear that the North had won the war on the battlefield, the nation's attention shifted to how this military victory should be constitutionally codified. A just war is not an eruption of meaningless violence. Rather, a just war has a just purpose, and true victory in such a war involves the attainment of this purpose—this proper and just war aim. Lincoln himself spoke in these terms at Gettysburg when he promised that "these dead shall not have died in vain."

But what had they died for, ex post? What had they been fighting for, ex ante? At the outset of hostilities, Lincoln and his allies defined the war aim narrowly. In 1861, it was a war for union and democracy. Having lost at the ballot box in 1860, disaffected Americans could not properly resort to bullets to undo the election, for such a precedent of bullets trumping ballots, if allowed to stand, would doom popular government. If a secessionist minority whenever it felt disgruntled could simply disregard elections and unilaterally quit (and take American land with it), then democratic self-government would be at an end. The secessionists' claim to an extreme minority veto was nothing less than an assault on the idea of democracy itself—"government of the people, by the people, for the people."

As the war dragged on, Lincoln and his fellow Republicans redefined the war aim. In effect, it became an abolitionist war. Since slavery had been the root cause of the conflict (as Lincoln reminded his audience in his hauntingly beautiful Second Inaugural), the conflict's just resolution required an end to slavery. Whereas the 1860 Republican Party platform had foresworn federal interference with slavery as it existed in the several states—and whereas Lincoln himself had given even further assurances to this effect in his First Inaugural—the 1864 Republican platform signaled a decisive shift, promising to amend the Constitution so as to effect the "utter and complete extirpation" of slavery from "the soil of the Republic." After American voters resoundingly supported this platform in the 1864 elections, an abolitionist amendment was proposed by Congress and duly ratified.

But with the adoption of the Thirteenth Amendment abolishing slavery in late 1865, it quickly became apparent that still more would be needed to safeguard the war's true purpose, lest the defeated slavocracy undo emancipation and perhaps even try to secede anew or to regain control of the federal government and undermine the deepest commitments of the new order. Thus, what had started as a war for union and democracy and had ended as a war of emancipation became after Lincoln's death a war for civil rights and additional national power. (Later in the decade, the war's constitutional meaning would expand still further; by 1869–1870 it retroactively became a war for political rights.)

Let's recall the situation as of late 1865. Many southerners, though defeated in battle, remained defiant in law. Free speech had yet to be assured on the ground in the Old South; Unionists and racial egalitarians were still being stifled in many places. Southern Black Codes had sprung up, demeaning free blacks and depriving newly freed slaves of the ordinary rights and privileges enjoyed by whites. Nowhere in the Old South were blacks being allowed to vote; yet the southern states were now claiming a right to be seated in Congress—and were eventually expecting to have *more* seats than they had before, with blacks being counted at a full five-fifths rather than the discounted antebellum rate of three-fifths. Such blacks, after all, were no longer slaves, and thus under the antebellum Constitution's rules these blacks would translate into extra political power for their white former masters, even though these blacks were not being allowed to vote and even though their former masters were bent on repressing them rather than representing them.[5]

In order to win the peace as they had won the war, Reconstruction Republicans realized in late 1865 that the Thirteenth Amendment would not suffice. New federal legislation and/or new constitutional amendments would be needed. But this dawning realization raised difficult questions about whether to involve the ex-Confederacy in the legislative and/or amendment process, and if so, how. Let us now move beyond the substantive enormity of the Reconstruction transformation and ponder the *process* of this transition.

In December 1865, despite Lincoln's insistence throughout the war that the South remained part of a single indivisible Union, postwar congressional Republicans refused to allow the South's elected representatives and senators to take their claimed seats in Congress. Over the course of the next year, Congress continued to exclude virtually all the alleged representatives and senators from the former Confederacy, yet this regional "rump" Congress nevertheless deemed itself entitled to draft and propose the Fourteenth Amendment. Never before had America witnessed widespread congressional exclusions such as this, and it seemed to many at the time that the plain meaning of Article I gave each state an obvious right to two senators and to its proportionate share of the House of Representatives. A year later Congress conditioned each southern state's readmission to Congress upon that state's ratification of the Fourteenth Amendment, and when southern states eventually said yes, these congressionally induced yes votes were counted as valid parts of the Article V amendment ratification process. No antebellum amendment had ever been ratified in anything like this fashion, with a large number of states in effect told to ratify an amendment . . . or else! If southern states in fact had a plain right to be seated in Congress, wasn't the Republicans' condition the constitutional equivalent of extortion?[6]

Not according to some of the best legal minds of the 1860s, who spearheaded the Fourteenth Amendment. As they saw it, the process that generated the amendment was not a lawless break with the past and its practices but, to the contrary, was continuous with prior and proper constitutional understandings, rightly understood and rightly applied to an admittedly unique and unprecedented constitutional crisis. On this issue, two of the Republicans' most incisive constitutional theoreticians were Senator Charles Sumner of Massachusetts and Representative John Bingham of Ohio—both accomplished lawyers. Here, we shall focus especially on Bingham, zeroing in on one particularly elaborate and interesting speech that has not received the careful analysis that it deserves.[7] As we shall see, this speech offers up a remarkable case study in high-stakes transitional lawyering.

As did Senator Sumner, Representative Bingham argued as follows. First, southern regimes could properly be excluded from their seats in Congress—seats that were ordinarily guaranteed by Article I—because these ex-Confederate regimes failed to meet the Constitution's requirements of republican government under Article IV. Second, clearly established Supreme Court case law supported the right and power of the House and Senate to serve as the proper judges of congressional elections and thus to make the relevant determinations of republicanism—determinations legally binding on the other branches of government. Third, what was true for the Article I congressional seating issue was also true for the Article V amendment process. Unrepublican states should simply be excluded from the Article V calculus, which generally required that a congressionally proposed amendment win the approval of three-quarters of the states.

In other words, Sumner and Bingham essentially argued that when Article V (and other parts of the Constitution, for that matter) spoke of "states," this word most sensibly meant "states with proper constitutional standing"—that is, states with operational and valid republican governments. On this reading, unrepublican southern states should simply not count in either the numerator of ratifying-states or the denominator of total states under Article V, just as territories should not count and just as the District of Columbia should not count. In effect, each southern state had reverted to a status akin to that of a western territory. Each lapsed state was part of Lincoln's indivisible Union, to be sure, but until each ex-gray state restored a proper republican government it could not rightfully claim all the rights or discharge all the duties of proper states in good constitutional standing.

In the end, Congress did not fully embrace the reduced-denominator theory of Sumner and Bingham. Nevertheless, this theory explains why Congress was in fact authorized to refuse to seat the South. This theory can also explain, as a lesser-included implication, why Congress was also authorized to condition southern state readmission upon each ex-gray state's ratification of the Fourteenth Amendment, if that amendment was truly germane to state republicanism—as indeed it was, we shall argue. Thus, as events actually played out, the process by which the Fourteenth Amendment sprang to life was not a case of lawless extortion, but rather a case of extremely aggressive, even unprecedented (depending on how one defines that word)—*but ultimately faithful*—transitional lawyering enforcing the deep principles of American republicanism, principles whose under-enforcement in the antebellum period had disastrously emboldened the slave power and nearly destroyed the American Republic.

In a key speech to the House on January 16, 1867, Bingham exemplified the transitional lawyer par excellence, invoking utterly orthodox legal rules and precedents to legitimate a proposal that many of his lawyerly adversaries doubtless deemed utterly unorthodox, illegal, unruly, and unprecedented.

At the core of Bingham's argument was a simple but powerful claim based on constitutional text and structure as applied to the recent unpleasantness. Though secession had been wholly unconstitutional, southern secessionists had in fact "succeeded in overturning their own local constitutional State governments."[8] Proper republican governments had yet to be reestablished in the ex-gray states (except Tennessee). Until that reestablishment, which would require the approval of Congress, the southern "states" were not proper "states" within the meaning of the federal Constitution: "By the express terms of the Constitution, ... there can be no constitutional States in this Union, save States duly admitted, obedient to the Constitution and laws of the United States, whose governments are republican, and all the legislative, executive, and judicial officers of which are bound by an oath to support the Constitution of the United States. Thus, sir, it is written."[9]

With these words, Bingham wrapped himself in the cloak of constitutional fidelity to the old order, rightly understood, even as he was proposing something that his critics saw as a radical rupture. Bingham invoked the words "Constitution" and "constitutional" four times in a single sentence, and reminded his audience that he was appealing to the "express terms" of the document: "Thus, sir, it is written." In his key sentence, he wove together references to three of the written document's seven articles. Proper states, he explained, are only those states "duly admitted" under Article VII (as original states) or Article IV (as new states); proper states obey the supremacy clause (Article VI) and the supremacy oath (ditto); proper states are states with republican forms of government (another provision of Article IV).

Elsewhere in his speech, Bingham invoked all the document's other articles and elegantly threaded them into his constitutional tapestry. Under Article I, the ex-gray states did not need to be—and in fact were not at that very moment being—seated: "There can be no representative body of the people of the United States in Congress save through organized State governments and elections therein held. There can be no senatorial body of the legislative power of this nation save by the direct legislative assemblies of organized States."[10] If ex-grays could be—and had been and were being—properly excluded from the House and the Senate under Article I, why shouldn't these same states properly be excluded from the numerator and denominator of Article V? In Bingham's words, "A Congress that can lawfully legislate can lawfully propose amendments and States that can lawfully elect to Congress can lawfully ratify amendments to the Constitution of the United States."[11] Here was a powerful legal point appealing to both constitutional logic and current practice.[12]

Ditto for Article II. In Bingham's words: "There can be no election of a Chief Magistrate of the United States save through electors appointed in such manner as the Legislature of the respective States may direct."[13] As Bingham knew—and as he knew his audience knew—although some ex-gray states had purported to participate in the presidential election of 1864, all these states had been pointedly excluded from the numerator and the denominator of the Article II electoral vote when Congress officially tallied the electoral votes.[14] Here, then, was another powerful legal point about logic and practice: Why should the rules for Article V's numerator and denominator in 1867 be any different from the rules for Article II's numerator and denominator in 1865?

Thus, Bingham drove to his two-pronged bottom line regarding Article V. First, Congress could exclude—and in fact Congress had already excluded—ex-gray states from the process of proposing the Fourteenth Amendment: "[T]his Congress had full power, without the consent and against the consent of every insurrectionary State in this land, to propose the pending amendment to the Constitution to all the organized States of this Union for recognition."[15] Second, what was true of Article V proposal—and of Article I and Article II, for that matter—was equally true of Article V ratification: "[T]hose insurrectionary States have no power whatever as States of this Union, and cannot lawfully restrain for a single moment that great body of freemen who cover this continent from ocean to ocean, now organized States of the Union and represented here, in their fixed purpose and undoubted legal right to incorporate the amendment into the Constitution of the United States."[16] Thus, "if three fourths of the organized and represented States put this amendment into the Constitution of the United States, it will bind the insurgent States and give them the benefits of it as well."[17]

In just a handful of sentences, then, Bingham managed to canvas and connect, with powerful legal logic, Articles I, II, IV, V, VI, and VII. And lest anyone think he overlooked it, he elsewhere explained how his core idea—that unrepublican ex-gray states were not proper "states" within the meaning of the Constitution—drew strength from, and applied to, the Constitution's final remaining article (Article III).[18] More generally, his entire speech was prefaced, as the written Constitution itself was prefaced (in the Preamble), with a poetic ode to the sovereignty of the People of the United States: "[T]he American nationality as a political organization never existed, but by means of organized State governments[.] Your Constitution begins to be through that instrumentality." In other words, We, the people ordained and established the Constitution via acts of proper conventions organized by proper republican state governments.

For Bingham, American popular sovereignty, Preamble-style, was no small point but the essence of the thing, for if the American people had a sovereign right to ordain and establish, they had an equal sovereign right to alter or abolish *at any time*. To allow secessionist conspirators to obstruct or delay the amendment process would be precisely contrary to this elemental sovereign right—and contrary to the basic war aim of preserving popular sovereignty, including the transcendent right of the popular sovereign to make fundamental alterations at any time as needed.[19] Thus, when Bingham early on apotheosized "guarantees embedded in the Constitution by the sovereign act of the people,"[20] he was referring not to the Founding document or even the long-established Bill of Rights, but rather to the pending Fourteenth Amendment. Near the close of this speech, he returned to this theme, once again claiming for himself the rightful mantle of constitutional fidelity. Despite the seemingly radical nature of his approach, he and not any of his conservative critics was the faithful son of George Washington: "I do not forget, sir, the words of Washington, transmitted to us. When about to surrender his public trusts he declared 'the basis of our political system is the "right of the people to make and alter their constitutions of government.""[21]

In addition to his textual and structural constitutional *tour de force* and *tour d'horizon*, Bingham brilliantly invoked a series of nonjudicial precedents and analogies. True, nothing like the massive secession and continental Civil War of the early 1860s had ever happened before under the

Founders' Constitution. In this sense, Bingham understood that he and his colleagues were sailing into uncharted waters as they tried to improvise a sensible constitutional response to what was a singularly unprecedented event in its magnitude and meaning. But good transitional lawyers look for and often find plausible precedents and analogies—familiar if dim stars to steer by and barely glimpsed landmarks on the distant horizon that might guide the journey ahead.

Even though the ex-Confederacy (Tennessee excepted) lacked proper republican state governments, Bingham insisted—as had Lincoln and his party throughout the war itself—that the South was surely still part of an indivisible American Union. The Constitution, after all, was the law of *the land,* and the land had never left: sharply taking issue with the extremist "conquered province" theory being floated by true radicals such as Thaddeus Stevens, Bingham—reaching back in time to maintain proper continuity with the prior legal order in classic transitional fashion—insisted that at no moment had "any rood [a Scottish land measure—roughly a quarter-acre] of the Republic [become] dissevered from the rest and made foreign territory."[22]

But if South Carolina (for example) was not a proper state in January 1867, exactly what was she and how should she be treated? Here, Bingham's intuitive analogic skills as an accomplished lawyer shone through. South Carolina was, he said, rather like Washington, D.C.—which had no seats in the House or the Senate or the electoral college and which did not participate in the Article V amendment process, but was surely part of the American constitutional system. Hence Congress could legislate directly over South Carolina until proper republican government was restored there—just as Congress could legislate directly over the District: "[F]rom the day treason did its work in South Carolina to this hour, the legislative power of the United States was as exclusive within the State of South Carolina as it is this moment within the District of Columbia."[23]

Precisely because both South Carolina and the District of Columbia were part of "the land" under the supremacy clause, Bingham expressed lawyerly outrage—here, the outrage of a *conservative* transitionist—in response to the efforts of Stevens and other radicals to "decitizenize" southern Americans and deprive them of their various rights. "[T]he Congress of the United States has no color of authority for providing by law . . . that a million persons, natural-born male citizens of this Republic and resident therein, are no longer citizens of the United States."[24] Stevens's approach, like "the utterance of an unlimited and crowned dictator," would

mean that "a million men in this land shall not peaceably assemble and petition this Government."[25]

Another Bingham analogy: South Carolina was akin to a western territory. Akin, but not identical, because Congress had not officially terri-
torialized the South, and if it were to do so, then presumably Congress
could redraw traditional state boundaries at will. Although Bingham believed that as a constitutional matter Congress could indeed choose to go
that far, he explained (again, in the voice of a conservative transitionist)
that official territorialization would be unwise because it would go further
than necessary to solve the problem at hand, namely, reestablishing proper
republican government in South Carolina and each of the other lapsed
states. "I recognize our authority to reduce those States to Territories; but
you have not so reduced them, neither is it made to appear that it is necessary so to partition and dismember them."[26]

Another element of Bingham's moderation: While he believed that the
ex-gray states could be excluded altogether from the Article V ratification
process, he also favored inducing ratification by these regimes. Through
this ratification, ex-gray states could evidence their good faith and genuine
republicanism, thereby giving Congress important assurances as it decided
when and how to readmit them as states in good standing.[27]

But how would this odd transition work? If South Carolina was not a
proper state, how could it "ratify" the pending Fourteenth Amendment
and have that ratification count under Article V? Just like a territory, Bingham, the transitional lawyer-analogist, argued. Prior to winning admission
as formal states, territories had sometimes elected would-be U.S. senators
and territorial voters had sometimes elected would-be congressional representatives. When past Congresses had decided to admit such territories
as new states under Article IV, Congress had typically agreed to seat the
previously picked senators and representatives under Article I. In effect,
via the process of admitting a new state, Congress had retroactively (*nunc
pro tunc*, as lawyers might say) conferred true-state status on the previous
territorial action. What had already worked for Article I and Article IV,
Bingham argued, could equally work for Article V.[28]

Yet another Bingham analogy: a kind of secession had in fact occurred
at the very moment of the Constitution's Founding, with eleven of the
original independent thirteen states ratifying the Constitution in 1787–
1788 and the remaining two states declining to do so. Yet, as Bingham the
lawyer-analogist cleverly noted, these two regimes, North Carolina and
Rhode Island, had in effect been allowed to ratify the Constitution and re-

join the Union in 1789 and 1790, respectively, even though at the moments of their ratification, they had not been proper states within the constitutional Union.[29] What had worked shortly after the Revolutionary War, Bingham argued, could work again after the Civil War.

In some ways, then, South Carolina in 1867 was analogous (though admittedly not identical) to North Carolina in 1789. In some ways it was analogous (though, again not exactly identical) to the Kansas Territory in the 1850s, when it had been up to Congress to decide whether Kansas's territorial elections were indeed fair and square enough to warrant Kansas's admission as a proper republican-government state. One other suggestive analogy provided still further support for Bingham's approach. In thinking about the southern Civil War of the 1860s, good transitional lawyers like Bingham found useful guidance not only in the western Civil War of the 1850s (also known as Bleeding Kansas) but also in the eastern Civil War of the 1840s—also known as Dorr's Rebellion.

In that rebellion, two rival regimes had each claimed to be the lawful government of Rhode Island, and a military struggle had ensued. In 1849, the Supreme Court, in the case of *Luther v. Borden,* had declined to decide for itself which of the two camps deserved federal recognition as the state's proper republican government. That issue, opined Chief Justice Taney for the court, was a "political question" that Congress should decide by determining which camp's leaders to seat in the House and Senate: "For as the United States guarantee to each State a republican government, Congress must necessarily decide what government is established in the State before it can determine whether it is republican or not. And when the senators and representatives of a State are admitted into the councils of the Union, the authority of the government under which they are appointed, as well as its republican character, is recognized by the proper constitutional authority. And its decision is binding on every other department of the government."[30]

As had Sumner and others before him, Bingham in his speech of January 16, 1867, took the *Luther* case and ran with it: "Whether a State of this Union has levied war against the United States or has a republican constitutional State government, or is entitled to representation in Congress, . . . or can rightfully exercise any of the powers of an organized State of the Union, are political not judicial questions, and can be decided only by the political department"—namely, Congress.[31] "Even the Supreme Court has always affirmed this. That tribunal so affirmed in *Luther vs. Borden.*"[32]

Although some have quibbled that the Supreme Court had not quite said all that—or at least had not quite said all that in as clear a fashion as Bingham contended[33]—*Luther* was an undeniably big gun in Bingham's argumentative arsenal. Thus, not only did Bingham have on his side the explicit text of Article I making each house the proper "judge" of "elections" to that house; not only could he forcefully invoke the actual practice of each house, which had indeed wielded this election-judging power to exclude the ex-gray states seeking admission in December 1865; but he could also invoke the authority of the Supreme Court itself for the proposition that Article I and Article IV interlocked just as he claimed: It was up to Congress, via its Article I election-judging and seating authority, to decide whether a putative state was indeed in compliance with the Republican Government Clause of Article IV.

Bingham and his audience surely relished the irony: Here was a leading representative of the antislavery party that had come to national power by attacking the pro-slavery Roger Taney—here, indeed, was the author of a proposed amendment whose first sentence openly repudiated Taney's most notable decision *(Dred Scott)*—advocating an extraordinarily aggressive procedure to win ratification of that proposed amendment by invoking as his ultimate judicial authority . . . Roger Taney!

And if that weren't delicious enough, Bingham also grabbed hold of Taney to swat away suggestions that the current Supreme Court might at some future time challenge the validity of any amendment that had been adopted by only true-blue states, with the ex-gray states (Tennessee excepted) simply excluded from both the numerator and denominator of the Article V tally. "It is not a judicial question; it is a political question in the decision of which the Supreme Court can in nowise interfere."[34] As far as Bingham was concerned, the basic logic of America's constitutional structure sufficed to establish his point. Yet he buttressed his structural reasoning by explicitly invoking the "political question" phraseology and philosophy of the very Supreme Court whose irrelevance he sought to underscore. Better still, this concession that the court should defer to Congress on the question of state status had arisen in an analogous context (of a civil war, albeit a localized one), had been framed in suggestively universal terms, and had emerged from the most prominent jurist from the other side of the political aisle, a man whom none of Bingham's enemies could ever dismiss as a Republican Party stooge.

And then Bingham added one final turn of the screw—in which a glint of iron may be seen peeking out from behind the velvet glove of the classic transitional lawyer. If a future court ever gave Congress grounds for thinking that the justices might indeed try to invalidate the Fourteenth Amendment on procedural grounds, Congress should respond by stripping the court of all appellate jurisdiction: "If, therefore, gentlemen are at all apprehensive of any wrongful intervention of the Supreme Court in this behalf, sweep away at once their appellate jurisdiction in all cases, and leave the tribunal without even color or appearance of authority for their wrongful intervention."[35] This was a truly drastic proposal, but by describing it as actually faithful to the court's own holding in *Luther*, Bingham managed to make his most extreme suggestion appear a little kinder and gentler. After all, given that the court itself had previously foresworn interference on issues such as the present one, what was the harm in holding the court to its word?[36]

In this single speech by Bingham, we see on display a remarkable array of legal and political tropes, tools, and techniques, as one notable transitional lawyer sought to impose legal order on the chaos swirling around him. Bingham used generally conservative legal techniques to advocate a policy that was anything but conservative. Yet Bingham's method and his bottom line were far more lawyerly and far more continuous with the legal past than extremist alternatives, such as Stevens's "conquered provinces" theory, that were also in the air as Americans debated just how much of the old order to carry forward into the uncertain future.

III. Reconstruction as Reinterpretation: Republicans Redefining Republicanism

One final set of issues deserves attention: the amendment process in the mid-1860s pivoted a remarkable reinterpretation of an old Founding text. In this reinterpretation, we see another aspect of classic transition, as Congress clearly innovated yet did so within the broad outlines of a preexisting constitutional framework. Before turning directly to this old text—the Republican Government Clause of Article IV, the Constitution's "sleeping giant" that Sumner and Bingham awakened and rode—let's consider with more precision how Congress ultimately induced the ex-gray states back into their proper relation to the Union.

In the First Reconstruction Act, Congress outlined what the ex-gray states should do to regain admission to Congress.[37] The act, which became law on March 2, 1867, applied to the entire ex-Confederacy except Tennessee, which had been welcomed back to Congress in July 1866, immediately after having voted to ratify Congress's proposed Fourteenth Amendment—the only ex-gray state to say yes to the amendment prior to 1868.

Three closely related congressional instructions formed the foundation of the First Reconstruction Act. First, each ex-gray state should adopt a new state constitution via an electoral process enfranchising virtually all adult male residents, regardless of race.[38] Second, each new state constitution should guarantee a right to vote in ordinary elections to this same broad swath of adult male residents. Third, the new governments elected under the new state constitutions should ratify the Fourteenth Amendment, which Congress had proposed in June 1866, and which had already been ratified by three-fourths of the loyal states, plus Tennessee.

How should we understand the legal status of this intriguing transition statute? To the strict constitutional textualist, the First Reconstruction Act lies entirely outside the written Constitution. Yet surely the act was a critical part of the very process by which the Fourteenth Amendment was eventually adopted. Without this landmark statute, it is doubtful that ex-gray states would have practiced and promised universal male suffrage; and without this broad suffrage base, it is doubtful that these states would have ever agreed to ratify the Fourteenth Amendment (or, for that matter, the later Fifteenth Amendment guaranteeing race-blind suffrage in every state). Even more obviously, the First Reconstruction Act plainly directed ex-gray states to ratify the Fourteenth Amendment with all deliberate speed. Properly understood, the statute was thus part of the public meaning of that amendment as an embodied enactment.

From this perspective, Americans in the 1860s should be understood as having given birth to a new constitutional principle, albeit one that did not explicitly appear in the Fourteenth Amendment's text. Under this new unwritten principle, the federal government would properly enjoy sweeping authority to hold state governments to the highest contemporary standards of democratic inclusiveness.

While this is not the only possible interpretation of the Fourteenth Amendment enactment process, it is more explanatory than alternative accounts, which are on one side unduly complacent and on the other utterly crazy.

Under a too-complacent view, the Fourteenth Amendment's enactment created no new constitutional norm because the Founders themselves had already provided the federal government with authority to hold states to proper democratic standards. Article I, section 5, allowed each house of

Congress to judge elections to its house, and Article IV instructed the federal government to "guarantee to every State in this Union a Republican Form of Government." Together, these clauses empowered Congress to refuse to seat any representative or senator if Congress deemed the underlying election constitutionally inadequate under correct principles of republican government.

True enough, but many Framers would have been startled to learn that Congress could use these clauses to require states to enfranchise blacks—indeed, illiterate, unpropertied ex-slaves, at that! State franchise law, as defined by state constitutions and traditional state practice, underpinned the federal system as originally designed. Thus, Congress would not rest on a nationally defined suffrage base, but would simply piggyback on state suffrage law. The federal House of Representatives would be chosen by those persons in each state who were eligible under state law to vote for state assemblies. Likewise, the United States Senate would be chosen by state legislatures who ultimately derived their powers from voting rules established by state law.

At the Founding, the Article IV Republican Government Clause was widely viewed as reinforcing this state-law bedrock, not undermining it: the federal government would simply guarantee existing state constitutional practices against the possibility of unrepublican amendment or violent overthrow—as might happen, for example, if a governor's minions revised the state constitution to create a hereditary dictatorship, or if a state military cabal wrested control from duly elected civilian authorities. On this narrow non-retrogression view of Article IV, a state could be prevented from backsliding whenever agitators tried to transform an existing republican regime into an unrepublican one, but no state would be obliged to make any great democratic leaps forward. So long as states faithfully followed the basic structural practices in place in 1787, the federal government would not interfere.

In the 1780s and in every decade thereafter, a significant number of states had denied free blacks the vote. Many Founding-era states also had property requirements for voting. Before the Civil War some states began to experiment with franchise-restricting literacy tests. By what right, asked President Andrew Johnson and his conservative allies in the mid-1860s, did the Reconstruction Congress claim authority to impose on the ex-gray states an utterly novel federal requirement of race-blind universal male suffrage? Would the state ratifying conventions in 1787–1788—especially in the South—have agreed to the federal Constitution had ratifiers clearly understood that Congress could radically redefine the most basic and jealously protected political structures of state constitutions?

Honest answers to these questions require us to admit that the enactment of the Fourteenth Amendment pivoted on a novel interpretation of the Republican Government Clause, an interpretation that had not been firmly established by the Founding Fathers. The too-complacent view misses the key fact that a new principle of broad national control over undemocratic state franchise law was born as part of the Fourteenth Amendment's enactment process.

Enter the crazies, who claim that because the Fourteenth Amendment was ratified by dint of a congressional statute that went beyond the Constitution as understood by the Framers, the amendment was never properly adopted. The supposed Fourteenth Amendment is therefore a nullity![39]

To be clear: no justice on the current court takes this position. Nor has any justice in history ever publicly written anything of the sort in *United States Reports.* Nor has any president proclaimed this view, if we put aside the curious case of Andrew Johnson, who said all manner of things while the amendment was pending, but ultimately allowed his own secretary of state to proclaim the amendment validly enacted. Nor does any mainstream constitutional scholar today deny the Fourteenth Amendment's legal validity.

This universal consensus reigns for a reason. Without this consensus, the project of American constitutionalism as we know it might well self-destruct. That project revolves around a canonical text—the written Constitution—that all (non-crazy) citizens and public servants acknowledge as the official supreme law of the land. Though interpreters may sharply disagree about the document's meaning, all point to the same basic text, which provides firm common ground for constitutional conversation and contestation. This text—with countless millions of copies in circulation, all of which include the words of the Fourteenth Amendment—is the national focal point, the common denominator for all constitutionalists, whether Democrat or Republican, liberal or conservative, private citizen or public servant.

Granted, some small imprecision at the outer edges of the text would not doom the project of written constitutionalism. But the Fourteenth Amendment stands at the very center of the Constitution, both textually and functionally. In 1955, Justice Felix Frankfurter remarked that "claims under the Fourteenth Amendment" were "probably the largest source of the Court's business."[40] Since then the practical significance of the amendment has only grown—indeed, skyrocketed. The amendment was the vehicle by which the post-1955 Supreme Court eventually (and correctly) came to apply virtually all the provisions of the original Bill of Rights against state and local governments. Today the lion's share of "Bill of Rights" cases litigated in courts are, strictly speaking, Fourteenth Amendment cases. The Fourteenth Amendment was also the truest source of congressional power to adopt sweeping civil rights laws in the late twentieth century, laws that changed the course of world history.

Long before the Warren Court revolution and the Second Reconstruction of the 1960s, the validity of the Fourteenth Amendment was definitively established. All three branches of the federal government pledged allegiance to the Fourteenth Amendment in the late 1860s and early 1870s, as did the citizenry and state governments at the time. Ever since, the amendment's legality has been a basic premise of the American constitutional system. For example, the federal income tax amendment was explicitly proposed by Congress and ratified by state legislatures as "Article XVI" of the amendments, plainly indicating that "Article XIV" and "Article XV"—the Fourteenth and Fifteenth Amendments—were already valid parts of the Constitution. Not even crazies can claim that the Sixteenth Amendment, adopted in 1913, was itself procedurally infirm on the theory that its enactment process was also somehow tainted by the First Reconstruction Act of 1867. (The Reconstruction Act's endorsement of universal male suffrage in the South had lapsed well before the turn of the twentieth century, and much of the Fifteenth Amendment's promise of race-neutral suffrage also lay dormant in the early twentieth century.)

To see the point yet another way, recall that the Civil Rights Act and Voting Rights Act of the 1960s were themselves notable efforts to enforce the Fourteenth and Fifteenth Amendments. Without the epic changes wrought by these laws, Americans in 2008 would never have elected Barack Obama president. If these amendments are truly invalid, then presumably the Second Reconstruction of the late twentieth century was likewise invalid and the results of that Reconstruction are also illegitimate. On this view, the very status of Barack Obama as president would be constitutionally dubious.

Only crazy people think this way.

The crazies fail to understand how the Reconstruction generation faithfully interpreted the Founders' project, even as Reconstructors went beyond various specific expectations that were widespread in the late 1780s. True, the First Reconstruction Act did supplement the Founders' rules.

But it did not supplant them. Rather, it interpreted and extended them in the unique context of a Civil War that, constitutionally, should never have happened because the original Constitution emphatically denied states authority to unilaterally secede. To the extent that Reconstructors stretched the text of various Founding-era clauses, Reconstructors did so in order to make the best sense of—and ultimately to preserve—the document as a whole.

Whatever various Framers may have expected or predicted, the *text* of the Republican Government Clause did not unambiguously limit the federal role to merely policing against state retrogression. Even if it had, the southern states had indeed regressed in obvious ways between 1789 and 1866.

In 1789, antislavery speech was broadly allowed, whereas in the late antebellum period it was officially outlawed and/or suppressed by massive extralegal violence in much of the South, where the Republican Party had in effect been criminalized in the 1850s. To repeat: in 1860 Lincoln received not a single popular vote—not one!—south of Virginia. One does not find such perfectly one-sided election returns or such savagely skewed public debates in true republics. Prior to the Founding, no large set of colonial or state officials had ever taken up arms to assail a freely elected government. In the years just before Reconstruction, a vast conspiracy of southern officials had done just that in arrogant defiance of the free-election essence of republican government. In 1789 southern states did not lag miles behind most northern states in the percentage of free males eligible to vote. By 1866 a yawning chasm had abruptly opened up between the ex-gray states and most true-blue states. In many a northern state, the law circa 1866 barred only a tiny proportion of free adult males—often less than 3 percent—from voting. In the ex-Confederacy before the First Reconstruction Act, comparable disenfranchisement rates ranged from about 25 percent to over 50 percent—roughly ten to twenty times the typical northern rate.

Thus, even though the ex-gray states claimed that they were simply perpetuating suffrage rules of long standing—in many places, free blacks had never been allowed to vote—the perpetuation of these old voting rules in the late 1860s threatened to create a wholly new and qualitatively different sort of disfranchisement. Free blacks accounted for a minuscule proportion of the total free population of most southern states prior to 1860. But once slaves won emancipation thanks to Lincoln's proclamation and the subsequent Thirteenth Amendment, free blacks mushroomed almost overnight to become a vastly larger segment—a significantly greater proportion of free folk than had ever been excluded from the franchise in the antebellum era.[41]

Though it cannot be said that the Founders' Republican Government Clause clearly required that these new freemen be enfranchised, neither can it be said that the clause clearly blessed the *unprecedented* disfranchisement of a *vast* number of *free* men. The written text did not clearly specify what should happen in this unanticipated scenario, and the unwritten non-retrogression principle could also be interpreted either way. Contrary to the too-complacent view, the First Reconstruction Act represented a new principle that was not clearly established in 1789; but contrary to the crazy view, the act reflected a plausible application of Founding texts and principles to a situation that the Founders had simply failed to address with specificity.

Three special factors added further support to the constitutional propriety of the Reconstruction Act. First, the nation needed strong medicine to ensure that recently rebellious states would never again commit the ultimate act of unrepublicanism by waging war on a freely elected regime. Even if universal male suffrage was not an *intrinsic element* of republican government, it was an *appropriate instrument* of republican government and thus good enough for government work, under *McCulloch v. Maryland.* Just as a continental bank, though not intrinsically necessary for a continental army, was nevertheless quite useful to support such an army, so black suffrage in the South would be quite useful to buttress the wholly proper republican-government project of ensuring due southern respect for the results of free elections. With blacks voting in the South, a second unilateral secession movement would be highly unlikely to prevail in any foreseeable state election.

Second, beyond the issue of enfranchisement, the Reconstruction Act's additional directive that ex-gray states ratify the Fourteenth Amendment was also an appropriate instrument to further the republican government ideal. Key parts of the amendment required every state to honor concrete elements of a proper republican government, such as equal citizenship, free speech, free assembly, free religious exercise, and fair trials. Although in 1789 these concrete elements were perhaps not universally understood as necessary components of republican government, neither were they universally understood as wholly beyond the proper meaning of republicanism. Here, too, Reconstructors did not violate Founding principles even as they went beyond them, clarifying what the original text and late-eighteenth-century history had left unclear. The Founders' question mark properly gave way to the Reconstructors' exclamation point.

Third, Congress adopted the Reconstruction Act only after three-quarters of the true-blue states had already ratified the amendment—enough to make the amendment fully valid had Congress followed Bingham's advice and chosen simply to exclude ex-gray states from the Article V amendment tally. Although the Reconstruction Congress ultimately opted to include ex-gray states in the amendment process, Congress need not have done so, as Bingham and Sumner had carefully explained. Read holistically, the Constitution envisioned a federal union of republican states, and states without proper republican governments could not justly complain if they were simply excluded from the Article V state count and instead treated as de facto federal territories pending reestablishment of proper republican governments.

As previously noted, Congress ultimately did not go this far. Instead, Congress improvised a two-stage strategy that relied heavily on the verdict of true-blue states in the first stage of enactment, but then gave ex-gray states an important role during the final stage of enactment. The pivot in this two-stage enactment process was the First Reconstruction Act, an act that was adopted only after a deep and wide democratic consensus had been reached in the only states where true republicanism—with free speech, broad electorates, and fair elections—had generally prevailed in the preceding decade.[42] Via the First Reconstruction Act—an extraordinary exemplar of transitional law—Congress ingeniously used the constitutional amendment process itself both as a good test of the South's genuine commitment to republican government and as a good vehicle for restoring truly republican southern states to their proper status as constitutional entities in good standing.

IV. Some Concluding Thoughts about Form and Reform

What explains the size and shape of the momentous transition of the 1860s? We conclude with a few general observations prompted by this case study.

First, American presidents are change agents and constitutional catalysts.[43] The pivotal decade of the 1860s started with a bang when Abraham Lincoln was elected as the first openly antislavery president in American history, winning in spite of an electoral college system that had been designed in 1787–1788 and redesigned in 1803–1804 to give the slaveholding South the inside track.

The Constitution's general design highlights the president's capacity to catalyze large-scale reform. Of the four leading institutions of federal power—the House, the Senate, the presidency, and the Supreme Court—only the House and the presidency turn over all at once, a design feature that conduces to large policy shifts in a small time span. And unlike the hydra-headed House, composed of many minds perhaps tugging in opposite directions, the presidency is vested in one person who presumably knows his own mind and can act quickly.[44] While Article II offers remarkably few specifics about the president's actual job description, it does draw explicit attention to the president's capacity to embody and define a reform agenda: "He shall from time to time give to the Congress Information on the State of the Union, *and recommend to their Consideration such Measures as he shall judge necessary and expedient.*" Although Lincoln himself played no formal role in the drafting or ratification of the momentous Thirteenth Amendment,[45] this extraordinary triumph of abolition surely could not have come about without President Lincoln's antislavery proposals and proclamations.

In this respect, Lincoln was hardly unique. Several of America's most momentous transitions were portended and/or precipitated by the elections of "realigning" presidents, presidents whose ascensions marked the arrival of a distinctively new dominant national political coalition. Jefferson, Jackson, Lincoln, FDR, and Reagan may all be seen in this light, as their elections embodied and/or prefigured the "Revolution of 1800," the "Age of Jackson," the "Reconstruction," the "New Deal," and the "Reagan Revolution," respectively.

But if presidents are by personal temperament and/or by structural design often change agents, many presidents have left office as *failed* change agents, whose grand visions of a new order have ultimately been mocked by the gods.[46] Lincoln himself might well have ended up as a failed one-term president—one of many, post-Jackson—had his opponents simply held their noses, held their fire, waited four years, and politically regrouped in 1864 to send him packing. After all, Lincoln's party did not win decisive control of either the House or the Senate in the 1860 election; over 60 percent of the electorate had actually voted against Lincoln; and the Supreme Court was firmly in the grip of slavocrats. (We should remember that it was none other than Roger Taney, Lincoln's nemesis, who swore him in.)

Of course, Lincoln's anti-republican opponents did not simply hold their noses and hold their fire. Rather, despicable anti-republican extremists—and here we mean not merely anti-GOP, but "anti-republican" in the deepest sense; we could just as easily describe these despicable extremists as "anti-democratic" or "anti-Constitutionalist"—took up arms against a duly elected government. In this sense, the 1860s "started with a bang" less because northern voters elected Abe Lincoln and more because southern traitors assaulted Fort Sumter.

Which brings us to our second general observation: wars and regime failures or near-failures can precipitate massive reform and realignment. Wars often create or accelerate large-scale economic, technological, social, cultural, and demographic changes, which in turn reshuffle political patterns and invite large legal reforms.

In a Westphalian world of nation-states, constitutional law and other domestic law typically track national boundaries that are in turn shaped by the shadow of war. Anyone who doubts this should remember the Alamo—or remember Canada for that matter. In many ways, today's Californians are culturally closer to today's Canadians than to today's Alabamians. But in places such as Vietnam, Iraq, and Afghanistan, Americans from every state have been siblings in arms; and the Canadians have not always been at their side. Indeed, Americans fought against Canadians in the French-and-Indian War, the Revolutionary War, and the War of 1812—and might have done so yet again had America actually decided to "fight" when it got less than its desired "Fifty-four Forty" in the mid-nineteenth century.

If Constitutions are war machines of sorts—legal systems that must be able to defend borders against other legal systems, or risk extinction—then it is no surprise that some of the biggest transitions in the American system have closely tracked American wars. The Constitution itself came to life because America had almost lost the Revolutionary War and was at risk of losing the next one, whenever and however that next war might arise. When the Founders' system was almost destroyed by another devastating war on American soil in the 1860s, it is not surprising that this near-failure precipitated a major legal overhaul—a Second Founding.

Though America's wars have often threatened liberty, they have also often expanded equality. Unpropertied men who were typically ineligible to vote in the colonies before 1776 won voting rights in many post-Independence states because as soldiers and militiamen these Americans had fought for the patriot cause. In a word, they were loyal. In the 1860s blacks won first freedom and then civil equality and eventually political equality because they too had been loyal to, and had fought for, the Union. Black men got the right to vote long before white women in part because blacks had earned their rights on the battlefield of glory. A half century later, American women secured a federal suffrage amendment during and partly because of World War I. America's professed war aim was to "end all wars"—which in turn meant that once the fighting ended, there would need to emerge a proper antiwar League of Nations, in which America would need to take a leading antiwar role. But America could not play this intended role unless America had moral credibility in the eyes of the world, and this ultimate war aim—American world moral leadership—required American woman suffrage. Or so President Woodrow Wilson explicitly argued in September 1918, when he officially recommended (in keeping with Article II) that Congress fashion a Woman Suffrage Amendment as, in his words, "a vitally necessary war measure." Even more recently, the ending of Jim Crow was linked to an American Cold War effort to win hearts and minds in Africa and Asia, and the voting age was constitutionally lowered because any American old enough to fight in Vietnam was also old enough, it was agreed, to vote on whether America should even be in that war.

A third general observation prompted by the great transition of the 1860s is that one good turn often begets another. What in retrospect might seem one great leap forward actually comes about by a series of discrete legal/political steps, sometimes not quite linear. As mentioned earlier, the Republicans' war aims evolved in response to changing conditions, and various limited reforms early on often led to further reforms, not all of which were envisioned from the start.

Thus, Lincoln's Emancipation Proclamation led to massive black enlistment in the Union army, which helped the Union achieve decisive military victories, which in turn helped Lincoln and his party win by a landslide in 1864. That electoral landslide led directly to the Thirteenth Amendment. But that amendment, in turn, boomeranged far harder and faster than most had anticipated. As three-fifths became five-fifths, it became increasingly clear that the southern master class might end up with even more seats in Congress—and that dawning recognition ultimately inspired black suffrage. But black suffrage could not politically be achieved in one jump—the political chasm between here and there was simply too wide in 1866. The ultimate reform was thus accomplished in two neat crab steps. First, the Reconstruction Act required that all ex-gray states[47] enfranchise blacks. And then, once that goal had been won, southern black voters and southern congressmen who had to answer to southern black voters helped push through Congress a black suffrage amendment—an amendment that probably could have never passed so long as Congress answered to a virtually all-white electorate, as had been the case from the Founding until 1868.

Fourth and finally, we note that revolutions ultimately end and that resistance to them should not be underestimated. Though the constitutional changes promised in the 1860s were far larger than occurred in just about any other decade of American history, many of these constitutional promises were not fulfilled fully, immediately, and enduringly. On the contrary, much of what was promised only materialized long afterward—in some cases, more than four score and seven years later.

The worst features of American slavery were indeed abolished in the 1860s, but large-scale peonage systems lingered for decades, and a widespread system of sexual slavery still stains our land—though this system lacks some of the intergenerational and racial atrociousness of its antebellum precursors. Most provisions of the Bill of Rights did not reliably come to be protected by the federal government against states until the mid-twentieth century. Sweeping congressional power to enforce civil rights was not recognized by the federal judiciary until the Warren Court era (and even today's court seems willing to cavil at certain congressional civil rights laws—a practice with a disgraceful history of which many of today's justices seem unaware). Genuine black civil equality did not enduringly come to pass before the landmark cases and statutes of the mid-twentieth century. Full black equality in voting, jury service, and office-holding likewise was not achieved until long after all this was promised by the Fifteenth Amendment. From one perspective, this promise was not completely redeemed until 2009, when another constitutional lawyer from Illinois—this time a biracial American—took the presidential oath of office.

Here, too, the general point radiates beyond the case study of the 1860s. For example, the First Amendment promised that Congress would make no law abridging the freedom of speech. Yet less than a decade after this promise was made, Congress broke it, in the Sedition Act of 1798, and federal courts cheerfully enforced that perfidious law. Even in the early twentieth century—more than a century after the adoption of the First Amendment—the Supreme Court continued to enforce federal sedition laws that violated that amendment's central meaning.

The old order dies hard, whether that order be a thin-skinned officialdom that tries to stifle antigovernmental criticism, or a racially oppressive oligarchy that tries to deny civil liberty and birthright equality. Epic changes often take much longer than promised. Still, the ability to inscribe a promise—even a radical one, one that may not be fully realizable any time soon—in a written Constitution can create a long-term dynamic in which the arc of history is more apt to bend toward justice. Even during decades when they lie unenforced, the words of a written Constitution remain written—patiently waiting to be dusted off and redeemed when redemption becomes possible, and in the meantime quietly subverting the corrupt legal order that tries to pretend that these bold words do not exist and that these grand promises were never made.

Notes

1. Of course, the concept of "extra" seats presupposes a baseline. From a contrasting point of view, slave states did not get *extra* seats because of their slaves but instead received *fewer* seats because slaves counted for less than did free persons—three-fifths rather than five-fifths. For a detailed discussion and defense of the baseline implied by the word "extra," see Akhil Reed Amar, *America's Constitution: A Biography* (New York: Random House, 2005), 91–95. In a nutshell:

> The basic argument for [counting nonvoters in the apportionment process was that] voters could with a straight face claim to virtually represent the interests of the larger free population—their minor children; their mothers, daughters, wives, and sisters; their unpropertied adult sons and brothers; and so on. But masters did not as a rule claim to virtually represent the best interests of their slaves. Masters, after all, claimed the right to maim and sell slaves at will, and to doom their yet unborn posterity to perpetual bondage. . . . [If] Parliament could not plausibly claim to represent Americans, surely masters could not plausibly claim to represent slaves. If George III had no right to speak for Americans after he sought to deny them their "unalienable Rights" of "Life, Liberty, and the Pursuit of Happiness," to "reduce them under absolute Despotism," and to deprive them of jury trials and legal protection, surely slaveholders had no right to speak for their slaves.
>
> The candid 1787 argument for counting slaves was not that masters sincerely *represented* them but that masters, rightly or wrongly, *owned* them. They were property, and property, many openly argued, deserved representation alongside population. On this account, however, the interests to be represented were not the slaves', but the masters'. With this claim, Southerners decisively distinguished slaves from free dependents. . . .
>
> Though candid, the Southern property argument was neither neutral

nor democratic. As antislavery men repeated time and again at Philadelphia and throughout the ratification debates, Article I treated slavery as *preferred* property. Animal chattel didn't count, land didn't count, buildings didn't count, jewels didn't count, securities didn't count, specie didn't count—only slave property would count. . . . [C]ounting only slave property permanently skewed apportionments and spawned perverse incentives. Southern governments would be rewarded for promoting slaveholding vis-à-vis other forms of property acquisition. The extreme vice of such a system snaps into focus when we notice that in 1787 no *slave* state counted slaves as preferred property for state apportionment. Even South Carolina promised to count all "taxable property," not just slaves.

More generally, it is fair to ask why property should have been counted at all in the federal apportionment formula. Nowhere else did the federal Constitution concede so much political power to property per se. True, voters for the House had to meet modest state-law property thresholds in most places, but the man who owned fifty times the minimal property threshold would get exactly the same single vote as the man who barely cleared the bar. By contrast, the three-fifths clause gave a state extra credit for each new unit of slave property it could breed, buy, or steal. Among the states, only rotten South Carolina openly included property as an ingredient of lower-house apportionment. Under the Articles of Confederation, wealthy states faced higher requisitions, but were not thereby entitled to more votes in Congress.

2. For an argument that this "taking" was nevertheless not a "using" and thus properly lay beyond the scope of the Fifth Amendment just-compensation clause, see Jed Rubenfeld, "Usings," *Yale Law Journal* 102 (1993): 1077.

3. See David Brion Davis, *Challenging the Boundaries of Slavery* (Cambridge, MA: Harvard University Press, 2003), 76.

4. Woodrow Wilson had boyhood roots in the South, but ran for president as the former president of a northern university (Princeton) and the current governor of a northern state (New Jersey).

5. Here again, baseline issues arise, see note 1. The key point to understand is that, in the absence of a new amendment, southern white voters and southern white elected officials were due to gain political power thanks to disfranchised blacks in their midst even though the whites could not with straight faces claim to be fairly representing the interests of these blacks. For

more discussion and documentation, see Amar, *America's Constitution*, 605–607 n. 49.

6. See Bruce Ackerman, *We the People: Transformations* (Cambridge, MA: Belknap Press of Harvard University Press, 2000), 99–119, 207–234. But cf. John Harrison, "The Lawfulness of the Reconstruction Amendments," *University of Chicago Law Review* 68 (2001): 398; Amar, *America's Constitution*, 366–380.

7. Several leading commentators have either missed or mangled Bingham's general views and his January 16, 1867, remarks in particular. For one especially notable but slanted account, see Ackerman, *We the People: Transformations*, 195–197.

8. *Congressional Globe*, 39th Congress, 2nd Session (1867): 501.

9. Ibid., 502.

10. Ibid., 501.

11. Ibid., 502.

12. Some readers will recognize that here and elsewhere in his speech, Bingham used a form of constitutional argument that has come to be known as "intratextualism"—in which the meaning of words in one part of the Constitution can cast light on the meaning of these words elsewhere in the Constitution. See generally Akhil Reed Amar, "Intratextualism," *Harvard Law Review* 112 (1999): 747.

13. *Congressional Globe*, 39th Congress, 2nd Session (1867): 501.

14. Amar, *America's Constitution*, 378; Joint Resolution of February 8, 1865, 13 Statutes at Large 567. For some of the background behind this resolution, see, for example, *Congressional Globe*, 38th Congress, 2nd Session (February 2, 1865): 551–552 (quoting Lyman Trumbull), 584 (February 3, 1865) (quoting James Lane); 40th Congress, 2nd Session (February 4, 1868): 954–955 (quoting George Williams and Charles Buckalew).

15. *Congressional Globe*, 39th Congress, 2nd Session (1867): 501.

16. Ibid.

17. Ibid., 505.

18. Ibid., 504.

19. "[T]hose insurrectionary States have no power whatever as States of this Union, and cannot lawfully restrain *for a single moment* that great body of freemen who cover this continent from ocean to ocean, now organized States of the Union and represented here, in their fixed purpose and undoubted legal right to incorporate the amendment into the Constitution of the United States." Ibid., 501 (emphasis added).

20. Ibid., 501.

21. Ibid., 504.

22. Ibid., 502.

23. Ibid., 501.

24. Ibid., 503.

25. Ibid., 502.

26. Ibid., 504.

27. Although Ackerman seems to suggest that Bingham quickly recanted his true-blue-only approach to Article V, this suggestion is erroneous. Compare Ackerman, *We the People: Transformations*, 196 ("By February, he [Bingham] abandoned radical mathematics."), with *Congressional Globe* 40-1-64 (March 11, 1867) (quoting John Bingham) ("To my mind nothing is clearer than that the organized represented States of this Union are the Union; and twenty of those states [nineteen true-blue states plus Tennessee], being three-fourths of the whole number represented, having ratified the [Fourteenth] amendment to the Constitution proposed by the Thirty-Ninth Congress, that amendment has now become part of the fundamental law."). For a later statement by Bingham to the same effect, see *Congressional Globe* 40-4-75 (January 13, 1868); see also Joseph B. James, *The Ratification of the Fourteenth Amendment* (Macon, GA: Mercer University Press, 1984), 278–279, 282–283; Harrison, "The Lawfulness of the Reconstruction Amendments," 412 n. 199; Amar, *America's Constitution*, 602 n. 32. For a still-later Bingham statement hedging his bets and urging the admission of Alabama and other states so as to establish the Fourteenth Amendment's validity "upon every theory," see *Congressional Globe* 40-2-3094 (June 12, 1868). For Ackerman's account of this speech, see Ackerman, *We the People: Transformations*, 231. It is also worth noting that Ackerman may mislead many non-expert readers when he characterizes Bingham as engaging in "radical" mathematics. Bingham's and Sumner's moderate lapsed-state views were quite different from Stevens's "conquered provinces" approach, yet Ackerman generally conflates the two to serve his polemic purposes. Ackerman does not appear to understand—or at least, does not help his readers understand—how Bingham's and Sumner's views were wholly consistent with Lincoln's insistence that the Union was indivisible and that southern land never lawfully left the Union. For a pointed corrective on this precise issue, see Amar, *America's Constitution*, 379, 608 n. 63. The detailed analysis provided today of Bingham's January 16, 1867, speech (including Bingham's sharp criticism of Stevens in this speech) provides further support for this earlier pointed corrective of Ackerman's misleading account.

28. *Congressional Globe,* 39th Congress, 2nd Session (1867): 501.

29. Ibid., 501.

30. *Luther v. Borden,* 48 U.S. (7 How.) 1, 42 (1849). In its famous 1869 decision in *Texas v. White,* the Supreme Court prominently quoted from and paraphrased this passage in *Luther* to provide context for the seating decisions made and Reconstruction laws passed by the Thirty-ninth and Fortieth Congresses—decisions and laws that were not under direct review in *White* itself. See *Texas v. White,* 74 U.S. 700, 730–733 (1869).

31. *Congressional Globe,* 39th Congress, 2nd Session (1867): 501.

32. Ibid., 502.

33. See Ackerman, *We the People: Transformations,* 442–444 n. 23; Harrison, "The Lawfulness of the Reconstruction Amendments," 424 (arguing that "[a] s announced in *Luther,* however, the political question doctrine is too coarse-grained to resolve the issues presented during Reconstruction, when the President and Congress were not of one mind as to the legality of different state regimes"). But see Amar, *America's Constitution,* 602–603 n. 32, and sources cited therein.

34. *Congressional Globe,* 39th Congress, 2nd Session (1867): 501.

35. Ibid., 502.

36. Echoes of Bingham can be heard in Justice Hugo Black's concurrence in the 1939 case of *Coleman v. Miller,* 307 U.S. 433 (1939). It is possible that Black had Bingham in the back of his mind when drafting this concurrence. Later decisions penned by Black, especially his dissent in *Adamson v. California,* 332 U.S. 46 (1947), reveal Black's close attention to other speeches of Bingham concerning the Fourteenth Amendment.

The court's opinion in Coleman invoked precedent to suggest that, after some reasonable period of time, the opportunity for additional states to add their approval to a still unratified amendment would close. The court proceeded to suggest that it was up to Congress to determine the length of this reasonable period. The court also noted certain aspects of the interesting process by which the Fourteenth Amendment was ratified, invoking various determinations made in the 1860s as evidence that some Article V issues were to be decided by the "the political departments." 307 U.S. at 449. This discussion—published more than seventy years after the relevant Reconstruction events occurred—stands as the most direct engagement of the Fourteenth Amendment's unusual ratification process to be found in the *U.S. Reports.*

Black agreed that the issue before the Coleman Court was nonjusticiable, but offered an even broader view of Article V nonjusticiability "To the extent that the Court's opinion in the present case even impliedly assumes a power to make judicial interpretation of the exclusive constitutional authority of Congress over submission and ratification of amendments, we are unable to agree." Ibid., 458 (Black, J., concurring in the result). Any suggestion by the court of "an ultimate control over the amending process in the courts" was, to Black, utterly contrary to a process "intrusted by the Constitution solely to the political branch of government," namely Congress. Ibid. "Article V ... grants power of the amending of the Constitution to Congress alone. Undivided control of that process has been given by the Article exclusively and completely to Congress. The process itself is 'political' in its entirety, from submission until an amendment becomes part of the Constitution, and is not subject to judicial guidance, control, or interference at any point. Since Congress has sole and complete control over the amending process, subject to no judicial review, the views of any court upon this process cannot be binding upon Congress." Ibid., 459.

If, indeed, Black had been reading Bingham, the justice arguably over-read the representative. Bingham, it will be recalled, stressed the nonjusticiability of the Republican Government Clause found in Article IV, section 4, and his main Article V argument piggybacked on his Article IV analysis. Thus, Bingham did not discuss in detail whether various Article V issues unrelated to the denominator question were also nonjusticable.

In one brief rhetorical flourish, however, Bingham did seem to gesture toward a broad argument for the general nonjusticiability of the amendment process. *Congressional Globe,* 39th Congress, 2nd Session (1867): 501 (suggesting that it would be outlandish for the "Supreme Court of the United States to undertake to adjudge the power of Congress to propose a constitutional amendment and the power of the people to affirm it"). It's also worth noting that a broader contextual similarity linked Bingham and Black. Bingham urged Congress to strip the Supreme Court of appellate jurisdiction should the court try to thwart the Fourteenth Amendment. When Black was in Congress, he too was not afraid to challenge the court; as a senator, Black had backed President Franklin Roosevelt's court-packing plan. Much as the Reconstruction-era court avoided a showdown with Congress—accepting, for example, a withdrawal of the court's jurisdiction in *Ex parte McCardle,* 74 U.S. 506 (1869)—so the New Deal–era court in Coleman avoided a showdown with Congress by declaring various aspects of Article V off limits for the judiciary. For further discussion of the connections between Reconstruction and Coleman, see Ackerman, *We the People: Transformations,* 261–266.

37. Act of March 2, 1867, 14 Statutes at Large 428. Strictly speaking, the act did not require the excluded states to do anything; it merely mapped out a safe

harbor. If states did the things specified in the statute, they would thereby win readmission.

38. The act envisioned disfranchisement of certain felons and rebels.

39. See, e.g., Pinckney G. McElwee, "The 14th Amendment and the Threat That It Poses to Our Democratic Government," *South Carolina Law Quarterly* 11 (1959): 484.

40. Felix Frankfurter, "John Marshall and the Judicial Function," *Harvard Law Review* 69 (1955): 217, 229.

41. See *Congressional Globe,* 39th Congress, 1st Session (January 25, 1866): 430 (quoting John Bingham) ("There was then [at the Founding] no State in this Union wherein any considerable portion of the free citizens of the United States, being male persons over twenty-one years of age, were disfranchised."). For more statements, see Amar, *America's Constitution,* 603–604 n. 37.

42. Leading Republicans were indeed aware that the Fourteenth Amendment had been ratified by a sufficient number of true-blue states in early 1867. See note 27.

43. See generally Stephen Skowronek, *The Politics Presidents Make* (Cambridge, MA: Belknap Press of Harvard University Press, 2000).

44. Two other papers in this symposium are directly relevant here. See Beermann, this volume; Mendelson, this volume.

45. Lincoln appended his own signature to the Thirteenth Amendment, on February 7, 1865, but the Senate resolved that Lincoln's signature had been unnecessary and "should not constitute a precedent for the future." *Congressional Globe,* 38th Congress, 2nd Session (February 7, 1865): 629–631. See generally Herman Ames, *The Proposed Amendments to the Constitution of the United States* (1896): 295–296.

46. See generally Skowronek, *The Politics Presidents Make.*

47. Except Tennessee, which enfranchised blacks on its own motion soon enough.

Commentary on Chapter 3
Ordinary and Extraordinary Transitions
Paul Horwitz

> The old order changeth, yielding place to new.
> — Alfred, Lord Tennyson, "The Passing of Arthur"
> in *Idylls of the King* (1869)

Introduction

Every great moment contains paradoxes, and transitions are no exception.[1] Transitions are both crowded and lonely. They require the consensus of many shifting constituencies to succeed, but they also regularly depend on the words and deeds of a few great individuals, who act in the teeth of the old order to bring about a new one. Transitions involve both discontinuity and continuity: they require a rupture with the *ancien regime,* but their legitimacy often depends on finding a way to keep faith with older traditions while forging new norms. They are both slow and sudden: like an avalanche, they depend on the steady accumulation of details and conditions, and then happen with a terrible swiftness. They regularly require violence in order to bring peace. They seek to bring justice from injustice, but often find that "[t]o do a great right," they must "do a little wrong."[2]

In their contribution to this volume, Akhil Reed Amar, Lindsey Ohlsson Worth, and Joshua Alexander Geltzer write about one such transition: the move from "America's antebellum Constitution" to its "postbellum Constitution," a transition that involved both the bloody violence of the Civil War and the uneasy ratification of the Civil War amendments that were its aftermath.[3] "The decade of the 1860s," Amar writes, with a touch of American exceptionalism, "was the proverbial mother of all transitions."[4]

Amar is right that the Civil War and the consecration of the Union victory through the amendments to the constitutional text is one of the great moments of American transition. Along with the *ur*-moment of American constitutional change—the American Revolution and the writing and ratification of the United States Constitution—and perhaps just one or two other moments,[5] it is one of the central examples that American constitutional theorists turn to when they try to describe and understand the concept of legal and political transition.

In this brief commentary on Amar's fine article, I will not take on Amar's historical arguments in a direct fashion. Instead, I want to use it as an occasion to examine a variety of questions raised by legal and political transitions. As it turns out, Amar's piece evokes many of the questions that recur throughout this volume, and throughout the legal literature on transitions more generally. Although he focuses on one particular transition, and a specifically American one at that, both the episode he describes and the *way* that he describes it have broader implications for those who want to think about the nature and role of transitions in legal and political orders, American or otherwise.

Amar's perspective is apparent in the very first sentence of his article, in which he describes the move from the antebellum Constitution to the postbellum Constitution both as involving a "sharp[ ] depart[ure]," and as an effort by "legal reformers" to "maintain formal continuity with the prior legal and institutional order."[6] Amar acknowledges the "sharp departure," but his emphasis throughout the paper is on "formal continuity." He concludes with the observation that even when "they lie unenforced, the words of a written Constitution remain written—patiently waiting to be dusted off and redeemed when redemption becomes possible."[7] The ratification of the Fourteenth Amendment, in this view, was primarily a restorative or redemptive action, not a revolutionary one.

This gives rise to the three questions this comment will explore, using Amar's paper as a jumping-off point. We might think of them as embodying three modes of response to Amar's paper, and to the broader question of transitions: evaluation, generalization, and domestication.

First, evaluation. Why the emphasis on continuity? Why is it so important to Amar to demonstrate that "the process that generated the [Fourteenth Amendment] was not a lawless break with the past and its practices but, to the contrary, was continuous with prior and proper constitutional understandings"?[8] What is gained—or lost—by focusing on continuity rather than discontinuity?

Second, generalization. What lessons, if any, does the American historical experience with the Civil War amendments hold for the many examples of legal transitions across the globe in our own age?

Finally, domestication. Whether transitions like the one America underwent in the 1860s are loyal or disloyal to the legal orders that they redeemed or superseded, why focus on such radical ruptures? In addition to thinking about *extraordinary* transitions, what observations can we make about the nature and frequency of what we might call *ordinary* transitions? Are they a different creature altogether, or is there a closer link than we usually imagine between ordinary and extraordinary legal transitions? I will examine each of these questions in turn.

I. Evaluation: Continuity and Legitimacy

No one questions the monumental and transformative nature of the Fourteenth Amendment, and very few people doubt its legitimacy. But some constitutional scholars question whether the process of ratifying the Fourteenth Amendment is genuinely consistent with the rules of the legal order from which it emerged.

The most famous of these is Amar's colleague, Bruce Ackerman. Ackerman argues that the process of ratifying the Fourteenth Amendment, which the southern states were forced to endorse as a price of their full readmission to the Union, was inconsistent with the amendment procedures set out in Article V of the Constitution.[9] Ackerman rescues the Fourteenth Amendment from illegitimacy by arguing that its legitimacy did not depend alone on its faithfulness to Article V, but on a broader series of affirmations of the amendment by the president, Congress, and courts that ultimately became a "constitutional moment"—one in which the Constitution was transformed regardless of whether it followed its own textual requirements for change.[10]

Amar rejects this maneuver. He acknowledges that both the process and the result of ratifying the Fourteenth Amendment were "anything but conservative."[11] But he is at pains to emphasize that the Fourteenth Amendment ratification process was "not a lawless break with the past and its practices but, to the contrary, was continuous with prior and proper constitutional understandings, rightly understood."[12] To that end, he focuses on a speech by Representative John Bingham of Ohio, arguing that the exclusion of "[u]nrepublican states . . . from the Article V calculus" was justified under a proper understanding of the Constitution.[13] Bingham's speech, he writes, is a "textual and . . . constitutional *tour de force*," a "remarkable case study in high-stakes transitional lawyering" that "has not received the careful analysis that it deserves."[14] It employs "generally conservative legal techniques" and is "continuous with the legal past."[15]

Doubtless Amar and Ackerman's debate will continue. But it raises a question, one that Ackerman writes will inevitably be asked by "hard-line lawyer[s]": "'Who cares?'"[16] Whether the Fourteenth Amendment ratification process followed proper Article V procedures or not, the deed is done. Arguing over it now is like standing in the middle of a henhouse and debating which came first, the chicken or the egg. It is of historical interest only, and lawyers are not, first and foremost, historians.

Ackerman has an answer to this question, one that I suspect Amar would share: namely, that "constitutional lawyers are in the legitimation business."[17] Constitutional lawyers need to be able to explain to "their fellow citizens why the Thirteenth and Fourteenth Amendments are properly part of the Constitution."[18] This seems an odd response. In truth, neither "hard-line lawyers" nor citizens in general seem much interested in this question. Despite the relative lack of interest in this issue, however, both Ackerman and Amar seem to be entranced by it.

Why, then, is it necessary to expend so much time and intellectual firepower on the question of the legitimacy or illegitimacy of the ratification of the Fourteenth Amendment, and on whether its legitimacy comes from the Article V process or something beyond it? How important is it, really, whether the Fourteenth Amendment and the process that birthed it was "ultimately faithful" to the "deep principles of American republicanism,"[19] or utterly faithless? In his book *America's Constitution: A Biography,* Amar compares the language of the Preamble to the Constitution, in which "We the People . . . do ordain and establish this Constitution," to a wedding vow, in which the words spoken "perform[ ] the very thing they describe[ ]."[20] But marriages, like constitutional orders, are temporally extended commitments. Whether a marriage *begins* for reasons of true love, calculation, religious or cultural constraint, or necessity may say less about the long-term legitimacy of that relationship than does everything that takes place *after* the vows have been spoken. What the couple said in their wedding vows is of some interest, but not much, in evaluating the marriage itself.

This, it seems to me, is the first fundamental question that Amar's chapter raises about transitions: how do we evaluate them? When, if ever, is it necessary for those transitions themselves to be "legitimate," or faithful to the old order—and why? And from what standpoint should we evaluate legal transitions?

Most of the time, and out of necessity, we evaluate transitions from an *ex post* perspective, and we focus less on legitimacy than on efficacy. To anticipate the next section of this comment, when we examine transitions such as the move from apartheid-era South Africa to post-apartheid South Africa, we are less concerned with whether the transition was legitimate than with whether and how it worked. We ask, did the transition process achieve the goals it set out to achieve—say, widening the franchise and providing solid grounds for the exercise of democratic authority? What compromises were necessary to achieve them? What problems, anticipated or unanticipated, did the transition raise, and how should they be addressed? These are all fairly conventional questions about transitional orders within democratic states. Even when the analysis takes place *ex ante,* it often takes the same form: we do our best to look forward into the future, and imagine a transition process that will achieve the goals we have in mind.

What is striking about Amar's chapter, by contrast, is that it attempts to analyze the success of the Fourteenth Amendment, viewed as a transition project, *in media res*—in the middle of the action. It focuses on "the situation as of late 1865" and the period immediately following it.[21] From this historicist perspective, it is impossible to say whether the project will ultimately succeed or fail, although in reality we have the answer to this question. Instead, the question becomes whether the transition, and the measures used to achieve it, were compelling or at least plausible *at that moment in time.*

From this vantage point, Amar's focus on Bingham and his 1867 speech is understandable. If Bingham, using the constitutional materials available to him at the time, could frame a persuasive set of reasons for ratifying the Fourteenth Amendment despite the obvious obstacle of southern intransigence, and precisely by excluding those intransigent voices from the decision-making process, then the forces that supported ratification at the time, even if they employed arguably draconian measures, were justified in doing so. They were "faithfully interpret[ing] the Founders' project"; "supplement[ing] the Founders' rules" but "not supplant[ing] them."[22] In short, Amar's focus is on the *legitimacy* of the Fourteenth Amendment and its procedures, viewed from within the transitional moment itself.

This is an interesting project, but in some ways an odd one. It is not quite history and not quite political theory. In both those disciplines, we are privileged to know how the story ends (so far, at least), and our analysis is inevitably affected by this knowledge. Amar's perspective, by contrast, is Edenic. His narrator, like Bingham himself, has not yet tasted of the fruit of the tree of knowledge; he does not yet know how things will turn out, although, of course, we do.

By tracking closely Bingham's own analysis, Amar performs a splendid act of imaginative reconstruction.[23] Students of constitutional history should be grateful to him. For most of us, however, it is not clear that this is the most productive way to understand legal transitions more broadly, or even the particular legal transition represented by the Fourteenth Amendment and the process surrounding its ratification. If we are interested in understanding, assessing, and modeling legal transitions, our focus should not be on legitimacy at the time of transition, but on the effectiveness of the transition in the long run.

That is not to say we should be utterly unconcerned with whether or not a particular legal transition is "continuous with prior . . . constitutional understandings."[24] Usually, we must take this into account. Not always: if we think the prior constitutional order is fatally flawed, or worse,[25] we may conclude that a sharp rupture with the prior order is just what is needed. As a practical matter, however, we should be concerned with any factors that will contribute to the success of the transitional enterprise—and continuity with the past will often be one such factor. But if our primary goal is a successful transition itself, an *ex post* assessment of these questions makes more sense than one that takes place *in medias res*.

If that is our concern, then we might ask a number of questions about any act of legal transition, including the ratification of the Fourteenth Amendment. We might, to be sure, ask how fair or sound the transition process was at the time—not for its own sake, but for the purposes of evaluating what effect that process would have on the long-term chances for a successful transition. Against the question of how fair or sound a transition process was, we might pose the question of how *necessary* a particular process was, regardless of its underlying fairness. We might ask how well reasoned the arguments for a particular transition process were at the time, especially to the extent that well-reasoned arguments might ease the transition process and assure general agreement with it over time. Of greater concern than the quality of the reasons, however, would be the simple question whether those reasons, whether they were good or bad, *stuck*. Certainly, too, we would ask the *realpolitik* question captured in Stalin's famous inquiry about the Pope: "And how many divisions has [he]?"[26] The Pope's unspoken rejoinder to Stalin's question reminds us that moral authority can be a source of power in and of itself, whether or not it is backed by military force; but that does not mean we should be uninterested in the frank question whether a transition can be enforced effectively.

All of these strike me as the right kinds of questions to ask about the ratification of the Fourteenth Amendment—or about *any* legal transition, at least if we are interested in drawing conclusions about it that can be exported to other contexts.[27] They're not terribly high-minded questions, but they *are* useful.[28] And what they share in common is that they are not terribly interested in the kinds of questions of legitimacy and continuity with the past that so concern Amar. They're not indifferent to the concerns he raises, but their interest in them is essentially instrumental. They do not suppose, as Amar seems to, that it is centrally important that the reasons supplied for a particular transition and its processes be *legitimate.* Instead, they think what counts is that those reasons succeed over time in *legitimating* that transition.

In the long run, I am not convinced that any other approach makes complete sense. The legitimacy of legal transitions—and constitutions— is in large measure a function of their ability to perform and to stick. It is more a practical question than an abstract one—although, to be sure, what it means for a transition or a constitution to perform effectively will depend on contested questions about what justice or efficiency require. But these questions will ultimately have to be resolved from the perspective of the post-transition present, not *in media res.*[29] Both legal transitions and constitutions, like marriages, are temporally extended projects.[30] Whether they are "ultimately faithful"[31] to their broader goals can finally only be decided after the dust has settled.

None of this is meant to detract from the value of Amar's skillful reconstruction of Bingham's arguments. Amar makes powerful arguments for the validity of Bingham's position; if they do not satisfy his colleague Ackerman, surely the Constitution, and Yale Law School, are big enough for both of them. I do mean to suggest, however, that whether or not Bingham's arguments for the validity of the ratification process he advocated are "legitimate" or "faithful" to the Constitution may depend less on how "faithful" they were at the time, and more on practical considerations and the verdict of history.

II. Generalization: The 1860s and Transitional Justice

I have already suggested that there is a note of American exceptionalism in Amar's reference to the American transition of the 1860s as the "mother of all transitions."[32] From an American perspective, this statement is unobjectionable. Others might have named different moments, like the American Revolution itself or the ratification of the Constitution in 1787, but none will deny that the 1860s is a genuine contender for the title. But it *is* an American perspective, one that sees the events of the 1860s as significant largely because of their importance for "the meaning of the *American creed*."[33]

In a book on transitions, it *is* important to consider the lessons offered by the Civil War and the constitutional amendments that it occasioned. Among other things, it serves as a most un-exceptionalist reminder that the American experience is not unique, but rather is of a piece with events—civil war, reconstruction, and constitutional change—that many nations have experienced, and continue to experience. But if we are to draw conclusions about transitions that can be generalized to other contexts, we must expand our focus beyond the American experience. Amar draws a number of conclusions from the events of the 1860s, and these conclusions are indeed generalizable to other legal transitions.[34] Still, it may be worth asking more specifically whether we can take some lessons from the American experience in the 1860s that can be applied to transitional justice more broadly: lessons that can be applied to legal transitions in other times and places, especially in post-conflict societies.[35]

Elsewhere in this volume, Ruti Teitel discusses transitional justice more effectively than I can hope to.[36] But perhaps we can use the American experience in the 1860s to identify some considerations that will figure in any attempt to generalize from the American experience to the global experience of high-stakes legal transitions.

The first is the role of different constituencies. Transitional justice models must regularly negotiate among the different stakeholders in the transitional society, not least those groups that previously held power. In doing so, they may have to trade off some of the goals of the transition in order to secure the *ancien regime*'s accession to the new order. At the same time, they cannot ignore utterly the interests of the previously powerless group. They may find that they have to sacrifice a measure of justice for that group, including some reparative justice for the wrongs they have suffered, in order to ensure that this group can move into a position of greater power without giving rise to rear-guard resistance by the old leaders. South Africa, with its denial of complete reparative justice for the black African majority and its substitution of the partial fix of a Truth and Reconciliation Commission, is one example.[37]

We can say the same thing about the Fourteenth Amendment transition. It had to balance the interests in justice, security, and power of a variety of interest groups, including the victorious northern states, the defeated southern states, the political parties, the president, the Supreme

Court, and most certainly the newly emancipated African Americans. It may have succeeded in this goal in the long run, but not without cost— some of the reparative aspects of the transition were quickly undone by opposing forces, prejudice, and the need for civil order—and not without significant resistance, resistance that continued for a century after the Civil War. This complex web of interests and constituencies makes it difficult to evaluate the "legitimacy" of a transition, if by that we mean whether that transition truly kept faith with the presuppositions of the existing legal order, or even with the goals of the new order. Whether Bingham happened to be "right" or "faithful" in his arguments for the constitutional fidelity of the ratification process he advocated is, from this perspective, less important than whether that process could effectively achieve its goals without causing significant problems of implementation. So it is with any transition, which is always a move from one imperfect order to a new order that is hopefully more just but still imperfect.

Another question we can ask about transitions is the role of what Amar calls "large-scale economic, technological, social, cultural, and demographic changes, which in turn reshuffle political patterns and invite large legal reforms."[38] Amar observes correctly that one source of these tectonic shifts in social conditions is war, including the Civil War itself. That is true, of course; it's no accident that many examples of transitional justice occur in post-conflict societies. But we may observe more broadly that conflicts not only cause, but are caused by, the kinds of social changes that Amar enumerates. Transitions occur both slowly and quickly: before the sudden thunderclap of revolutionary change, conditions on the ground must also change, both to precipitate the conflict and to make post-conflict victory and transition possible. Again, this was true of the Fourteenth Amendment transition: technological, economic, and demographic change was as much a part of the story of the slow move to civil war, and the long move away from it, as any argument about constitutional fidelity.[39] So, in evaluating the prospects for legal transition and the likelihood that such transitions will succeed, we must ask how important these factors are compared to the role of law and politics viewed more narrowly.

Another question we might ask about the Civil War transition in particular, and about transitions in general, concerns the role played by written constitutions. Amar places our own written Constitution in the foreground of his story, arguing that because we have "a canonical text—the written Constitution," the "project of American constitutionalism as we know it might well self-destruct" unless we admit the legal validity of the

Fourteenth Amendment.[40] And he sees a powerful role for written constitutions in both "subverting the corrupt [old] legal order" and redeeming the new one.[41]

But we could say more about written constitutions and legal transitions. It may be that written constitutions, by giving the old order something to cling to, can retard or complicate legal transitions. Conversely, by setting out "grand promises"[42] that the previously disempowered groups insist on redeeming, written constitutions may simultaneously galvanize those groups and, because those promises cannot fully be kept, disappoint them. Tradeoffs are inevitable,[43] and not always welcome. Finally, we may ask whether, by demanding that new wine be poured into old bottles, written constitutions provide some stability and continuity, which is conducive to a successful transition, but also tax the transition process by requiring advocates of transition to expend effort in demonstrating continuity with the past that would be better spent elsewhere. Our own Constitution is arguably an example of this. The relative infrequency of its amendment has helped it survive for two centuries and counting, but its canonical nature may deter efforts to secure much-needed amendments to cure serious defects in its structure.[44]

Another question we might ask is how we should balance the need for *political* change against the desire for reparative or retributive *justice*. This is a common question in transitional justice, from ancient Athens down to our own time.[45] There is no one right answer here, "no one simple solution capable of addressing the complexities and subtleties inherent in a range of different factual situations."[46] But it is likely always to be a part of the calculation that transitional justice must make. It is certainly one that has figured prominently in discussions of the Fourteenth Amendment itself.[47]

Last on this list, but surely first in any consideration of transitions and transitional justice, is the question of what *goals* are meant to be served by the transitional justice model one chooses and the transitional process one selects. Those goals, and the processes that serve them, will change from place to place. As Judge Richard Goldstone has written, "The peculiar history, politics, and social structure of a society will always inform the appropriate approach to [the] question [of transitional justice] in any given context."[48] Just as important, they will change from time to time, even within the same state; a transitional society may cycle through a variety of goals and models before all is said and done.

This is why, to reiterate the general theme of this comment, it is difficult to come up with a generalizable picture of transitional justice by focusing on the abstract *legitimacy* of an argument for transition, or a particular transition process, especially if one focuses on the "faithfulness" of that argument at a single moment in time. The legitimacy of Bingham's arguments depended in part on "prior and proper constitutional understandings" as viewed from the vantage point of the 1860s.[49] But in the long run, they depend far more on the goals of that transition, on how those goals may have changed over time, and on our own changing views of what constitutes a "proper constitutional understanding." If we are to generalize from the 1860s in a way that might offer general insights into legal transitions, we must avoid the American temptation to think of the Civil War and its aftermath as utterly extraordinary, as the "mother of all transitions." We should think of *all* transitions as siblings, with a similar genetic makeup but different traits and widely differing outcomes.

III. Domestication: Of Ordinary Transitions

Let us suppose, however, that the 1860s was indeed the mother of all transitions. What about her children? Transitional justice studies generally focus on major ruptures with the past legal order, of which the Civil War and its aftermath is certainly one example, whether it was continuous with the sweeping promises made by the Constitution and the Declaration of Independence or not. Amar's colleague Bruce Ackerman, in his study of "constitutional moments," likewise focuses on major ruptures with the prevailing legal order by distinguishing between ordinary lawmaking and rare moments of "higher lawmaking."[50]

But, as some have argued, the distinction between ordinary and extraordinary transitions may not be as clear or as great as all that. Thus, Mark Tushnet has suggested that it is difficult to distinguish between the "determinate indeterminacy" of constitutional law in ordinary times and the "profound fissures" in constitutional law during extraordinary times.[51] Similarly, Eric Posner and Adrian Vermeule have argued that "theorists of transitional justice commonly err by treating regime transitions as a self-contained subject" that is distinguishable from "the wide variety of transitions that occur in consolidated democracies"; in fact, "legal and political transitions lie on a continuum, of which regime transitions are merely an endpoint."[52]

This seems right to me. Amar's chapter focuses usefully on a major rupture in the American constitutional order, and seeks to bring out a sense of its continuity with the past. But it is also possible to focus on ordinary transitions in American constitutional law and politics, and see discontinuities in them. In doing so, we may find a new way of thinking about so-called ordinary transitions that helps us rethink both these moments and moments of extraordinary transition.

Consider the election of President Barack Obama, the first African American to hold that office. The fact of his election is momentous, and Amar links it to the 1860s, writing that without the "epic changes wrought" by the civil rights laws of the 1960s, which were themselves the eventual product of the Civil War amendments, "Americans in 2008 would never have elected Barack Obama president."[53]

That's true, but Obama's ascension to power is significant in other ways, ways that may be more mundane but are potentially no less momentous. Among other things, he represented a switch in the party holding the presidency after eight years under another leader—a period that saw terrorist attacks on American soil, the pursuit of major wars in two countries, an economic crisis, and major disputes about the meaning of the Constitution, particularly the scope of executive power during times of war or emergency. When he took the presidential oath, Obama committed himself at least to the *possibility* that he would revisit each of the presidential decisions that surrounded these crises, charting a new path in accordance with his own independent understanding of the Constitution.

Whether he ultimately charts such a new path depends on a host of factors. His understanding of the Constitution might not differ substantially from the last officeholder's own vision. Even if it does, he may consider himself constrained by circumstances and by prudential or pragmatic political judgments about how strong a turn to take.[54] What matters is that he is oath-bound to consider the possibility of doing so. As Amar writes, "American presidents are change agents and constitutional catalysts."[55]

In this sense, as I have written elsewhere, "every presidential transition is a constitutional moment."[56] Because constitutional meaning does not reside in the courts alone, but also (among other places) in the oath-bound views of the chief executive, "each presidential transition is a moment in which at least one branch of the federal government must consider anew what the Constitution means and what it demands."[57] A new president, every time he takes the oath and long after that, is "confronted with all the questions of constitutional meaning and obligation that have been with us since Philadelphia"—and that certainly includes the questions raised by the dramatic transition of the 1860s.[58] Our constitutional past, as William Faulkner would remind us, is never dead; it's not even past.[59]

This is especially true for stable constitutional democracies, like the

United States. In thinking about the Constitution and constitutional change, we can be so focused on the stability-enhancing function of a written constitution, on its seeming permanence, that we fail to appreciate sufficiently the ways in which it derives stability not from its fixed nature but from its capacity for change and adaptation—both through extraordinary processes like the shift we saw in the 1860s, and through the vehicle of "ordinary" political and constitutional change. But if, as Jean Hampton has written, democratic change is a form of "controlled revolutionary activity,"[60] then it will not do to ignore the little revolutions that occur along the way.[61]

A focus on ordinary transitions may seem to take us far afield from Amar's own subject of the 1860s, which was surely no ordinary transition, and from Teitel's contribution on transitional justice, which generally involves large-scale ruptures in emerging democracies. It may bring us closer to the more mundane, if important, contributions to this book by Jack M. Beermann and Nina Mendelson, who write about the law of ordinary presidential transitions.[62]

But the point of this commentary has been precisely that the differences among them are narrower than they may seem at first. For some purposes, it may make sense to distinguish between ordinary and extraordinary transitions. In other respects, though, the distinction is misleading. If we want a general theory or understanding of transitions—and that is surely the goal of this book—we must focus on both ordinary and extraordinary transitions, and treat them as the same phenomena, albeit under substantially different circumstances. If Amar wants to focus on aspects of continuity in the extraordinary transition of the 1860s, by the same token we can find aspects of *dis*continuity in *ordinary* transitions: transitions in which political power passes in a more peaceful and well-regulated fashion, but constitutional meaning changes, or may change, just the same. Posner and Vermeule are right to say that every transition lies on a continuum. And every transition, ordinary or extraordinary, "embodies the tension inherent in constitutional moments—the tension between consistency and change."[63]

Conclusion

Amar has written a valuable contribution to this volume. Anyone who is interested in his broader project of constitutional history and interpretation will find an important piece of the puzzle here. The extraordinary transition of the U.S. during the 1860s is surely a vital text for students of transitions and transitional justice.

If we are interested in a general understanding of transitions, however, we will want to pay some attention to how this moment, and every other transitional moment, can be analyzed, generalized, and domesticated. That focus may pull us away from the moment of the 1860s itself, and away from the question whether the process of transition represented by that moment, as captured in Bingham's powerful speech, was "continuous with prior and proper constitutional understandings" at the time.[64] It may lead us away from a tendency to think of the 1860s, or any other period of transition, as unique, as a "mother of all transitions" that requires a mother of all justifications. Instead, to properly understand the effectiveness and the long-term legitimacy of transitions, ordinary and extraordinary, we will have to focus on how well those transitions dealt in the long run with the complex relationship between continuity and change in legal orders.

Notes

1. See, e.g., Fionnula Ni Aolain and Colm Campbell, "The Paradox of Transition in Conflicted Democracies," *Human Rights Quarterly* 27 (2005): 172.

2. William Shakespeare, *The Merchant of Venice* IV.1.213, ed. Jay Halio (Oxford, UK: Clarendon Press, 1993).

3. Akhil Reed Amar, Lindsey Ohlsson Worth, and Joshua Alexander Geltzer, "Reconstructing the Republic: The Great Transition of the 1860s," in this volume," 98–100. For simplicity's sake, and because this work is clearly a part of Amar's larger project of exploring the Constitution and its history, see, e.g., Akhil Reed Amar, *America's Constitution: A Biography* (New York: Random House, 2005), I refer to Amar as the author in the main text. I intend no slight to the contributions of Worth and Geltzer.

4. Ibid., 98.

5. Amar's colleague, Bruce Ackerman, would add to this list the New Deal. See Bruce Ackerman, *We the People: Foundations* (Cambridge, MA: Harvard University Press, 1991); Bruce Ackerman, *We the People: Transformations* (Cambridge, MA: Harvard University Press, 1998).

6. Amar et al., "Reconstructing the Republic," 98.

7. Ibid., 123.

8. Ibid., 102.

9. See, e.g., Ackerman, *We the People: Transformations,* 99–252.

10. Ibid.

11. Amar et al., "Reconstructing the Republic," 111.

12. Ibid., 102.

13. Ibid., 103.

14. Ibid., 106; 103.

15. Ibid., III.

16. Bruce Ackerman, "Revolution on a Human Scale," *Yale Law Journal* 108 (1999): 2279, 2300.

17. Ibid., 2302.

18. Ibid.

19. Amar et al., "Reconstructing the Republic," 104 (emphasis omitted).

20. Amar, *America's Constitution: A Biography,* 5.

21. Amar et al., "Reconstructing the Republic," 101–2.

22. Ibid., 115–16.

23. Pun intended.

24. Amar et al., "Reconstructing the Republic," 102.

25. The abolitionist William Lloyd Garrison called the antebellum Constitution "a covenant with death, and an agreement with hell." See generally J. M. Balkin, "Agreements With Hell and Other Objects of Our Faith," *Fordham Law Review* 65 (1997): 1703.

26. George Weigel, "The Pope's Divisions," *Washington Post,* September 22, 1996, Book World, at 1.

27. See part II below.

28. I have taken a similarly unromantic position on similar questions elsewhere. See Paul Horwitz, "Democracy as the Rule of Law," in *Prosecuting the Bush Administration: What Does the Rule of Law Require?* ed. Nasser Hussain and Austin Sarat (New York: New York University Press, 2010).

29. See, e.g., Richard H. Fallon Jr., "Legitimacy and the Constitution," *Harvard Law Review* 118 (2005): 1787, 1789 (arguing that "the legal legitimacy of the Constitution depends more on its present sociological acceptance than on the [questionable] legality of its formal ratification").

Fallon does not count out the importance of legal legitimacy altogether, nor would I. But he does suggest—and I agree—that "[r]ealistic discourse about constitutional legitimacy must . . . reckon with the snarled interconnections among constitutional law, its sociological foundations, and the felt imperatives of practical exigency and moral right." Ibid.

30. This is a subject on which Amar's colleague Jed Rubenfeld has written powerfully. See, e.g., Jed Rubenfeld, *Freedom and Time: A Theory of Constitutional Self-Government* (New Haven, CT: Yale University Press, 2001). For a conversation between Amar and Rubenfeld that discusses some of their differences on this point, see Akhil Reed Amar and Jed Rubenfeld, "A Dialogue," *Yale Law Journal* 115 (2006): 2015.

31. Amar et al., "Reconstructing the Republic," 104 (emphasis omitted).

32. Ibid., 98.

33. Steven G. Calabresi, "'A Shining City on a Hill': American Exceptionalism and the Supreme Court's Practice of Relying on Foreign Law," Boston University Law Review 86 (2006): 1335, 1398. See generally Deborah L. Madsen, *American Exceptionalism* (Staffordshire, UK: Keele University Press, 1998); Seymour Martin Lipset, *American Exceptionalism: A Double-Edged Sword* (Bridgewater, NJ: Replica Books, 1996).

34. See Amar et al., "Reconstructing the Republic," 118–23. All but one of these conclusions are phrased in broadly generalizable terms. The first—that "American presidents are change agents and constitutional catalysts," ibid., 118, is not, but it can easily be abstracted in a way that is applicable to other nations.

35. See generally Ruti G. Teitel, *Transitional Justice* (Oxford, UK: Oxford University Press, 2000).

36. See Ruti Teitel, "Global Transitions, New Perspectives on Legality, and Judicial Review," in this volume. For my own brief thoughts on transitional justice in general, see Horwitz, "Democracy as the Rule of Law."

37. See, e.g., Christine Bell, "Transitional Justice, Interdisciplinarity, and the State of the 'Field' or 'Non-Field,'" *International Journal of Transitional Justice* 3 (2009): 5, 13; Robert I. Rotberg and Dennis Thompson, eds., *Truth v. Justice* (Princeton, NJ: Princeton University Press, 2000) (collected essays discussing the South African Truth and Reconciliation Commission and its proceedings). For other examples, see Horwitz, "Democracy as the Rule of Law."

38. Amar et al., "Reconstructing the Republic," 120.

39. For just one example, see Peter Kolchin, *American Slavery 1619–1877* (New York: Hill & Wang, 1993), 94–95 (arguing that the invention of the cotton gin helped extend the institution of slavery in the South).

40. Amar et al., "Reconstructing the Republic," 114.

41. Ibid., 123.

42. Ibid.

43. See, e.g., Jon Elster, *Closing the Books: Transitional Justice in Historical Perspective* (Cambridge, UK: Cambridge University Press, 2004), 190 ("The incoming forces often have two conflicting desires: for a peaceful transition and for transitional justice. When negotiating with the outgoing leaders to achieve the first goal, they may have to sacrifice the second.").

44. See, e.g., Sanford Levinson, *Our Undemocratic Constitution: Where the Constitution Goes Wrong (And How We the People Can Correct It)* (Oxford, UK: Oxford University Press, 2006).

45. See Horwitz, "Democracy as the Rule of Law"; Elster, *Closing the Books.*

46. Richard Goldstone, "Preface," in *Human Rights in Political Transitions: Gettysburg to Bosnia,* ed. Carla Hesse and Robert Post (New York: Zone Books, 1999), 9.

47. See, for example, Symposium, "The Jurisprudence of Slavery Reparations," *Boston University Law Review* 84 (2004): 1135.

48. Goldstone, "Preface," 9.

49. Amar et al., "Reconstructing the Republic," 102.

50. See, for example, Ackerman, *We the People: Foundations,* 230–265.

51. Mark Tushnet, "Treatise Writing During Constitutional Moments," *Constitutional Commentary* 22 (2005): 251, 254.

52. Eric A. Posner and Adrian Vermeule, "Transitional Justice as Ordinary Justice," *Harvard Law Review* 117 (2004): 761, 762–763.

53. Amar et al., "Reconstructing the Republic," 115.

54. As of this writing, a few weeks before the midterm elections of 2010, the prospects for change seem even more distant than they did in the spring of 2010, when this symposium took place.

55. Amar et al., "Reconstructing the Republic," 118.

56. Paul Horwitz, "Honor's Constitutional Moment," *Northwestern University Law Review* 103 (2009): 1067.

57. Ibid., 1067–1068.

58. Ibid., 1080.

59. William Faulkner, *Requiem for a Nun* (New York: Garland Publishing, 1951), 92.

60. Jean Hampton, "Democracy and the Rule of Law," in *The Rule of Law: Nomos XXXVI,* ed. Ian Shapiro (New York: New York University Press, 1995), 13, 34.

61. See generally Horwitz, "Democracy as the Rule of Law" (discussing the relationship between the rule of law, transitional justice, and political change in stable democracies).

62. See Jack M. Beermann, "Midnight Deregulation," in this volume; Nina Mendelson, "Midnight Rulemaking and Congress," in this volume.

63. Horwitz, "Honor's Constitutional Moment," 1068.

64. Amar et al., "Reconstructing the Republic," 102.

4
Transitional Disclosures
What Transitional Justice Reveals about "Law"
David Gray

Introduction

For secular humanists there are few idols in the pantheon that are the object of more fervent claims of faith than "law." Law, and its procedural bodhisattva the rule of law,[1] play a central role in the utopian visions of philosophers, and the absence or perversion of law and the rule of law occupy a central place in the dystopian visions of cinema and literature. It is no surprise, then, to find that much of the academic writing and practical engagements in the field of transitional justice is preoccupied in one way or another with sorting out the role of law before, during, and after transitions to democracy. Much of this work relies on a presumption that law and the rule of law is a nearly unadulterated good, the idea being that mass, institutionalized, and targeted human rights abuses reflect the absence or failure of law and that the best hope for peace, stability, and justice going forward lies with a return to the true faith. This collection means in many ways to complicate some of these assumptions about the nature and role of law; so, too, will this chapter.[2]

Transitional justice asks what a successor regime committed to democracy, human rights, and the rule of law can and should do to achieve peace, stability, and justice in the wake of targeted violence and institutionalized human rights abuses perpetrated by and under a predecessor regime.[3] The questions are not new. As Jon Elster has pointed out, they date back at least two thousand years to the fall of the twelve tyrants in Athens.[4] More recently, "Third Wave" democracy movements[5] have led to an explosion in the literature on transitional justice, spawning wide-ranging interdisciplinary exchanges, dedicated journals, specialized centers, and nongovernmental organizations.[6] As Austin Sarat suggests in his introduction to this volume, the experiences of abusive regimes, their democratic heirs, and the transitions that occupy the liminal space between them have many lessons to teach us about law and the rule of law.[7] In this chapter I attempt to derive but a few by engaging some of the unique circumstances that lead to transitions and transitional justice.

One account of abusive regimes holds that, in them, law is absent. According to this view, the kind of targeted violence and human rights violations characteristic of abusive regimes are only possible in lawless societies. Part I challenges this view, arguing that law plays a central role in organizing and justifying the atrocities perpetrated by and under abusive regimes. In some abusive regimes, black-letter law, statutes, and other sources of public norms that even ardent positivists would identify as "law" demand, sanction, or at least do not punish murder, rape, assault, and expropriation of property when directed against members of a targeted group. In most abusive regimes, however, the positive law, read with a cold and foreign eye, appears to prohibit these acts of violence and theft no matter the victim. In these circumstances, understanding the role of law in abusive regimes requires that we view law and laws in a broader context as participants in paradigms of law, defined as constellations of norms, practices, and institutions that implement, inform, and engage with law, laws, and the law as it rules.

Part II builds on this expanded notion of "law" to describe an account of social crisis and collapse. Here I argue that social stability is not a function of consensus fidelity to a shared norm, ideal, or institution. To the contrary, that kind of unanimity is a formula for atrocity. Rather, stability in most relatively peaceful societies is maintained as a consequence of contests among paradigms and dynamic tension between overlapping group associations and oppositions. Crisis and breakdown occurs when one paradigm achieves hegemony and is able to erase the cross-sectional pathways of dynamic stability. Here again, law as paradigm, law as field of contest among paradigms, and law as an object of those contests appears to play a significant role in crisis and collapse.

Having spilled considerable ink in parts I and II arguing that law is not an unadulterated good, in part III I suggest some lessons that the study of transitions may teach us about the potential for "law" to play a positive role in achieving, sustaining, and maintaining peace and stability. Central among these is that "law" ought to adopt internal structures, meta-norms, and operational roles in society consistent with the goal of maintaining the robust web of overlapping associations and oppositions necessary to sustain dynamic stability. After reviewing the conclusions reached by prior work on religion, part III returns to the idea that "law" is a secular religion to conclude that law's greatest potential as an agent of peace is to remain a legitimate field of—and object for—contests among competing groups and paradigms. This suggests that, for example, robust public debates in the United States about the Constitution and constitutional law ought to reassure rather than be a cause for concern because these debates bespeak the persistence of background dynamic stability. We need only start to worry about social collapse if those debates are settled and one party or another wins the unchallenged right to dictate how the Constitution should be read and what it means.

While well beyond the scope of this chapter, part III concludes with some tentative comments about constitutional debates in the United States. It takes no position in perennial debates among, for example, originalists and living constitutionalists. Rather, I suggest that we ought to celebrate the fact that we have passionate contests over the true meaning of the Constitution, its application, the proper mode of interpretation, and the proper role of judges. These debates were bequeathed to us by the drafters of our Constitution, who embedded in that text a host of maddeningly enigmatic phrases. Their choice—or inability to make choices—has left us with considerable space for heated and meaningful constitutional debate. Those debates provide an important field for contests among competing social groups and therefore for the reinforcement and extension of dynamic stability through the inevitable fissions and fusions that accompany multiparty public contests.

I: Law as Paradigm

In this part I examine transitions and the abusive regimes that precede them in order to expose a multidimensionality in "law" that is often lost, forgotten, or denied in stable states where the central distraction frequently is black-letter law. In particular, I argue that the concept "law" includes elements of a broader social paradigm in which law participates and affects what law is such that to talk about "law" is really to talk about a broader set of norms, practices, and institutions constitutive of what I will here call the paradigm of law. This basic insight is hardly new for students of debates among positivists, realists, and naturalists of various stripes. However, the path to illumination here is less familiar. It focuses on an assessment of a common claim in transitional justice debates: that abusive regimes are "lawless." Here I argue that pre-transitional abuses are "extraordinary"[8] precisely because they express and extend a paradigm of law that justifies and often demands targeted violence.

On April 6, 1994, then-president of Rwanda Juvenal Habyarimana died when his plane crashed during its approach into Kigali airport under suspicious circumstances. During the months and years prior to his death, his government, the larger Hutu Power movement associated with his regime, and the civilian militia known as the interahamwe, spent considerable time and energy preparing the rhetorical and material resources necessary for genocide. Habyarimana's death unleashed that potential, and in less than four months between 500,000 and 1,000,000 Rwandan Tutsis, moderate Hutus, and others designated as "ibyitso"[9] were shot, hacked to death with hand tools and farming instruments, or simply beaten to death with sticks by former friends, neighbors, and spouses.

The first shot in Argentina's "Dirty War" was fired with the abduction and execution of General Pedro Aramburu by the left-wing Perónista Montoneros in May 1970.[10] The abduction and murder of General Aramburu ushered in an era of abductions, armed robberies, bombings, and terrorist attacks perpetrated by a variety of groups boasting colorful acronyms.[11] By 1974, and the rise of Isabel Perón, institutional violence had become a staple of the new right regime. Under the guidance of José López Rega, the Argentine Anticommunist Alliance (AAA) set about a nationwide program of assassinations and disappearances in order to protect the nation from the "plague" of communist insurgents.[12] Students, priests, lawyers, teachers, activists, journalists, and politicians were all targets for organized death squads. Despite the hundreds killed, however, not a single assassin was arrested, much less prosecuted. Relying on the evidence of continued violence, the survival of leftist paramilitary groups, and the resonate rhetoric of the cold war,[13] the military stepped into Argentine politics in 1976,[14] organizing executive control under the first in a series of military juntas. From 1976 to 1983 tens of thousands of Argentines identified as "subversives" were murdered, tortured, and disappeared.[15]

From the early seventeenth century into the nineteenth, millions of Africans were taken by force to the Americas as chattel slaves. A substantial number of those millions were brought to the British colonies of North America and later the United States. By the time President Abraham Lincoln issued his Emancipation Proclamation on January 1, 1863, the total number of Africans and Americans of African descent enslaved in the United States topped four million. Inhumane by definition, chattel slavery in the United States was also notoriously brutal. Torture and rape were routine. Murder was not in the slightest uncommon. While passage of the Reconstruction amendments ended the institution of slavery, discrimination and violence targeted against Americans of African descent abated only slightly, now directed through systems of economic and political disenfranchisement, segregation, and targeted violence including, most notoriously, lynching.[16] While the forms and institutionalized pathways of systemic racial injustice have changed, racial injustice persists today in various forms in criminal justice systems, education, housing, economic access, and radical disparities in social status—leaving the United States with seemingly indelible marks of its slaveholding past.[17]

In cases such as these, it is tempting to think that law was absent or otherwise was powerless to stop atrocities or to protect members of targeted groups. If that is right, then the challenge in transitions is a straightforward one with a simple solution: bring law and the rule of law to the lawless. While practical difficulties surely abound, there would seem to be few, if any, knotty conceptual challenges or significant theoretical lessons to be learned about the nature, structures, and role of law. While this view is tempting, due in no small part to the distinct flavor of universalism, it fails to take seriously the key role played by law and the rule of law in targeted and mass violence.

In a provocative article titled "The New Imperialism: Violence, Norms, and the 'Rule of Law,'" Rosa Ehrenreich Brooks[18] takes on the fable that abusive regimes are characterized by and perhaps are a consequence of the absence of the rule of law. As she argues, "most of our standard assumptions about the relationship between law, order, and violence cannot be justified at all."[19] To the contrary, conceived as a set of formal structures for the promulgation and regular enforcement of public and private law, "the rule of law" can be a terrible tool indeed. For example, the rule of law was central to the genocidal designs of the Third Reich, which used the formal structures of law and legalism to organize and justify discriminatory policies, forced movement, nationalization of property, slave labor, and, eventually, genocide.[20]

Rule of law devotees may shrug off these examples as instances of perversion, arguing that the true faith requires not just respect for formal structures but an understanding of those structures as linked to a form of universalism that packages human nature, law, and the rule of law together with an onto-teleological conception of human rights.[21] Ehrenreich Brooks rightly challenges this view as well, pointing out that, not only is there "little correlation between law, order, and violence,"[22] "some of the time at least, people actively prefer violence and suffering to peace and prosperity,"[23] "in part because many people value moral meaning more than they value safety and prosperity."[24] To put it mildly, this is a disturbing proposition, and deserves a bit more attention.

The German philosopher and psychiatrist Karl Jaspers in his famous lectures on "German Guilt" pointed out that "[e]very human being is fated to be enmeshed in the power relations he lives by."[25] That Jaspers put this idea at the center of a heroic effort to come to terms with his role and the role of his fellow Germans in the Holocaust grants his claim weight and salience in the present context. Particularly important is Jaspers's recognition that our common subjective notions of freewill must at least recognize that we each, as agents, are socially, culturally, and politically embedded. That we are "enmeshed" in these power relationships does not, as Maggie Grace has argued, mean that we must abandon our closely held notions of freewill or the possibility of moral and legal responsibility.[26] Rather, the point is that we are by nature social beings. In the context of mass atrocities, which require the coordinated actions of thousands or millions, understanding the conditions and effects of social forces is fundamental to our understanding of targeted violence, its agents, and ourselves.

In his work on social processes, Victor Turner strikes a contrast between "consensual power" and "coercive power."[27] On Turner's view, coercive power is distinguished by its use of force or the threat of force to achieve its ends. Coercive power may be brutal, but it is often more subtle. For example, utilitarian approaches to criminal law understand power as a tool of coercion. In particular, utilitarians seek to change, alter, or manipulate behavior by using threats of force to shift personal calculations of risk and reward.[28] By contrast, consensual power "is a symbolic medium"[29] that creates links between subjects, a worldview, an ideology, and complementary life ways.[30] Consensual power creates links between subjects' senses of themselves and the production and maintenance of social states of affairs.[31] Consensual power therefore conceives of its subjects not as objects for manipulation by threat of force, but as a supple medium that can be shaped and formed into willing instruments.[32] Consensual power seeks not to force subjects to perform, but rather aspires to produce effects from within. As compared to coercive power, consensual power pursues patterns of conformance by creating subjects who find fulfillment and meaning in the production and maintenance of a particular vision of the world as it is, ought to be, can be, and will be.[33] To return to Ehrenreich Brooks's vocabulary, consensual power achieves results by shaping its subjects' conceptions of moral meaning and ethical value so those agents will engage in desired forms of conduct not to avoid unwanted consequences but as positive expressions of ethical commitments to self and to the world as it ought to be.

A similar conception of power is at the heart of Michel Foucault's historical archaeologies. Foucault argues that power's most significant preoccupation is with the production of subjects within "regimes of truth."[34] Foucault defines regimes of truth as circular relationships among "truth"—conceived as "systems of ordered procedures for the production, regulation, distribution, circulation and operation of statements,"—"systems of power"—"which produce and sustain [truth],"—and "effects of power"—"which [truth] induces and which extend [truth]."[35] In his view, truth and power are linked through public institutions and practices where truth is elaborated and established by the production of phenomena, including subjects, which in turn reinforce and sometimes alter the norms of inclusion and exclusion, right and wrong, good and bad, which constitute truth as a system for ordering descriptive, ontological, normative, and teleological claims.

While somewhat elusive on first review, Foucault maintains that this conception of truth and power as regime is far from metaphysical. To the contrary, for him "Truth [as] a thing of the world . . . induces regular effects of power."[36] Principal among those effects are status relationships between individuals and structural relationships between individuals and institutions, all of which are, on his view, mutually constitutive.[37] That is, by being "enmeshed" in regimes of truth, we are captured in a multi-lectical web of relationships among institutions, people, and values in which we create others and institutions just as we are created by others and institutions.

Foucault pursued this account of truth and power at length in his archaeologies, where he documents the interactions between normative systems and institutions in the creation of subjects.[38] The core lesson of this work is that, while the general structures of truth and power are largely universal, its participant and consequent effects are highly contingent. So, as Foucault puts it, "Each society has its regime of truth, its 'general politics' of truth."[39] Further, societies at all levels are constantly in flux, engaged in the process of establishing, developing, and using institutions to sort truth claims, create norms, histories, teleologies, and social ideologies that regulate, order, and thereby create subjects.[40]

By way of ethnography rather than social archaeology, Turner reached a similar view, though he used the vocabulary of "paradigms" instead of truth regimes. According to Turner, "paradigms" are "sets of 'rules' from which many kinds of sequences of social action may be generated but which further specify what sequences must be excluded."[41] Paradigms draw and maintain the boundaries of society and designate the roles and positions of individuals within society.[42] In addition, because paradigms regulate the terms of acceptable conduct and describe the content and categorization of social identity, they are both the subject and the object of social action. That is, in addition to generating their own subjects, paradigms enter into contests with competing paradigms.[43] Paradigms are, therefore, not just sources of meaning, but provide fields of contest among groups and among groups' competing moral, political, and cultural truth claims.

More recently the notion that subjective experiences of moral meaning and ethical values are linked contingently to experience, political commitments, socioeconomic status, and institutional context has provided the motivating superstructure of the highly engaging cultural cognition project led by Dan Kahan, Donald Braman, David Hoffman, and others.[44] Contributing researchers to this project have conducted several comprehensive surveys and have drawn data from many more to demonstrate that, for example, subjects' ranking of crime seriousness and assessments of what conduct violates "core" moral or legal norms are highly dependent on collateral cultural, social, religious, gender, and class affiliations.[45] While the debate over moral universalism and legal naturalism is far from settled,[46] the efforts of these scholars and researchers provide persuasive evidence that our ethical and moral commitments, and even our core assessments of self, are developed in a broader social context that is both affective and effective.

While far too fast, this brief survey is sufficient to claim some credibility for a fairly straightforward proposition: societies feature internal identity norms that are developed, established, and extended through public and private institutions, practices, rituals, and patterns of behavior. These norms are fundamental to society and its members. They mark boundaries of inclusion and exclusion, and therefore play a central role in constructing identity.[47]

Thinking of identity as a function of norms, practices, and institutions leads to the conclusion that identity is, to borrow from Benedict Anderson, "imagined."[48] However, for most folks identity is both fundamental and experienced as "true" from a subjective point of view.[49] Internal assessments of self-worth and external dignity claims are also grounded in notions that not only identity, but also the constellation of norms, practices, and institutions that participate in the circular processes of mutual production described by Foucault's regime of truth, are natural, necessary, and right. This socio-ethical dimension of "moral meaning" incorporates conceptions of relative ontological position and teleological entitlement endorsed by historical narrative, linking self-image and assessments of self-worth to broader systems of truth and power.

This last point is critical. Social paradigms and regimes of truth are not abstract. They require terrestrial footing. They exist and persist only to the extent that they can and do produce subjects who internalize core values, act in ways that reflect and extend dominant social ideologies, and who are willing to pursue a transcendent view of the end of history.

We are now in a better position to make sense of Ehrenreich Brooks's claim that, for some people "in some places, some of the time, violence and suffering are actually more attractive than peace and prosperity, not simply because violence offers a chance to gain power and wealth, but because killing (or dying) for a cause can seem far more important—indeed more appealing—than mere survival or acquiring wealth."[50] The kind of violence and atrocities at the center of conversations about transitional justice are not like most acts of violence perpetrated in stable states.[51] Events of mass atrocity are much more than a coincidental collection of murders, rapes, and assaults perpetrated by independent agents. Thousands of Hutus did not just wake up on a spring day in 1994 and simultaneously decide to murder their neighbors.[52] What distinguishes these atrocities from common murders and assaults in stable states is the role played by the constituents of social paradigms or truth regimes, which together give targeted violence "moral meaning."[53] Taking this descriptive claim seriously has important consequences for conversations about transition, transitional justice, and, as we shall see, "law."

As John Rawls points out, transitional states are heirs to abusive paradigms and therefore are "burdened."[54] The paradigms that hold sway in pre-transitional regimes provide a view of the world for abusers in which murder, rape, and assault targeted against members of a specific group[55] are moral, ethical, or historical imperatives. At the very least, those abusive paradigms posit an ontological account of society that exempts members of the targeted group from the universe of "persons" who can be "murdered," "raped," or "assaulted."[56] On Daniel Goldhagen's description, this public sanction often manifests subjectively as a sense of entitlement on the part of abusers: "Who doubts that the Argentine or Chilean murderers of people who opposed the recent authoritarian regimes thought that their victims deserved to die? Who doubts that the Tutsis who slaughtered Hutus in Burundi or the Hutus who slaughtered Tutsis in Rwanda, that one Lebanese militia which slaughtered the civilian supporters of another, that the Serbs who have killed Croats or Bosnian Muslims, did so out of conviction in the justice of their actions?"[57] Perpetrators of atrocities are "willing executioners," as Goldhagen describes them, because they are defending their view of the world as it ought to be and carrying out their destiny as a people, group, or society.[58] Their acts of violence are therefore pregnant with "moral meaning."

While abusive paradigms vary in the details, they share a few salient features. First, they tend to divide members of the society into one of two groups.[59] Second, following this "bipolar logic,"[60] abusive paradigms engage an ontology that provides grounds for members of one group to characterize members of the other group as subhuman,[61] naturally subservient,[62] or at least not people "like us" deserving of full respect and equal treatment.[63] Third, abusive paradigms endorse a teleological view of history that identifies the members of one group as a persistent and emergent threat against the survival of the dominant group and a barrier against the dominant group's succeeding to its rightful place at the end of history.[64] At the intersection of these features, abusive paradigms allow perpetrators to attach moral meaning if not ethical necessity to violence.[65]

The role of an abusive paradigm at the core of pre-transitional abuses is widely recognized.[66] For example, Roy Brooks points out that "atrocities can only occur when the perpetrator fails to *identify* with [his] victims and fails to recognize a common humanity between [him] and [his] victims."[67] Laurel Fletcher and Harvey Weinstein reach a similar conclusion.[68] In an essay on the Balkans, Richard Rorty notes that those who participate in mass atrocities do not regard their victims as "fellow human beings," but as "animals" or "pseudohumans."[69] Daniel Goldhagen has argued that perpetrators of atrocities are "willing executioners" who "th[ink] that their victims should die" and who kill "out of conviction in the justice of their actions."[70] Philip Gourevitch has described genocide as "an exercise in community building."[71] W. E. B. Du Bois tied racial oppression to a bipolar logic, highlighting the role of intergroup fear in racial violence.[72] Echoing Du Bois, Sherrilyn Ifill has linked lynching in the United States during the early twentieth century to a background racism that cast those with dark skin as dangerous, prone to violence, and lesser evolved.[73]

"Law" has a significant role in the construction, extension, and expression of abusive paradigms. In stable states, prohibitions on violence are so commonly, regularly, and relatively equally enforced that we often feel comfortable talking about universal legal norms.[74] In these comfortable environments, violence and theft are the exception because they are labeled and prohibited by established and regularly enforced legal prohibitions on murder, rape, assault, and larceny. By contrast, in abusive regimes, violence and expropriation of property targeted against particular groups is both the norm and is normalized.[75] In these ancién regimes,[76] black-letter law frequently fails to condemn, supports, or even demands acts of abuse.[77] Public officials participate, either directly or by sustaining an environment in which targeted violence is tolerated or encouraged.[78] Police and the military join local officials in organizing and perpetrating offenses in the name of the state.[79] Other public officials organize programs of systematic discrimination.[80] These official acts form part of a paradigm of law that provides license for the targeted violence at the center of most conversations about transitions and transitional justice. In recognition of the role played by paradigms of law in abusive regimes, transitions must focus on personal and institutional reforms designed to give material dimension to the rhetorical commitments to democratic ideals, human rights, and the rule of law that so often comprise the raison d'être of transitions to democracy.[81]

"Paradigm of law" as I use the phrase here, is not identical to or exhausted by black-letter law. In some regimes, black-letter law requires abuse. This is not always the case, however. In many regimes, laws on the books prohibit murder, rape, and other acts of violence.[82] Unfortunately, as another contributor to this volume, Ruti Teitel, has pointed out, in abusive regimes "there is commonly a large gap between the law as written and as it is perceived."[83] Those perceptions are not due to the idiosyncratic views of particular agents, but reflect that fact that black-letter law out of context is at best random markings upon the page. Those pen strokes and type strikes only gain meaning and the capacity to produce effects in the world if they are embedded in a paradigm or regime of truth.[84] In abusive regimes, "law" is regulated by social and institutional elements of legally engaged paradigms, which affect perceptions of *what* is and is not legal[85] and, perhaps more important, *who is* and *who is not* a proper beneficiary of legal protections.[86] So, while there were laws on the books against murder in antebellum slave states, killing slaves was a crime against chattel, not murder.

To sum up a bit, in abusive regimes mass violence is not random but reflects the targeting of certain classes of victims. That targeting reflects and expresses prevailing "paradigmatic" beliefs about who is and who is not included in the class of beings who enjoy the protections afforded by laws against murder, rape, assault, and theft. Those who participate in violence do so both because the "law" grants them leave, but also to express in clear terms their moral endorsement of—and ethical attachment to—the vision of reality and the end of history described and defended by the prevailing abusive paradigm of law. For the moment, it does not matter where the "truth" that underlies and sustains abusive regimes comes from. Whether it is a result of colonial occupation, political strategy, or timeless narrative, the effect is the same: there is a rational social grounding for the mass, institutionalized, and targeted violence at the center of conversations about transitional justice.[87]

While it is impossible in this chapter to be completely responsible from an anthropological or historical point of view, a couple of examples are in order:

Nazi crimes, and the support provided by ordinary Germans during the Holocaust, were sponsored by an "eliminationist anti-Semitism"[88] that foretold a complete eradication of European Jews.[89] An abusive paradigm of law, disseminated and enforced by bureaucratic, executive, and military agents, played a critical role in the targeting of Jews and Gypsies for death in Nazi occupied Europe from 1935 to 1945.[90] From early experiments with targeted violence that preceded passage of the Nuremberg Laws, to *Kristallnacht,* to full-scale mechanized genocide, Nazi atrocities carried moral meaning for perpetrators, who, through their engagements with the constituents of the prevailing abusive paradigm of law, were invited to conclude that their acts of targeted violence put them on the right side of the law, the right side of right, and the right side of history.[91]

The Nazis were not the only perpetrators of atrocities to deploy historical teleology, social ontology, and institutional practice as constituents of an abusive paradigm of law to guide and justify mass atrocity. In 1994, the Hutu Power government in Rwanda utilized the authority of the state in combination with broader media and social outlets to explain that killing Tutsis was essential to the preservation and survival of the state. That abusive paradigm further justified targeted violence by reference to a historical conception of Tutsis as foreign interlopers and a teleology that foretold their departure on the waters that brought them.[92] Within days of the call by Hutu Power leaders to send Tutsis back whence they came, the rivers leading north to Lake Kivu were clogged with tens of thousands of corpses.

In addition to being justified by pseudoscience on race, chattel slavery in the United States was explicitly endorsed by the Constitution as ratified in 1788.[93] Further, as Mark Graber has argued, judicial decisions upholding slavery, including the infamous *Dred Scott* case in the Supreme Court, were "rightly" decided to the extent that they accurately read not only laws on the books, but also the set of public norms, institutional practices, ontological beliefs, and teleological commitments constitutive of the prevailing paradigm of law.[94]

As these examples show, linking historical narrative and racial ontology to victim status is common among paradigms that inspire and justify targeted abuse.[95] It is also an essential piece of the puzzle posed by questions of law in transition. An abusive paradigm linked to law and system of laws is essential to projects of mass, institutionalized, and targeted violence. Calls for transition, and the institutional and social reforms that transitions entail, serve as further evidence of this descriptive claim. While acts of violence stand out against the backdrop of a stable state, the acts that characterize pre-transitional societies blend into a society whose pathology runs so deep that large-scale political, social, cultural, and legal change is necessary.[96] This defining demand for fundamental change in transition only makes sense if one recognizes that there is something deeply wrong with abusive regimes.[97] That something, the feature of abusive regimes that requires the hard work of transition, is the abusive paradigm that played a key role in rationalizing and sustaining the program of targeted abuse.

In abusive regimes, socio-ontological support provided by an abusive paradigm combines with actual laws on the books, official doctrine, and state practice to construct an abusive paradigm of law that affects interpretations of legal duty and establishes the conditions necessary for mass atrocities on a scale that requires systemic transition and transitional justice.[98] In some cases, state approval is tacit, manifested by passivity in the face of abuses.[99] In other cases, state support is active and organized.[100] In some cases laws against murder are not enforced or are interpreted as not protecting some groups.[101] In other cases black-letter law or official state policies require targeted violence.[102] In all cases, however, state support expressed by and through an abusive paradigm is a necessary corollary of mass atrocity. To conclude the contrary would be to claim that slavery in America, the Holocaust, the Argentine Dirty War, the abuses of Apartheid, and the Rwandan Massacre were no more than unhappy coincidences of independent evil acts of will.

This claim does not defend or rely on determinism. Those living under abusive regimes can choose not to participate in atrocities. In fact, many do; and all cases of mass atrocity feature stories of moral heroes who do what is right or refuse to do what is wrong, often at great personal peril. Those who participate in mass violence choose to become abusers, some grudgingly and some with frightening enthusiasm. The critical point defended here is that these choices are not made in solipsistic isolation. That is in part the point of Rawls's reminder that abusive regimes are "burdened" societies.[103] That burden is a function of the fact that atrocities committed by and under abusive regimes reflect an operating set of socially generated and publicly circulated beliefs that, in combination with institutional practices and government policies, form a paradigm of law that at least does not forbid violence against a victim group and often actively encourages it.

Neither does this account of atrocities imply that conformance with an abusive legal paradigm justifies abuse. Rape, murder, and torture are evils no matter what a contrary paradigm of law might say. The court in *Dred Scott* was most definitely wrong, even if the case was rightly decided. The only claim made here is that "law," as it appears to those living in abusive regimes, does not forbid, and frequently encourages, violence targeted against particular individuals and groups.[104] This official support distinguishes institutionalized mass violence from banal criminal activity or small-scale abuses of power perpetrated by cadres of opportunists—the conditions well understood by "ordinary justice."[105] It also distinguishes transitional justice from the "ordinary justice" concerns that distract most legislators and law enforcement officials in stable states.

Any attempt to deal with the challenges of justice in transitions that ignores this defining feature will always fail to satisfy.[106] It also will pose significant risks for the success of transitional movements by ignoring the need for sustainable reform of public norms and institutions. Only by taking normative account of the unique circumstances of pre-transitional abuses can practitioners and theorists hope to develop a practically sustainable and theoretically sound approach to transition and transitional justice. In so doing, those practitioners and theorists will advance our understanding of "law" as a set of normatively informed institutional practices embedded within broader social paradigms that inform the content, application, effects, and assessments of law. The perhaps not-so-humble suggestion here is that what those efforts have and will reveal is that "law" is not just words on a page, but the meaning and impact of those words in light of broader social paradigms manifested by subjects' conduct under law. "Law" in this sense is implicated in broader paradigms. "Law" also is often a paradigm of itself, host to its own fields of contest and participant in broader contests among competing paradigms. The lesson to be taken from transitions, then, is that law is not separate from, but is part of, implicated in, defined by, and made manifest in these contests. Law, like its subjects, is "embedded."

II: Mass Violence and the Collapse of Dynamic Stability

In addition to asking what transitions and the abusive regimes that precede transitions reveal about law, one of the goals of this collection is to examine the conditions that precipitate crisis and breakdown in legal authority. The first part of this chapter challenged the assumption underlying this question, which is that crisis in the form of mass targeted atrocities is a consequence of a breakdown of "law." In part I, I argued that, quite to the contrary, mass violence is linked to law and legal authority through an abusive paradigm such that law as paradigm becomes a participant in atrocities. Even if this account of abusive regimes is correct, however, the question of how abusive paradigms of law come to be and how they gain sufficient sway to organize mass violence is a worthy one and promises to deepen our understanding of law as paradigm.

Targeted and mass violence follows as a natural and necessary consequence of the collapse, not of law and legal authority, but of dynamic stability among competing and overlapping associations and oppositions. In keeping with the description of abusive paradigms in part I, the account of crisis and breakdown advanced here endorses an expanded definition of law as inclusive of broader social paradigms that inform, animate, and activate the proscriptive norms often identified as "law." This argument suggests that law only functions as a tool of peace and stability if it is cast in a broader social and political milieu that reinforces an overlapping array of oppositions and associations. In this respect, abusive regimes and transitions are not so much exceptional as revelatory. "Law," wherever it is found, exists and functions as a paradigm and is linked to a broader set of competing paradigms that affect how law functions and therefore what "law" is.

Complicating "law" to include the constituents of a broader paradigm of law risks implying that communities, states, and nations are homogeneous, inhabited by only one paradigm, truth regime, or source of consensual power. This is most certainly not the case. To the contrary, as Karl Jaspers has pointed out: "There is no such thing as a people as whole. All lines that we may draw to define it are crossed by facts. Language, nationality, culture, common fate—all this does not coincide but is overlapping."[107] As this suggests, most societies are not limited to a single fundamental and ubiquitous line or mode of association. Rather, all societies, and particularly stable states, are "segmented,"[108] constituted of many smaller groups and associations with each standing in opposition to at least one competing group or association.[109]

By definition, groups exclude some individuals and include others. Groups and their members are engaged in constant battles over where to draw boundaries of inclusion and exclusion, often in the context of efforts to recruit and retain members or to exclude nonmembers. In the midst of these contests opposition-based identity claims carry real force, often as literal or figurative calls to arms. The rhetoric of these claims on solidarity and efforts to defeat the agendas and efforts of opposed groups often rely on the same bipolar logic characteristic of abusive paradigms.[110] Members are encouraged to cultivate a sense of privilege and natural superiority and are emboldened by predictions that, at the end of the day, their group surely will prevail.

These appeals and exchanges occur at all levels of society as individuals and groups deploy competing paradigms in contests over scarce resources, political dominance, or identity itself. We argue about who we should hire into our workplaces and who we should include in our country clubs, churches, and cliques. We comment on how our friends' new loves are not worthy or deserving. We spin history to conform the world to our idiosyncratic conceptions of right. This is the stuff of society at all levels, and a mainstay for Tolstoy, Austen, and daytime dramas. These common line-drawing activities also follow the bipolar logic that drives abusive paradigms by indulging in ontologies of superiority and teleologies of entitlement. In other words, in all states lie the seeds of targeted violence and mass atrocity. Yet, somehow, qua stable states, most societies are able to maintain peace and to constrain the capacity of "moral meaning" attached to oppositional and associational identity to drive acts of violence, much less sustained targeted abuse.

Petty slights and minor intrigues aside, our common social engagements around group formation and maintenance seldom result in blood-letting more serious than fisticuffs between fans of opposing sports teams. On a larger scale, despite the fact that deep social and political oppositions are a given in most modern states, with few exceptions these divisions, no matter how deep and emotional, do not lead to social collapse. Even in the face of heated electoral contests underwritten by deep party divisions and fed by inflammatory rhetoric, in most countries, most of the time, members of political parties do not kill one another piecemeal, much less wholesale. "Why" may seem a riddle; but the answer is both transparent and profound: states maintain stability by preserving a diversity of overlapping oppositions and associations.

In the midst of heated public contests among groups, charismatic public figures often implore us to set aside our differences and to celebrate common interests, traits, or characteristics that suggest something shared and universal—a thread that unites us despite our differences. Some political scientists endorse these prescriptions, suggesting that identity based on opposition, particularly when drawn along racial or ethnic lines, is inherently destabilizing.[111] While in some ways tempting, these calls to unity are unrealistic and potentially dangerous.

Despite their obvious dangers, oppositions and oppositional identity are necessary by logic and unavoidable in practice. There is no association without opposition.[112] Inclusion by definition implies exclusion. Every time we lay claim to a colleague as someone "like us" we at least posit, but more often identify by implication, another person who is not. That is okay. While perhaps fraught, the processes and dynamics of oppositional identity are fundamental to our species and do not require a bloody end. That is because most people do not limit their conceptions of themselves to one line of association and opposition, and most societies contain a large number of associations and oppositions that overlap and cross-sect one another.

Identity, including ethnic and racial identity, is not "fixed, unidimensional, and exogenous to politics."[113] Rather, identity is "fluid, multidimensional," and responsive to public and private events.[114] Identity is, to revert to vocabulary developed earlier in this chapter, a product of subjects' engagements with social and legal paradigms by which they develop an ethical sense of what Ehrenreich Brooks calls "moral value." However, for most citizens of relatively stable states identity is not defined entirely by reference to a single association. Rather, most of us understand ourselves in relation to a multiplicity of intersecting associations and oppositions.[115] While some postmodernists view this multidimensionality as partial license to regard identity claims with a certain irony,[116] for most people, most of the time, oppositions and associations along gender, religious, racial, ethnic, cultural, class, sexual, and political lines are regarded as both essential and fundamental.

If this is right, then individuals have a more complex identity than their association with a particular group might suggest. Pulling back a bit to achieve a broader perspective reveals that this multidimensionality means that individuals mark points of intersection between different groups. The point in social space occupied by any particular person implicates multiple dyadic lines of opposition and association. Individual group members who occupy these points of intersection create lines of cohesion among groups with potentially conflicting agendas and, by virtue of their positions, limit the potential for groups to develop and sustain long-term opposition or to escalate normal conflicts to violence.[117] Perhaps paradoxically, then, a robust multiplicity and variety of segmentary oppositions actually allows societies to achieve and maintain stability.[118] Stability consequent of multiple overlapping associations and oppositions is by nature and necessity dynamic, supple, and flexible in the face of internal and external challenges.[119] It is by virtue of this dynamic stability that most societies maintain a relative level of peace.[120] By contrast, societies that reify a single exclusive thread of universal association and raise to preeminence a particular line of association are terrifyingly brittle, unstable, and poised on the precipice of disaster, awaiting only a trigger event to lead them into chaos.[121]

This account of stability as a function of dynamic cross-sectionality is not entirely novel. In fact, it is a centerpiece in many mid-twentieth century ethnographies.[122] E. E. Evans-Pritchard's work on the Nuer provides a ready example.[123] According to Evans-Pritchard, patriarchal lineage provides a primary source of identity among the Nuer, particularly in the context of feuds, where agnatic associations establish duties of defense and vengeance.[124] Members of agnate groups do not necessarily live in close proximity. Rather, as a consequence of exogenous marriage rules and other economic and social pressures, patrilineal affiliates frequently live some distance away from one another.[125] As a consequence, daily life is dominated not by patrilineal association and opposition, but by a variety of economic, social, political, and religious links that sometimes overlap agnatic lines, but often do not. These cross-secting group affiliations introduce fissures within agnate groups, but also bind members of otherwise opposed agnate groups to one another along collateral lines of association.[126] Exogenous marriage rules play a particularly important role, as reflected in the pithy phrase "they are our enemies; we marry them."[127] Social rules regarding child care create yet more structural cross-associations, linking children and maternal uncles.[128] Add to these various other economic, ritual, historic, and social associations, and a picture emerges of Nuer society as constructed of dynamic competing cross-associations.[129] As a consequence, even between sworn enemies, there exist associational forces of cohesion.

As Max Glucksman has argued, this overlapping structure of group association and opposition is essential to reducing and controlling violence.[130] Societies composed and recomposed by dynamic cross-sectional associations are far more stable than isolated groups or collections of unassociated individuals.[131] Intra- and intergroup conflict is, of course, inevitable. In Evans-Pritchard's terms, segmentary forces of fission constantly arise, emphasizing particular lines of opposition and association.[132] If individuals existed in a one-dimensional social universe there would be no hope of limiting conflict or constraining violence when fissures appeared. However, individuals who exist at the nexus of numerous different lines of association inevitably find that self-interest is far more complex than might appear in the face of an immediate fission within or between groups. Thus, countervailing, collateral forces of fusion drive members and groups together even as fissionary forces push them apart.[133]

This is a dynamic process. Different lines of association wax and wane, often in reaction to the source and nature of a conflict or threat.[134] Conflicts among nations drive intertribal conflicts into the background.[135] Clan rivalries are suffused in the face of intertribal conflict. Associational identities may even be forgotten in the absence of an activating opposition.[136] However, in functional and stable societies cross-sectional associations never disappear entirely. It is by virtue of this dynamism that conflict and violence underwritten by any particular opposition is controlled, regulated, and constrained.[137] Stability is maintained by offsetting vectors of association and opposition.[138]

Long before Evans-Pritchard's work on the Nuer, James Madison highlighted the stability of dynamic cross-sectional societies as an important reason to support the formation of a union among the thirteen colonies.[139] In Federalist Nine, Hamilton railed against factions as a present danger to the stability of the proposed union.[140] His fear was that, liberated to pursue their own interests, people would form insular groups and mobilize to pursue narrow agendas, thereby fragmenting and destabilizing the body politic with deleterious consequences to the fragile new union.[141] Madison was sympathetic to these concerns, but disagreed with Hamilton's assessment of the danger. Madison recognized that the only way to prevent political factions from forming was by tyrannical means. As a natural consequence of freedom, people will develop and pursue their own conceptions of the good life, forming associations with those who share their interests and goals.[142]

Unlike Hamilton, Madison did not see the demise of the union in these exercises of freedom. To the contrary, he argued that the union was more likely to survive and thrive if it encouraged diversification rather than consolidation of interests.[143] According to Madison, the real danger in any democracy is not factions, but the emergence of a single tyrannical faction. Interest groups forced to swim in a sea alive with competitors have a harder time forming uncomplicated, dominant, and persistent majorities. Anticipating Kanchan Chandra's work on ethnic politics, Madison argued that, in a broad and diverse union, factions are forced to adopt moderate policy positions in order to form majorities and to maintain the support of members who have cross-affiliations with other factions.[144]

The role that Madison predicted for dynamic cross-sectionality is evident in most stable democracies.[145] Social cohesion in modern nation-states is achieved not by ensuring fundamental loyalty to one shared norm, narrative, or institution. Rather, it is achieved through a complex interwoven web of competing and overlapping loyalties and associations.[146] The nation is stabilized by the overlapping communities within its borders through intersecting lines of interest and allegiance among members.[147]

John Venn might describe this account of social stability graphically as an extensive system of overlapping circles. Each circle would represent a group inclusive of its animating and legitimizing paradigm. Each of us is a member of multiple groups. We therefore occupy a unique space created by the intersecting spheres of the communities in which we are members. This account of dynamic stability therefore provides not only a description of society, but of personal identity as well. We *are* the space created by overlapping claims of existential sufficiency. Some of us are mothers, lawyers, Presbyterians, and Cubs fans. Others of us are child-free, photographers, Buddhists, and Cardinal fans.

It is by virtue of the intersectional identity of its members that most societies are able to maintain relative stability. Were a society to be definitively divided between two groups it would be a recipe for disaster. Fortunately, this seldom happens. In most societies most of the time, the members of opposed groups are linked directly or indirectly through collateral lines of association. Whenever a line of opposition is emphasized, pushing society to segment, collateral lines of association are activated, limiting the destructive potential of the divisive force. Cubs and Cardinal fans may spit venom at each other at the height of a divisional race, but also see each other in church on Sunday or at professional conferences where their shared group affiliations are emphasized. A similar phenomenon is evident on the international stage, where trade, treaties, immigration, and the maintenance of diplomatic ties serve as essential tools for regulating and controlling conflicts among sovereign countries by creating lines of interdependence and by building and maintaining bulwarks of affiliation against inevitable tides of conflict.[148]

So how do states collapse into cycles of mass violence? In most states, a robust system of overlapping associations provides overall stability by counterbalancing segmentary pressures with collateral sources of cohesion. What distinguishes abusive regimes from stable states is a catastrophic failure in this web of dynamic stability; a shift that is normally precipitated by crisis, often in the form of external threat.[149] Referring to the crisis, members of a group vying for dominance draw on their group's paradigm to claim that members of an opposing group are connected in an essential way to the threat. That move opens a critical gap between those with us and those against us and provides teleological justification for isolating members of another group. When these rhetorical strategies target groups defined by existential status, such as race, ethnicity, or religion, genocide is in the offing. The only task that remains is to assert control over law and legal institutions in order to provide a legitimate pathway for targeted violence as an expression of the now-dominant paradigm.

In contrast with stable states, where there is a dynamic balance of diverse associations and oppositions, this process of exploiting crisis reifies a single line of opposition. Now dominant, the paradigm that defines that line of opposition makes ontological connections between group identity and normative status to justify claims of inherent status inequality that render members of the targeted group not only as subhumans, but as emergent threats, and therefore proper targets for violence. That pathological status inequality also severely limits the ability of cross-secting terms of association and identification to preserve the broader and more inclusive systems of social cohesion that restrain violence.[150] The consequence of this crisis-driven pathological segmentation is an almost inevitable lapse in the "general need for peace, and recognition of a moral order in which this peace can flourish,"[151] which opens the door to violent realization of the normative and teleological projection of an abusive paradigm of law.

This pattern of crisis-driven collapse of dynamic stability was evident in Nazi Germany. While eliminationist anti-Semitism was a persistent thread in the social fabric of early-twentieth-century Germany, Aryans, Jews, Romani, and other non-Aryans lived in relative peace because lines of social, economic, and even family association cross-cut the racial divide.[152] What precipitated the Holocaust was the suppression of those cross-associations and the alignment of anti-Semitism with nationalism underwritten by widespread anxiety tied to economic crisis.[153] The exclusive claim on authentic national identity asserted by a core group obsessed with racial purity rendered any commitment to continued association with those not of Aryan descent unpatriotic—an act of faithlessness not just to race but to country as well.[154] Had race not assumed this position of dominance as the defining line of opposition and association then the Holocaust simply would not have happened.

The Rwandan genocide followed a similar pattern. There was a history of ethnic tension in the country long before 1994. There were even episodes of violence. However, that violence was constrained by innumerable cross-secting lines of association. Many Hutus married Tutsis, and vice versa. Hutus and Tutsis attended the same churches and schools. They were business associates and sat across from each other in government offices.[155] All that changed in early 1994 when rumblings about a Tutsi uprising from Burundi gave Hutu Power leaders in Rwanda the evidence they needed to bind national security to ethnic purity.[156] As in Nazi Germany, national identity in Rwanda was collapsed into ethnic identity as the paradigm of Hutu Power rose to dominance with its historical narrative and social ontology of ethnic supremacy. Those who retained a commitment to their Tutsi family, friends, and associates were identified as sympathizers and put to death alongside their loved ones because they chose to identify with the wrong side of the now hegemonic and defining line of social division.

While it is at least conceptually possible that a society may permanently fall prey to a paradigm of abuse,[157] far more common are cases of punctuated violence during which the paradigm—the truth regime—of one group gains temporary hegemony and exploits that dominance in an attempt to destroy permanently one or more opposing groups. In other words, mass atrocities mark moments of crisis. That crisis may be years or generations in the making, and may last months, decades, or even centuries. What is striking, however, is the near universal phenomenon of incomprehension among abusers and victims when the violence ends. In the wake of mass atrocity, participants frequently look in bewilderment at their bloody hands and destroyed lives and wonder how on earth this could have happened. That confusion signals the resurfacing of what had been forgotten, or at least suppressed: the lines of association between victims and abusers.

This moment of realization provides crucial guidance in transition. As we shall see, it also describes an important role for law and the rule of law in transitional and stable societies. The main task during the period of transition after mass atrocity is to construct or reconstruct the system of overlapping associations and oppositions characteristic of a stable society. Frequently this entails severing the claims of exclusivity and necessity made by an abusive paradigm during its rise to power and delinking that paradigm from law and legal institutions. To correct the pathological status disparities that allow abusers to see their victims as deserving of abuse or as subhumans unworthy of legal protection, transitions must create social pathways between the cohort of abusers and the cohort of victims through public institutions and civil society groups. In part III of this chapter I argue that "law" has a significant role to play in this enterprise as a set of normative guidelines, a collection of procedural pathways, and, perhaps most important, as a disputed field for contests among groups.

III: Law, Paradigms, and Overlapping Identities

It is tempting to think that the sort of targeted violence and mass atrocities that is prelude to transitions and transitional justice is only possible where law is absent or fails. Parts I and II of this chapter tested that instinct by arguing that violence on a scale that requires transition is organized and justified by a constellation of norms, institutional practices, social ontology, and historical teleology that give "moral meaning" to acts of violence directed against specific groups. Sometimes black-letter law and other sources of legal authority specifically endorse targeted violence; but laws on the books in abusive regimes frequently prohibit murder, rape, and assault. No matter their facial clarity, however, those familiar constraints on violence seldom provide any protection for members of targeted groups because abusive paradigms enforce status inequalities that relegate those in the targeted group to categories of "subhumans," "subversives," or others who are beyond the protections of black-letter law read with an eye made cold by removal from context. This account of mass atrocities indicated that law is not absent in abusive regimes. Rather, law participates in abuses by way of abusive paradigms. This examination of the role of law in abusive regimes supports a view of "law" as having a broader footprint than words on a page. At least in conversations about transitional justice, then, "law" takes on a more sociological dimension reflected in the phrase "law as paradigm."

For those who, like this author, put a lot of stock in the utopian potential of law and the rule of law, this description of the role of law in abusive regimes provides a moment of pause, but should not inspire despair. Part II holds the key to that hope. There it was argued that the main source of social stability is a diversity of overlapping oppositions. Social collapses that lead to transitions and the need for transitional justice occur where crisis events allow one particular line of opposition to assume a position of primacy, suppressing cross-secting lines of association, and attaching ontological significance to existential identity criteria that allow a rising paradigm to rationalize targeted abuse as necessary to bring about the proper end of history. This account of stability and collapse, in combination with an understanding of law as paradigm, suggests several important roles law can play in maintaining stability and preventing collapse.

First, in keeping with Madison's prescription in Federalist Ten, law and legal institutions should provide a normative structure that supports diversification of groups and group affiliation. In transitions, as in stable states, the key to maintaining social stability is preserving and extending a complex web of cross-secting associations and oppositions. Laws that reserve considerable space for civil society provide the opportunity for groups and associations to form, compete, and transform. The United States Constitution contains some valuable examples, including the right to free speech, the right to free association, and, as is discussed in more detail below, prohibitions against governmental infringement on religion. While a diversity of overlapping associations and oppositions provides dynamic protections against the development of hegemonic paradigms, law can build additional barriers against unproblematic claims of entitlement, dominance, and superiority. Equal protection laws are good examples of substantive legal norms attentive to this goal. Rules and governmental agencies that support access to justice provide critical procedural analogues to equal protection and offer some additional structural limits on the potential for routine status inequalities to become concrete and to produce sustained conditions of injustice.

Second, law should provide procedural alternatives to violence. It is sometimes said that litigation is war. Of course litigation is not war. Rather, litigation provides a field for contests among groups competing for scarce resources where violence is prohibited. Insofar as law can maintain its claim of legitimacy as a forum for these contests it provides a further limitation on the strategies competing groups can deploy to advance their goals. More important, it limits the scope of reasons deemed relevant in resolving these disputes. Law and lawyers often are criticized for their artificial vocabularies and the labyrinthine procedures in which they spend their professional lives. While often frustrating for litigants, the artificiality of law as a field for contests among parties and between groups plays an important role in controlling conflict. Before moving on, it is worth a moment to bring this point into clearer focus.

As described in part II, in the hurly-burly of public and private life we frame our claims of right by appealing to the normative ontology and social teleology of one or more social paradigms in which we and our audience are embedded. Counter claimants do the same. As a consequence, these contests over resources threaten to escalate into contests over group identity, dominance, and authenticity—familiar contests of "us vs. them." Because law has a somewhat abstract normative structure, it forces litigants to frame their claims in often arcane legal prose that is at least facially neutral with respect to larger contests among paradigms. As a consequence, law limits the utilitarian incentive to embed resource claims within encompassing social paradigms and therefore avoids linking disputes among individuals to larger contests among factions. Ideally, then, legal rules and procedures, properly conceived and realized, should be foreign, neutral, and should therefore render irrelevant and unnecessary the need for contestants to link damages claims, say, to narratives of ontological privilege and teleological entitlement. That constraint on reasons provides a valuable guard against the development of abusive paradigms.

Third, law should itself be a field and object of contest among groups and competing paradigms. This may seem somewhat in tension with the point just made. In some respects it is; but in keeping with the sociological approach to law advanced in this chapter, this reflects realities about the role played by law in social contests among groups.

Any student of the law knows that law is seldom completely neutral and that various groups at various times are able to embed their interests and the elements of the social paradigm that privileges those interests into the body and functions of law. This is dangerous. In fact, where too successful, this strategy can be a prelude to crisis and collapse because it creates permanent structures that enforce persistent status inequalities between groups. To guard against this tendency, opposed groups can and should engage in contests over the content and application of law. Whether as legislative battles or civil society debates, these contests provide a forum for explaining and exploring different visions of the world as it ought to be. Further, just as the artificial nature of legal processes impose some constraints on violence, the central role of communicative reason in the legislative process and in civil society debates imposes inherent constraints on the strategies groups can use to achieve their ends while placing a premium on consensus as intersecting interests and membership are identified.[158] By extension of this point, the formal rules of engagement in contests over law should maximize opportunities for participation by defending the conditions of what Justice Stephen Breyer calls "active liberty."[159]

While the present context does not allow an expansive discussion of these proposals, it is useful in the space remaining to consider briefly the examples afforded by religion and a secular analogue: contemporary debates in the United States about the role, meaning, and application of the United States Constitution.

A. Religion and Dynamic Stability

Societies collapse into cycles of targeted violence when a single line of opposition and association achieves dominance, creating an encompassing line of opposition, ossifying otherwise flexible social orders, and obscuring cross-secting lines of association. The best structural impediment against this kind of collapse is a robust web of diverse and highly contested associations and oppositions that make multiple and overlapping claims on individual identity. By preserving significant space for civil society and by affording protections for minority groups, law can play a crucial role in maintaining these basic structures of dynamic stability, which are essential to preserving overall social stability. Religion is historically one of the most promising and one of the most dangerous fields for these kinds of contests.

Religion, with race and ethnicity, tops the charts as a source for abusive paradigms.[160] It is at least nominally at the center of conflicts in Israel, Iraq, Iran, Afghanistan, and elsewhere in the Middle East.[161] Religious tension occupied a central place in the battle over Irish independence.[162] Ethnically tinged religious opposition motivated and organized conflicts in the Balkans during the 1990s.[163] Before these relatively modern crises, religion played a key role in the Crusades[164] and colonial movements the world over.[165]

Given this history, it is tempting to conclude that religion is inherently dangerous as a source for the kind of exclusive paradigms and truth regimes at the center of targeted atrocities. After all, religion—particularly in its fundamentalist forms—is committed to line-drawing. Religion defines the world and society in stark terms. In addition, common narratives internal to religious faith—including notions of deific favor, salvation, and prophesies of the end times—provide a natural source for the normative ontology and historical teleology that together frequently drive mass atrocities. Given this, the prospect of a completely secular society may seem pretty attractive.

Despite its dangers, religion is not all bad. Quite to the contrary, religion and religious figures comprise a prominent lineage among peacemakers. From Siddhartha Gautama, to Jesus Christ, to Gandhi, to Martin Luther King, the world-historical religious figures with public legacies of peace are too many to count. More privately, religion routinely motivates important acts of charity. In addition, many religious institutions play an important role in coordinating and directing good acts the world over. It seems, then, that there are good reasons for law to at least respect religion. Those reasons may extend even to justifying legal protections of religion generally.

There is, however, a deeper structural reason for law to encourage and preserve a place for religion in civil society. That reason is straightforward in light of the account of dynamic stability and collapse offered here. While religion is naturally and by definition exclusive, religious communities are, for the same reason, also inclusive. Implied in the marking of some as other is the acceptance of others as self. Inclusion implies exclusion by definition; and opposition by necessity entails association. However, very few religions trace the boundaries of inclusion and exclusion along collateral lines of race, gender, or class. To the contrary, most religions are doctrinally designed to welcome membership from a broad spectrum of individuals across other exclusive communities, thereby providing an important source for cross-secting association. Of course religions often are perverted by those who claim the contrary, but the willingness of some who identify themselves as holy men to bend religion to the purposes of injustice does not signal an inherent deficit in religion itself.

There are many other sources of ecumenical association, of course; but religion is quite unique in at least one crucial respect. Ethnicity, race, gender, and, to a large extent, class, are birthrights. For the most part, religion is not. Quite to the contrary, most religions are in one fashion or another evangelical and seek to grow by converting new members to the faith. Others are not so proactive, but nevertheless are open to those willing to convert. Because religious groups can accommodate a broad spectrum of individuals from diverse collateral cohorts, religion provides a field more hospitable to overlapping identities than is offered by more immutable group identities.

Religion, then, is an important player in the construction and maintenance of dynamic stability even though it, like many other sources of fission and fusion, implies its potential to destroy in its acts of construction. This suggests that any political society facing the architectural tasks at the fore in designing and maintaining broader structures of law should reserve a central place for religion because religion has the potential to limit the capacity of other exclusive communities to achieve dominance in society and to pursue programs of oppression and targeted violence. The design goal, then, is to preserve space for religion in civil society while guarding against its hegemonic leanings and destructive potential. The results are likely to look quite familiar: law should protect religion but should be keen on religious diversity. Law should not establish or endorse a single religion. Legal authorities should avoid adopting religiously based truth claims in justifying and advancing state policy, and should instead favor secular language and reasons.

This is hardly radical stuff, but the claim that law should preserve space for religion while promoting religious diversity is enticing in the context of the effort in this chapter to view law through the lens of social paradigms. One lesson to be learned from the dynamics of mass violence is that law can play an important role in maintaining stability by organizing, directing, and limiting violence. The point of this brief discussion of religion is that law can accomplish this peacekeeping function not only by providing an alternative to violence, but also by establishing a pattern of precommitments designed to affirm, extend, and maintain a system of overlapping oppositions and associations by preserving fields on which opposing groups can form, engage members, and stage open contests. Of course, taking seriously that claim leads quickly to a more radical conclusion: that law itself is an important field for such contests on par with religion.

B. Constitutional Contests and Dynamic Stability

In many transitional societies the most important public debates are not about the possibility of criminal prosecutions or reparations for victims, but about constitutional design and legal commitments to democracy and human rights.[166] Parties to these contests of course try their best to promote legal architectures that will directly advantage them and their group affiliates; but in an open design contest these gambits are met by the opposing efforts of competing groups. The result is usually stalemate, which may last for some time, but frequently leads to outcome-neutral compromises on representation, division of power, preservation of local control, ambiguous language, and so forth, so that competing parties are comfortable that, while they did not win, they have not lost either. At the very least, these compromises usually reassure parties that they have not been relegated permanently to the margins of society.

While the outcomes of these foundational debates about legal and constitutional texts during transition are important, far more critical are the model they create for public contests over law going forward and the stage they set for diversity in those contests. To the extent that transitional debates over "law" reach at least a temporary compromise, they establish an important precedent showing that political contests are not zero-sum. Competing groups can both win and lose. By preserving space for future contests, competitors gain some reassurance that if they did not win this time, they may win in the future. That is the same solace those of us who live in relatively stable societies take away from ongoing policy debates in our home countries, where our political structures often favor the middle and almost always leave open the possibility that those whose views lie farther to the margin can advance their agendas "next time."

Contemporary debates about the meaning of the United States Constitution, its application, the role of federal judges, and the proper interpretation of the Constitution offer useful examples. Particularly since the failed nomination of Judge Robert Bork to the Supreme Court seat later occupied by Justice Anthony Kennedy, these have been hot topics in political and civil society arenas in the United States. At the center of many of these discussions are complex discussions about how the Constitution should be interpreted. While these contests often are framed in bipolar terms as between "originalists" and those who regard the Constitution as a living document, both the academic and the public debates are far more nuanced.

It is not necessary for present purposes to dive into these complex academic, legal, and political debates. Rather, all that is necessary is to highlight the fact that these debates happen. In fact, they have been a feature of politics in the United States since the Constitution's adoption. Different groups have entered these contests about the meaning of the Constitution, the proper mode of interpretation, and the role of judges with an eye toward linking those claims to group interests. They have also linked their positions to broader visions of society as it was, is, and ought to be. As a consequence, debates about "law," here as constitutional law, have provided fields for contests among groups from across the political, social, and class spectrums. During these debates members have often found themselves conflicted and pressed to point out ecumenical complexities posed by the exclusive fundamentalist claims of their cohorts. Debates about "law," like debates about religion, therefore have provided a field in which groups have expanded, multiplied, diversified, overlapped, joined, and fragmented. As a consequence of this dynamism, constitutional debates in the United States have provided an important structural contribution to overall stability.

While worthy of further reflection, this brief account of the stabilizing role of constitutional debates in the United States suggests an intriguing perspective on linked debates about constitutional and statutory interpretation. One form of "orignalism" privileges the original intent of those who drafted the text. "Original intent" has met considerable resistance in academic debates, and most influential originalists on the bench have by now rejected it.[167] One of the principal reasons for the demise of original intent is the simple fact that it assumes as fact something that is demonstrably a fiction: that the process by which constitutions and legislation are drafted and passed bespeak a coherent intent.[168] To the contrary, these processes are quite messy. It is often the case that two people who vote for the same law or constitutional provision read it very differently. In fact, ambiguity is often an important tool for drafters of legal and constitutional texts because it allows them to move forward without needing to achieve substantive compromises or final resolutions of thorny problems. In many cases, then, it is folly to claim that a legal or constitutional text actually reflects any intention, much less a single intent. This is particularly true of abstract moral language, such as "due process" and "cruel," that is a feature of the United States Constitution.[169]

For many, losing the anchor of original intent is disconcerting. It should not be. To the extent that "law," like religion, represents an important field of contest among groups in a dynamically stable society, it is a good thing that definitive answers about the meaning of a particular constitutional passage are hard or impossible to discern. Just as an interest in dynamic stability recommends promoting and preserving diversity in the field of religion, so, too, does it recommend promoting and preserving diversity in contests over the meaning assigned to critical passages of the Constitution.

Debates about constitutional texts are often deeply emotional. That is because the competing interpretations advanced by parties to these contests implicate broader paradigms that both separate and link members of society. From the perspective of dynamic stability, this is a good thing. Debates about constitutional text are also hard or impossible to win, at least for very long. Again, from the perspective of dynamic stability, this is a good thing. Definitive clarity in constitutional debates, like definitive clarity on the word of god, is dangerous because it concretizes lines of opposition and sets the stage for further ossification and therefore instability. We should therefore be thankful that our Founders left us with these perennial and important messes.

Conclusion

In this chapter I have tried to draw some lessons about the nature and potential of "law" from the experiences of transitions to democracy and accompanying transitional justice movements. The analysis of social structures underlying abusive regimes, transitions, and transitional justice pursued in this chapter paints a picture of "law" as composed of a network of intersecting and overlapping socio-normative paradigms, which usually remain unnoticed by those of us in stable states who live among the edifices and spires of elaborate positive law. While this account of "law" has realist overtones, the goal is not to take a firm position in long-standing theory debates. Rather, this account of "law" is offered in a sociological mode to describe law as an embedded enterprise. The conclusion invited by this view is that examinations of law in transition should lead us to take seriously the claim that "law," phenomenologically if not conceptually, has a broader footprint than is suggested by exclusive focus on the words that appear on the pages of legal texts.

Taking seriously a vision of law as an embedded enterprise promotes some intriguing insights about the role of law in crisis and stability. Again drawing lessons from abusive regimes and the transitions that follow, this chapter advances an account of crisis centered on the collapse of dynamic stability. The claim is that social and political stability is a result not of consensus fidelity to a specific norm, institution, or practice, but is an artifact of diverse overlapping oppositions and associations. Mass and targeted atrocities are only possible when one line of opposition asserts exclusive dominance, allowing the underlying ontology and teleology endorsed by those on one side of a divide to assert hegemony. To guard against this possibility, I have suggested that "law" should preserve space for group diversity and should guard against ossification of group identities. I have also suggested that among the most promising fields for expanding and maintaining group contests that preserve and maintain dynamic stability are contests over "law" itself. These may be civil society and legislative debates over policy, but may also take the form of debates about the meaning of particular laws, including heated contests about how one ought to read foundational texts such as constitutions.

While by definition incomplete and provisional, these tentative conclusions should provide significant reassurance for those of us who live in relatively stable societies where passionate battles over "law" are perennial features of public and private life. There is certainly pathological potential in these debates as groups vie for the privilege of controlling "law." However, when conducted within carefully constructed legal structures built around precommitments against definitive victory, debates about "law" in relatively healthy societies serve as important forums for maintaining a robust web of cross-associations among members of competing groups. The process is most assuredly messy, maddening, frustrating, and often frightening, but when contrasted with the clarity at the heart of mass atrocities, "messy" is a wonderful and comforting thing.

Notes

1. The implied enigma captures the range of sects in the church of the rule of law, ranging from Lon Fuller, *Morality of Law* (New Haven, CT: Yale University Press, 1965), which attempts to naturalize the basic tenets of the legality principle, to contemporary efforts by international and development organizations to advance "good governance," which tend to view the rule of law more as a procedural precondition to economic growth and stability.

2. This chapter draws upon and extends prior work addressing various transitional justice issues, including David Gray, "A No-Excuse Approach to Transitional Justice," *Washington University Law Review* 87 (2010): 1043 (reparations); David Gray, "Constitutional Faith," *Maryland Law Review* 69 (2009): 26 (establishment of state religion); David Gray, "Devilry, Complicity, and Greed: Transitional Justice and Odious Debt," *Law & Contemporary Problems* 70 (2007): 137 (odious debt); David Gray, "An Excuse-Centered Approach to Transitional Justice," *Fordham Law Review* 74 (2006): 2621 (criminal trials); and David Gray, "What's So Special About Transitional Justice?" *American Society of International Law* 100 (2006): 147 (criminal trials).

3. Gray, "An Excuse-Centered Approach," 2621–2623; Laurel Fletcher and Harvey Weinstein, "Violence and Social Repair: Rethinking the Contribution of Justice to Reconciliation," *Human Rights Quarterly* 24 (2002): 573, 574.

4. Jon Elster, *Closing the Books* (Cambridge: Cambridge University Press, 2004), 3–23; Plato, *Apology*, trans. G.M.A. Grube (Indianapolis, IN:Hackett, 1981) 32b–e.

5. See generally Samuel P. Huntington, *The Third Wave: Democratization in the Late Twentieth Century* (Norman: University of Oklahoma Press, 1991).

6. Kieran McEvoy, "Letting Go of Legalism: Developing a 'Thicker' Version of Transitional Justice," in *Transitional Justice from Below*, ed. Kieran McEvoy and Lorna McGregor (Oxford: Hart, 2008) 15; Fletcher and Weinstein, "Violence and Social Repair," 574. Contemporary conversations about transitional justice began with a debate in print between Professors Diane Orentlicher and Carlos Nino published in the *Yale Law Journal*. See Diane Orentlicher, "Settling Accounts: The Duty to Prosecute Human Rights Violations of a Prior Regime," *Yale Law Journal* 100 (1991): 2537; Carlos Nino, "The Duty to Punish Past Abuses of Human Rights Put into Context: The Case of Argentina," *Yale Law Journal* 100 (1991): 2619; Diane Orentlicher, "A Reply to Professor Nino," *Yale Law Journal* 100 (1991): 2641.

7. Sarat, introduction to this volume.

8. See Gray, "A No-Excuse Approach," 1095–1099. Compare Eric Posner and Adrian Vermeule, "Transitional Justice as Ordinary Justice," *Harvard Law Review* 117 (2004): 761.

9. The meaning of the word "ibyitso" remains disputed, but has been translated as "foreigner," "accomplice of the enemy," or "cockroach." Hassan Ngeze, Jean Bosco Barayagwiza, and Ferdinand Nahimana, the defendants convicted in the "Media Trial," claimed the more benign "foreigner" or "accomplice of the enemy," while Alison des Forges, the author of the Human Rights Watch report on the Rwandan genocide, claims the more inflammatory "cockroaches."

10. Jaime Malamud-Goti, *Game Without End: State Terror and the Politics of Justice* (Norman: University of Oklahoma Press, 1996), 29; Carlos Nino, *Radical Evil on Trial* (New Haven, CT: Yale University Press, 1996), 51.

11. Among these were the Juventud Perónistas (JP), the Fuerzas Armadas Perónistas (FAP), the Fuerzas Armadas de Liberacion (FAL), the Fuerzas Armadas Revolucionarias (FAR), the Partido Revolucionaria del los Trabajadores (PRT), and the Ejercito Revolucionaria del Pueblo (ERP).

12. Nino, *Radical Evil on Trial*, 43.

13. This was reflected in the 1976 "Act Fixing the Purpose and Basic Objec-

tives for the Process of National Reconstruction," which called for the armed forces to "ensure national security" and "annihilate subversion."

14. Nino, *Radical Evil on Trial,* 53.

15. See Guillermo O'Donnell, "Modernization and Military Coups: Theory, Comparisons and the Argentine Case," in *Armies & Politics in Latin America,* ed. Abraham Lowenthal and Samuel Fitch (Teaneck, NJ: Holmes & Meier, 1986), 96; Nino, *Radical Evil on Trial,* 45, 54–57; Nunca Mas, Report of the National Commission on the Disappearance of Persons, Part V (1984).

16. Sherrilyn Ifill, *On the Courthouse Lawn: Confronting the Legacy of Lynching in the Twenty-First Century* (Boston: Beacon Press, 2007), 64–66.

17. Thomas McCarthy, "Coming to Terms with Our Past, Part II: On the Morality and Politics of Reparations for Slavery," *Political Theory* 32 (2004): 750, 758–764; Randall Robinson, "What America Owes Blacks and What Blacks Owe to Each Other," *African-American Law & Policy Report* 6 (2004): 1, 2.

18. Rosa Ehrenreich Brooks, "The New Imperialism: Violence, Norms, and the 'Rule of Law,'" *Michigan Law Review* 101 (2003): 2275.

19. Ibid., 2302.

20. Ibid., 2307.

21. This set of beliefs was famously advanced by President George W. Bush. While far more sophisticated and therefore reserved, Lon Fuller somewhat less famously argued that the rule of law implies its own internal moral structure such that the various conditions of legality, including prospectivity, accessibility, fair warning, clarity, regular enforcement, stability, etc., are not merely good policy, but defining and fundamental features of any system that could plausibly claim the mantle of "law." See Fuller, *Morality of Law,* 33–38.

22. Ehrenreich Brooks, "The New Imperialism," 2305.

23. Ibid., 2302.

24. Ibid., 2305.

25. Karl Jaspers, *The Question of German Guilt* (Bronx, NY: Fordham University Press, 1948), 28.

26. Maggie T. Grace, "Criminal Alternative Dispute Resolution: Restoring Justice, Respecting Responsibility, and Renewing Norms," *Vermont Law Review* 34 (2010): 563.

27. Marc J. Swartz, Victor Turner, and Arthur Tuden, "Introduction," in *Political Anthropology,* ed. Marc J. Swartz, Victor Turner, and Arthur Tuden (Chicago: Aldine, 1966), 14.

28. See *Economist,* August 8, 2009, at 71; Ernesto Verdeja, "A Critical Theory of Reparative Justice," *Constellations* 15 (2008): 208, 210; Ehrenreich Brooks, "The New Imperialism," 2321.

29. Swartz et al., "Introduction," 14.

30. Jürgen Habermas, *Lifeworld and System: A Critique of Functional Reason*, trans. Thomas McCarthy (Boston: Beacon Press, 1985), 119–152.

31. Swartz et al., "Introduction," 14–17; see also Cheryl Harris, "Whiteness as Property," *Harvard Law Review* 106 (1993): 1707, 1742–1777.

32. Swartz et al., "Introduction," 10.

33. Ibid., 15.

34. Michel Foucault, "Truth and Power," in *Power/Knowledge*, ed. Colin Gordon (New York: Random House, Vintage, 1980), 109, 133.

35. Ibid., 133.

36. Ibid., 131.

37. Michel Foucault, *The History of Sexuality: An Introduction*, vol. 1 (New York: Random House, Vintage, 1990), 94; Michel Foucault, "The Ethic and Care for the Self as a Practice of Freedom," in *Final Foucault*, ed. James Bernauer and David Rasmussen (Cambridge: MIT Press, 1987), 1, 11.

38. See, e.g., Michel Foucault, *Madness and Civilization: A History of Insanity in the Age of Reason* (New York: Random House, Vintage, 1988); Michel Foucault, *Discipline and Punish: The Birth of the Prison* (New York: Random House, Vintage, 1995); Michel Foucault, *The History of Sexuality*; Michel Foucault, *The History of Sexuality, Vol. II: The Use of Pleasure* (New York: Random House, Vintage, 1990); Michel Foucault, *The History of Sexuality, Vol. III: The Care of the Self* (New York: Random House, Vintage, 1988).

39. Foucault, "Truth and Power," 131.

40. Patricia Lundy and Mark McGovern, "The Role of Community in Participatory Transitional Justice," in *Transitional Justice from Below*, ed. Kieran McEvoy and Lorna McGregor (Oxford: Hart, 2008), 99, 109.

41. Victor Turner, *Dramas, Fields, and Metaphors* (Ithaca, NY: Cornell University Press, 1974), 17.

42. Swartz et al., "Introduction," 31.

43. Turner, *Dramas, Fields, and Metaphors*, 17.

44. See, e.g., Dan Kahan and Donald Braman, "The Self-Defense Cognition of Self-Defense," *American Criminal Law Review* 45 (2008): 65; Donald Braman and Dan Kahan, "Legal Realism as Psychological not Political Realism," in *How Does Law Know*, ed. Austin Sarat ((Stanford: Stanford University Press, 2006); Donald Braman, Dan Kahan, and David Hoffman, "Some Realism about Punishment Naturalism," *University of Chicago Law Review* 77 (2010) (arguing that moral intuitions underwriting conceptions of "core" crimes and natural right in punishment are linked to socioeconomic and political contingencies constituent of those who hold those intuitions).

45. See generally Braman et al., "Some Realism about Punishment Naturalism."

46. See, e.g., John Mikhail, "Is the Prohibition of Homicide Universal?" *Brooklyn Law Review* 75 (2010): 497.

47. Jaspers, *The Question of German Guilt,* 28–29. Husserl adopts a similar view in his account of "lifeworlds." See Edmund Husserl, *The Crisis of the European Sciences* (Evanston, IL: Northwestern University Press, 1970), 108–109, 133. See also Habermas, *Lifeworld and System,* 113–118.

48. Benedict Anderson, *Imagined Communities: Reflections on the Origin and Spread of Nationalism* (Brooklyn, NY: Verso, 1991); Ehrenreich Brooks, "The New Imperialism," 2316.

49. See Donald Horowitz, *Ethnic Groups in Conflict* (Berkeley and Los Angeles: University of California Press, 2000), 6–12, 17–18, 53.

50. Ehrenreich Brooks, "The New Imperialism," 2305–2306.

51. Hate crimes are an exception that proves the rule. As distinguished from most "normal" crimes, hate crimes are motivated or justified in the mind of perpetrators by claims of entitlement or justification that rely upon abusive paradigms that reinforce status inequalities between victim and abuser along lines of race, gender, sexuality, and so forth. See, e.g., Susan Estreicher, "Rape," *Yale Law Journal* 95 (1986): 1087 (arguing that rape is linked to background paradigms of patriarchy and gender discrimination). Hate crimes are, then, atrocities akin to those at the center of conversations about transitional justice, but on a smaller scale. The description of "normal" crimes implied here appears to be in some tension with Jean Hampton's work on punishment. See, e.g., Jean Hampton, "Correcting Harms Versus Righting Wrongs: The Goal of Retribution," *UCLA Law Review* 39 (1992): 1659, 1665–1685. However, Hampton's account of crime as an assertion of unjust entitlement by the criminal is pitched as a theoretical claim rather than a description of psychological states.

52. Daniel Goldhagen, *Hitler's Willing Executioners: Ordinary Germans and the Holocaust* (New York: Random House, Vintage, 1996), 15.

53. Ruti Teitel, *Transitional Justice* (New York: Oxford University Press, 2000), 18–20.

54. John Rawls, *The Law of Peoples* (Cambridge, MA: Harvard University Press, 1999), 5, 106.

55. Roy Brooks, "The Age of Apology," in *When Sorry Isn't Enough: The Controversy Over Apologies and Reparations,* ed. Roy Brooks (New York: New York University Press, 1999), 3–11; Richard Rorty, "Human Rights, Rationality, and Sentimentality," in *On Human Rights,* ed. Stephen Shute and Susan Hurley (New York: Basic Books, 1993), 111, 112.

56. *Prosecutor v. Banovic,* IT-02-65 (September 3, 2003): 1–5, 120–121; Rorty, "Human Rights, Rationality, and Sentimentality," 112.

57. Goldhagen, *Hitler's Willing Executioners*, 14–15.

58. Jaspers, *The Question of German Guilt*, 28–29.

59. Malamud-Goti, *Game Without End*, 29–99; see also Alex Boraine, *A Life in Transition* (Random House: Struik, 2008), 104, 110–112; Elster, *Closing the Books*, 93.

60. Malamud-Goti, *Game Without End*, 29–99.

61. Ehrenreich Brooks, "The New Imperialism," 2327; Fletcher and Weinstein, "Violence and Social Repair," 609.

62. Roy L. Brooks, "Getting Reparations for Slavery Right—A Response to Posner and Vermeule," *Notre Dame Law Review* 80 (2004): 267; Rorty, "Human Rights, Rationality, and Sentimentality," 112–115.

63. Ryan Fortson, "Collective Liability, the Limited Prospects of Success for a Class Action Suit for Slavery Reparations, and the Reconceptualization of White Racial Identity," *African-American Law & Policy Report* 6 (2004): 77.

64. Goldhagen, *Hitler's Willing Executioners*, 3–24, 49–50; Frank Chalk and Kurt Jonassohn, *The History and Sociology of Genocide* (New Haven, CT: Yale University Press, 1990), 29; Simon Wiesenthal, *The Sunflower: On the Possibilities and Limits of Forgiveness* (New York: Random House, 1997), 15; Ehrenreich Brooks, "The New Imperialism," 2327; Swartz et al., "Introduction," 15.

65. Fletcher and Weinstein, "Violence and Social Repair," 636.

66. Phillip Zizubando, *The Lucifer Effect: Understanding How Good People Turn Evil* (New York: Random House, 2007), 296; Ehrenreich Brooks, "The New Imperialism," 2313, 2327; Fletcher and Weinstein, "Violence and Social Repair," 581, 604–620; Roberta de la Roche Senechal, "The Sociogenesis of Lynching," in *Under Sentence of Death: Essays on Lynching in the South*, ed. W. Fitzhugh Brundage (Durham: University of North Carolina Press, 1997); Roberta de la Roche Senechal, "Collective Violence as Social Control," *Sociological Forum* 11 (1996): 97, 106.

67. Brooks, "Getting Reparations for Slavery Right," 267.

68. Fletcher and Weinstein, "Violence and Social Repair," 606–620.

69. Rorty, "Human Rights, Rationality, and Sentimentality," 112.

70. Goldhagen, *Hitler's Willing Executioners*, 14–15.

71. Philip Gourevitch, *We Wish to Inform You That Tomorrow We Will Be Killed with Our Families: Stories From Rwanda* (New York: Farrar, Straus, and Giroux, 1998), 95.

72. W. E. B. Du Bois, "The Shape of Fear," in *The Social Theory of W. E. B. Du Bois*, ed. Phil Zuckerman (Newbury Park, CA: Pine Forge Press, 2004), 56.

73. Ifill, *On the Courthouse Lawn*, 17, 43–44, 64–66; see also Ehrenreich Brooks, "The New Imperialism," 2327.

74. Paul van Zyl, "Dilemmas of Transitional Justice: The Case of South

Africa's Truth and Reconciliation Commission," *Journal of International Affairs* 52 (1999): 647, 661. But see Braman et al., "Some Realism about Punishment Naturalism."

75. van Zyl, "Dilemmas of Transitional Justice," 660–661.

76. I adopt this phrase from another contributor to this volume, Ruti Teitel. See generally, Teitel, *Transitional Justice.*

77. See Ehrenreich Brooks, "The New Imperialism," 2307; Goldhagen, *Hitler's Willing Executioners,* 27–163, 416–454; Gourevitch, *We Wish to Inform You,* 47–62, 96–131; Kosovo Report: Conflict, International Response, Lessons Learned (2000): 33–64; Malamud-Goti, *Game Without End,* 29–99; Nino, *Radical Evil on Trial,* 41–60; Samantha Power, *A Problem from Hell* (New York: Harper Perennial, 2002), 1–16; Rorty, "Human Rights, Rationality, and Sentimentality," 112–115; "Argentina Executive Decree No. 158/83, Dec. 13, 1983," in Nunca Mas, Report of the National Commission on the Disappearance of Persons, Part V (1984); see also Raul Hilberg, *The Destruction of the European Jews* (Teaneck, NJ: Holmes & Meier, 1961), 62.

78. Goldhagen, *Hitler's Willing Executioners,* 97; Simon Wiesenthal, *Every Day is Remembrance Day* (New York: Henry Holt & Co, 1987), 11–28; Eugene Davidson, *The Trial of the Germans* (Columbia: University of Missouri Press, 1966), 7.

79. Alan Rosenbaum, *Prosecuting Nazi War Criminals* (New York: Basic Books, 1993), 11–12.

80. Hilberg, *The Destruction of the European Jews,* 6.

81. Elster, *Closing the Books,* 83; Teitel, *Transitional Justice,* 29.

82. Sanford Levinson, "Trials, Commissions, and Investigating Commitees," in *Truth v. Justice: The Morality of Truth Commissions,* ed. Robert I. Rotberg and Dennis Thompson (Princeton, NJ: Princeton University Press, 2000), 211, 219.

83. Teitel, *Transitional Justice,* 19.

84. See Foucault, "Ethic of Care for the Self as a Practice of Freedom," 11.

85. Ibid., 18–20.

86. Rorty, "Human Rights, Rationality, and Sentimentality," 112–114.

87. Goldhagen, *Hitler's Willing Executioners,* 14–15.

88. Ibid., 49–128.

89. Rosenbaum, *Prosecuting Nazi War Criminals,* 11; Wiesenthal, *Every Day is Remembrance Day,* 15.

90. Wiesenthal, *Every Day is Remembrance Day,* 11–28; Davidson, *The Trial of the Germans,* 7.

91. Goldhagen, *Hitler's Willing Executioners,* 8, 11–13, 416–454; Rosenbaum, *Prosecuting Nazi War Criminals,* 11.

92. Gourevitch, *We Wish to Inform You,* 47–62; see also Collette Braekman, "Incitement to Genocide," in *Crimes of War,* ed. Roy Gutman and David Rieff (New York: W. W. Norton & Co., 1999), 192; Human Rights Watch, Leave None to Tell the Story (1999).

93. See the Constitution of the United States of America, Art. I, Sec. 2 (providing that "Representatives and direct Taxes shall be apportioned among the several States which may be included within this Union, according to their respective Numbers, which shall be determined by adding to the whole Number of free Persons, including those bound to Service for a Term of Years, and excluding Indians not taxed, three fifths of all other Persons.").

94. Mark Graber, *Dred Scott and the Problem of Constitutional Evil* (Cambridge: Cambridge University Press, 2006). The account of relationships between law and society that underwrites Graber's account is by now common currency among legal historians, including most prominently William Nelson, who has engaged in a sustained and persuasive effort starting with his groundbreaking book on the common law to document the close relationship between legal change and social movements. See William E. Nelson, *Americanization of the Common Law: The Impact of Legal Change on Massachusetts Society* (Macon: University of Georgia Press, 1975), 1760–1830.

95. Goldhagen, *Hitler's Willing Executioners,* 55, 66–69; Richard Lerner, *Final Solutions: Biology, Prejudice and Genocide* (Philadelphia: Pennsylvania State University Press, 1992); Robert Wistrich, *Antisemitism: The Longest Hatred* (New York: Schocken, 1991).

96. van Zyl, "Dilemmas of Transitional Justice," 661 (pointing out that criminal justice is more appropriate for stable states where abuses are the exception rather than the norm).

97. Bruce Ackerman, *The Future of Liberal Revolution* (New Haven, CT: Yale University Press, 1992), 5.

98. Elster, *Closing the Books,* 83; Teitel, *Transitional Justice,* 29.

99. Noam Chomsky, *Rogue States: The Rule of Force in World Affairs* (Brooklyn, NY: South End Press, 2000), 62.

100. Gourevitch, *We Wish to Inform You,* 85–96.

101. Teitel, *Transitional Justice,* 18–20; Goldhagen, *Hitler's Willing Executioners,* 97–98; Rorty, "Human Rights, Rationality, and Sentimentality," 112–115.

102. Gourevitch, *We Wish to Inform You,* 96, 123.

103. Rawls, *The Law of Peoples,* 5, 106 ff.

104. Goldhagen, *Hitler's Willing Executioners,* 14–15, 80–163; Gourevitch, *We Wish to Inform You,* 96, 110–131.

105. Posner and Vermeule, "Transitional Justice as Ordinary Justice," 761; Rajeev Bhargava, "Restoring Decency to Barbaric Societies," in *Truth v. Jus-*

tice: The Morality of Truth Commissions, ed. Robert I. Rotberg and Dennis Thompson (Princeton, NJ: Princeton University Press, 2000), 45, 46–50.

106. Fletcher and Weinstein, "Violence and Social Repair," 633.

107. Jaspers, *The Question of German Guilt,* 35.

108. Max Glucksman, *Custom and Conflict in Africa* (Indianapolis, IN: Blackwell Publishing, 1956), 8, 17; E. E. Evans-Pritchard, *The Nuer* (New York: Oxford University Press, 1940), 147–148.

109. Kanchan Chandra, "Ethnic Parties and Democratic Stability," *Perspectives on Politics* 3 (2005): 235, 236, 242; Glucksman, *Custom and Conflict in Africa,* 1–2, 24.

110. Alfred Brophy, "The Culture War Over Reparations for Slavery," *DePaul Law Review* 53 (2004): 1181.

111. See Chandra, "Ethnic Parties and Democratic Stability," 235–238 (describing this view and citing proponents).

112. W. F. Hegel, *Phenomenology of Spirit,* trans. A. V. Miller (New York: Oxford University Press, 1977), 11–19.

113. Chandra, "Ethnic Parties and Democratic Stability," 236–238.

114. Ibid. See also Harris, "Whiteness as Property," 1736–1737 (discussing the creation of "whiteness" in response to economic and political factors).

115. Nancy Fraser, "Social Justice in the Age of Identity Politics," in *Redistribution or Recognition,* ed. Nancy Fraser and Axel Honneth (Brooklyn, NY: Verso, 2003), 7, 55–56; Jessica Benjamin, "Recognition and Destruction: An Outline of Intersubjectivity," in *Like Subjects, Love Objects: Essays on Recognition and Sexual Difference* (New Haven, CT: Yale University Press, 1995); Anthony Appiah, "Multicultural Societies and Social Reproduction," in *Multiculturalism,* ed. Amy Guttmann (Princeton, NJ: Princeton University Press, 1994), 149, 150–151.

116. See generally, Richard Rorty, *Contingency, Irony, and Solidarity* (Cambridge: Cambridge University Press, 1989).

117. See Appiah, "Multicultural Societies and Social Reproduction," 150–151; Arnold Van Gennep, *Rites of Passage,* trans. Monika Vizedom and Gabrielle Caffee (Chicago: University of Chicago Press, 1960), 1–3; Glucksman, *Custom and Conflict in Africa,* 1–2, 25; Chandra, "Ethnic Parties and Democratic Stability," 241–245; Swartz et al., "Introduction, " 8.

118. Horowitz, *Ethnic Groups in Conflict,* 134, 135–136.

119. Verdeja, "A Critical Theory of Reparative Justice," 211; Chandra, "Ethnic Parties and Democratic Stability," 236–238.

120. Nicholas Sambanis, "Do Ethnic and Nonethnic Civil Wars Have the

Same Causes," *Journal of Conflict Resolution* 45 (2001): 259, 264; Chandra, "Ethnic Parties and Democratic Stability," 241–244.

121. Horowitz, *Ethnic Groups in Conflict*, 135–136; Sambanis, "Do Ethnic and Nonethnic Civil Wars Have the Same Causes," 280; Boraine, *A Life in Transition*, 104, 110–112; Harris, "Whiteness as Property," 1768 (noting the racial oppression of "colorblindness").

122. Fraser, "Social Justice in the Age of Identity Politics," 7, 51.

123. E. E. Evans-Pritchard, *Nuer Religion* (New York: Oxford University Press, 1956); E. E. Evans-Pritchard, *Kinship and Marriage Among the Nuer* (New York: Oxford University Press, 1951).

124. Evans-Pritchard, *Kinship and Marriage Among the Nuer*, 156–157; Evans-Pritchard, *Nuer*, 193–200.

125. Glucksman, *Custom and Conflict in Africa*, 11; Evans-Pritchard, *Nuer*, 209.

126. Glucksman, *Custom and Conflict in Africa*, 13–15; Evans-Pritchard, *Kinship and Marriage Among the Nuer*, 22–28; Evans-Pritchard, *Nuer*, 209–210.

127. Glucksman, *Custom and Conflict in Africa*, 13; Evans-Pritchard, *Nuer*, 225.

128. Evans-Pritchard, *Kinship and Marriage Among the Nuer*, 165–167.

129. Glucksman, *Custom and Conflict in Africa*, 17–18.

130. Ibid., 24–26.

131. Ibid.

132. Ibid., 8, 17; Evans-Pritchard, *Nuer*, 147–148.

133. Swartz et al., "Introduction," 8; Glucksman, *Custom and Conflict in Africa*, 24–26.

134. Evans-Pritchard, *Nuer*, 139–191.

135. Ibid., 142–143.

136. Ibid., 147.

137. Glucksman, *Custom and Conflict in Africa*, 8–9. See also Napoleon A. Chagnon, *Yanomanö* (Austin, TX: Holt, 1968), 185–189.

138. Glucksman, *Custom and Conflict in Africa*, 24–26; Evans-Pritchard, *Nuer*, 147–148.

139. Alexander Hamilton and James Madison, Federalist Nos. 9 and 10, in *The Federalist Papers*, ed. Clinton Rossiter (New York: Holt, 1961), 71–84.

140. Ibid., 71–73.

141. Ibid.

142. Ibid., 78–79.

143. Ibid., 81–84.

144. Ibid.; Chandra, "Ethnic Parties and Democratic Stability," 241–245.

145. Glucksman, *Custom and Conflict in Africa*, 4, 24–25.

146. Chandra, "Ethnic Parties and Democratic Stability," 241–245; Paul Schiff Berman, "An Observation and a Strange but True 'Tale': What Might the Historical Trials of Animals Tell Us About the Transformative Potential of Law in American Culture?" *Hastings Law Journal* 52 (2000): 123, 130–131.

147. Glucksman, *Custom and Conflict in Africa,* 24; Chandra, "Ethnic Parties and Democratic Stability," 243–245.

148. See Jack Goldsmith and Eric Posner, *The Limits of International Law* (Oxford: Oxford University Press, 2005), 83–106; Glucksman, *Custom and Conflict in Africa,* 4.

149. Chandra, "Ethnic Parties and Democratic Stability," 246.

150. Boraine, *A Life in Transition,* 104; Harris, "Whiteness as Property," 1741–1742, 1760, 1767 (discussing inability of whites living under Jim Crow to identify with black class peers).

151. Glucksman, *Custom and Conflict in Africa,* 25.

152. Martin Gilbert, *The Holocaust: A History of the Jews of Europe During the Second World War* (New York: Holt, 1987), 35.

153. Goldhagen, *Hitler's Willing Executioners,* 49–128; Rosenbaum, *Prosecuting Nazi War Criminals,* 11–12 (1993); Wiesenthal, *The Sunflower,* 15; Alan Davies, "The German Third Reich and Its Victims," in *When Sorry Isn't Enough: The Controversy Over Apologies and Reparations,* ed. Roy Brooks (New York: New York University Press, 1999), 24.

154. Goldhagen, *Hitler's Willing Executioners,* 8, 11–13, 416–454. See also "Testimony of SS Officer Otto Ohlendorf before the Nuremburg War Crimes Tribunal, Oct. 8–15, 1947," in *Trials of War Criminals before the Nuremberg Military Tribunals under Control Council Law* 10, no. 4, (1950): 283–287.

155. See Christina M. Carroll, "An Assessment of The Role and Effectiveness of the International Criminal Tribunal for Rwanda and the Rwandan National Justice System in Dealing with the Mass Atrocities of 1994," *Boston University International Law Journal* 18 (2000): 163, 166–167; Mark A. Drumbl, "Rule of Law Amid Lawlessness: Counseling the Accused in Rwanda's Domestic Genocide Trials," *Columbia Human Rights Law Review* 29 (1998): 545, 555.

156. Gourevitch, *We Wish to Inform You,* 47–62; see also *Prosecutor v. Nahimana, Barayagwiza, and Ngeze,* ICTR-99-52-T (December 3, 2003); Colette Braeckman, "Incitement to Genocide," in *Crimes of War,* ed. Roy Gutman and David Rieff (New York: W. W. Norton & Company, 1999), 192; Human Rights Watch, *Leave None to Tell the Story: Genocide in Rwanda* (1999).

157. See Derrick Bell, *Race, Racism and American Law* (Boston: Little Brown and Co., 1980), 29–30.

158. Habermas, *Lifeworld and System*, 53–60, 150–152.

159. Stephen Breyer, *Active Liberty: Interpreting Our Democratic Constitution* (New York: Knopf, 2005).

160. These thoughts on religion are explored at greater length in Gray, "Constitutional Faith," 2.

161. See, e.g., Edward Wong, "Top Iraq Shiites Pushing Religion In Constitution," *New York Times* (February 6, 2005).

162. See generally Claire Mitchell, *Religion, Identity and Politics in Northern Ireland: Boundaries of Belonging and Belief* (Farnham, UK: Ashgate Publishing, 2005).

163. See generally Michael Sells, *The Bridge Betrayed: Religion and Genocide in Bosnia* (Berkeley and Los Angeles: University of California Press, 1998).

164. See generally Jonathan Riley-Smith, *The Oxford History of the Crusades* (Oxford: Oxford University Press, 1999).

165. See generally David Chidester, *Savage Systems: Colonialism and Comparative Religion in Southern Africa* (Charlottesville: University of Virginia Press, 1996).

166. Ackerman, *The Future of Liberal Revolution*, 46–68.

167. Antonin Scalia, *A Matter of Interpretation: Federal Courts and the Law* (Princeton, NJ: Princeton University Press, 1997), 16–18.

168. Ibid.

169. Jessica Olive and David Gray, "A Modest Appeal for Decent Respect," *Federal Sentencing Reporter* 23, no. 1 (October 2009): 72; David Gray, "Why Justice Scalia Should Be a Constitutional Comparativist . . . Sometimes," *Stanford Law Review* 59 (2007): 1249, 1261–1265.

Commentary on Chapter 4

Power, Paradigms, and Legal Prescriptions: "The Rule of Law" as a Necessary but Not Sufficient Condition for Transitional Justice

Meredith Render

> In Rwandan history, everyone obeys authority. People revere power, and there isn't enough education. . . . The peasants, who were paid or forced to kill, were looking up to people of higher socio-economic standing to see how to behave. So the people of influence, or the big financiers, are often the big men in genocide. They may think they didn't kill because they didn't take life with their own hands, but the people were looking to them for orders. And, in Rwanda, an order can be given very quietly.
> — Philip Gourevitch, *We Wish to Inform You that Tomorrow We Will Be Killed With Our Families*, 1998

Introduction

It is difficult to reckon with human-rights abuses on a mass scale such as occurred in the Rwandan genocide, the Holocaust, and the Reconstruction-era American South. It is tempting to conclude that an abject abandonment of legal order lies at the root of such inhumanity, and that, consequently, a robust commitment to "the rule of law" can prevent such atrocities. It is comfortable for us to believe that states with an adequate commitment to the rule of law need not fear the slippery slope of ethnic, racial, religious, class, or ideological divisiveness, because an adequate commitment to the rule of law ably safeguards against the possibility of abusive regimes, genocide, and other mass atrocities.

This picture of "rule of law" as talisman against the unthinkable is challenged by David Gray in his excellent and provocative chapter, "Transitional Disclosures: What Transitional Justice Reveals about 'Law.'"[1] Gray offers two distinct insightful descriptive narratives and provides a prescription, in light of these narratives, of how law might better serve as a bulwark against abusive regimes. Gray's first descriptive narrative illuminates a "multidimensionality in 'law'" that is frequently overlooked in the context of transitional justice.[2] His second narrative examines the hegemonic risks of cross associations along multiple identity lines (such as class, religion, ethnicity, or ideology) within transitional societies and argues that although it may seem counterintuitive, a "dynamic stability among competing and overlapping associations and oppositions" is necessary to stave off abusive regimes.[3] Finally, Gray offers a prescription: transitional law would do well to build legal structures that support rather than dissipate multiple and overlapping lines of identity-based association and opposition.[4]

Gray's descriptive points underscore the nearly inscrutable web of factors that seem to contribute to the rise of abusive regimes, as well as the difficulties inherent in making both macro and micro causal claims about these types of complex—and heartbreaking—human events. In highlighting the "multidimensionality" of the meaning, role, and practice of law in the context of societies in crisis (or societies not yet in crisis but nonetheless vulnerable to the rise of abusive regimes), Gray presents a persuasive argument that placing too much reliance on the rule of law ignores the role that law itself plays in constructing and perpetuating human-rights catastrophes. Gray rejects the conventional view that it is primarily "lawlessness" that gives rise to atrocity, and he succeeds in providing an alternative narrative that locates the cause of atrocity within the collapse of the dynamic tension among intra-societal identity-based associations.[5]

Here, however, Gray is painting with very broad strokes across a number of important conceptual lines, each of which warrants distinct consideration before we can draw conclusions about the *nature* (or concept) of law, the *role* of law, and the *rule* of law in transitional and pre-transitional societies. In particular, in presenting his claim of "law as paradigm" Gray is necessarily making implicit claims about (1) law as a practice constituted by social norms; (2) law as constitutive agent and participant in social practice; and (3) the relationship of the "rule of law" (or legality) to the content of law and role of law in pre-transitional societies.

Therefore, I argue in this chapter that while Gray's descriptive picture is compelling, it also merits a closer parsing of three concepts that are central to his analysis: the *role* of law, the *rule* of law, and the concept of *law*. A closer examination of these concepts reveals that the relationship between law and the perpetuation of atrocity is more nuanced than Gray's broader strokes may suggest, and that in light of these nuances, a robust commitment to the rule of law remains as a necessary (yet not sufficient) condition of his prescription for a successful transitional regime.

Toward this end, in part I of this chapter I pursue some conceptual distinctions between the content of law and Gray's conception of the "law as paradigm." In part II I explore the role that law plays in pre-transitional and transitional societies. Part III considers the significance of the rule of law in the context of abusive regimes in light of the insights of parts I and II.

I. Abusive Norms and the Content of Law: Some Conceptual Parsing

Gray argues that the emphasis placed on the rule of law by those interested in transitional justice is premised in part on a misapprehension of the nature and role of law in abusive regimes.[6] In abusive regimes, Gray posits, law often plays not only a role, but a key role, in facilitating (and even, infrequently, requiring) atrocity.[7] To describe these regimes as "lawless" is inaccurate and, in Gray's view, obscures the powerful ways in which law acts to shape "moral meaning and ethic value," mark the boundaries of inclusion and exclusion within a society, and to otherwise aid in framing the bloody vectors of opposition that ultimately culminate in mass graves.[8] An exclusive focus on "black-letter law" (which most often expressly forbids the kinds of abuses committed or tolerated by the state) fails to account for these important aspects of law. Therefore, Gray argues, a better account of "the concept of 'law' includes elements of a broader social paradigm in which law participates and which affects what law is such that to talk about 'law' is really to talk about a broader set of norms, practices, and institutions constitutive of what [Gray describes as] the paradigm of law."[9]

As an initial matter, Gray is walking upon well-trod ground insofar as he takes the concept of "law" to extend in some way to the practices engaged in and the norms abided by legal actors.[10] Few (if any) legal theorists understand the concept of "law" to be coterminous with so-called black-letter law, and indeed legal positivists of all stripes generally adhere to some version of what is known as "the social fact thesis," which holds (in its broadest construal) that what *counts* as law in any particular society is fundamentally dependant upon certain social facts within that society.[11] By most positivists' lights, one of two types of social facts are potentially significant in determining the content of law in a given society: (1) social facts that relate to sovereignty (a theory premised upon Hobbes's ideas concerning sovereignty and political authority)[12] or (2) social facts that relate to the social rules that constitute the rule of recognition within that society (a theory most famously advanced by H. L. A. Hart).[13] The significance of a particular kind of social fact turns on the strand of positivism one embraces.

An extensive explanation of these two branches of positivist thought is not necessary here, but a consideration of the basic distinctions between these two kinds of social facts is helpful in evaluating Gray's claim that a "broader social paradigm [consisting of abusive 'norms, practices, and institutions' that lie outside the express letter of legislative or judge-made law] *affects what law is*" such that the concept of law itself incorporates these norms, practices, and institutions.[14] Gray's claim that these norms alter or constitute the *content of law itself* in transitional and pre-transitional societies is an important one, and is central to his claim that the conventional emphasis on the rule of law among proponents of transitional justice is misplaced. Therefore it is important to consider *how* (and, ultimately, whether) the abusive norms Gray identifies affect the content of law in transitional and pre-transitional societies.

It may be helpful to begin this inquiry with an explanation of why the demarcation between what does and does not "count" as law in pre-transitional societies is significant in the context of Gray's arguments. This explanation must begin with the perhaps obvious point that unless we can reasonably identify what counts as "law" we are not able to identify what is "lawless" or "unlawful."[15] The demarcation of what counts as law then is a necessary precursor to both claims of legality and claims of a departure from legality (or an abandonment of the rule of law). So, for example, in the context of Gray's example of the Reconstruction-era American South, if, as Gray hypothesizes, abusive social norms about the inherent inferiority and subhumanity of former slaves formed part of the law itself such that those norms succeeded in altering the content, application, or scope of other laws (such as the Equal Protection Clause and state laws against lynching), then it would be inaccurate to describe the widespread practice of lynching former slaves as "unlawful" within that society. It follows then that if the lynching of former slaves was not unlawful in the Reconstruction-era South, we cannot conclude that the targeted violence that occurred in that society resulted from an inadequate commitment to the rule of law. So if Gray is right that abusive social norms made their way into content of the law in the Reconstruction-era South, we can neither criticize the targeted violence that occurred in that society as unlawful, nor can we rely on a robust commitment to the rule of law to aid in the prevention of future abuses.

However, to evaluate Gray's hypothesis that what "counts" as law in pre-transitional societies includes abusive norms, practices, and institutions, we must be clear about the mechanism by which Gray contends that abusive norms are incorporated into the law of a given society. In Gray's view, abusive social norms are incorporated into the content of the concept of law by a mechanism of state sponsorship in which state officials "normalize" the abusive norms either by participating directly in targeted violence, or by encouraging or tolerating targeted violence.[16] "These official acts form part of the paradigm of law that provides license for the targeted violence."[17] This process of official "normalization" of targeted violence in turn affects the popular perception of the legality of targeted violence and the perception of who is (and is not) entitled to the benefit of legal protection.[18] Ultimately, this mechanism of state sponsorship contributes to the transformation of an act that is otherwise often expressly forbidden (by the state's black-letter law) into an act that is "legal" insofar as it is consistent with the "paradigm of law" that operates in that particular society.[19]

But is it accurate to state that the mechanism of state sponsorship described by Gray succeeds in transforming otherwise illegal acts into legal acts (or acts consistent with the content of the concept of law embraced by a given society)? As stated earlier, positivists generally understand the kinds of social facts that impact the *content* of law to be limited to either facts about sovereignty or facts about the rule of recognition. It is not immediately clear to which—if either—of these categories Gray understands the facts constitutive of the "paradigm of law" to belong, but a consideration of each construction of the social-fact thesis may aid in illuminating Gray's arguments.

A. The Sovereign Makes the Rules

It is possible that Gray's arguments are tacitly premised on an understanding that the concept of "law" in the pre-transitional societies he describes is consistent with the command theory of law.[20] Early legal positivists, relying on Hobbes's account of law as the command of the sovereign, understood social facts that relate to the existence or absence of sovereignty to inform the question of what "counts" as law in a given society.[21] In this understanding, "law" is the command of the sovereign backed by sanction, and therefore questions concerning what counts as law turn almost entirely upon social facts about who may validly lay claim to sovereignty and the content of the sovereign's commands.[22] Although most modern positivists have abandoned this construction of the content of "law" in favor of some version of Hart's more nuanced theory of the rule of recognition, this earlier position is worth mentioning in the context of Gray's analysis because much of Gray's ideas concerning abusive norms as part of the concept of law seems to turn on the behavior of agents of the state: state officials.

Gray believes that his multidimensional understanding of the concept of law in pre-transitional societies is warranted by the fact that officials in pre-transitional societies often embrace and participate in paradigms of abuse.[23] Officials fail to enforce laws that prohibit targeted violence (or even directly participate in targeted violence) and thereby express and extend the belief that individuals targeted for violence fall outside the class of individuals protected by the law.[24]

The fact that *officials* engage in this expression and extension of abusive norms seems significant to Gray's account in a way that may suggest that Gray embraces two underlying premises about the pre-transitional societies he discusses. First, Gray may construe state officials to be "sovereign" in some pre-transitional societies. Second, Gray may understand the concept of law itself within those societies to be aligned with the idea that law (in those societies) consists of the command of the sovereign backed by the credible threat of sanction.[25] If Gray adheres to the command theory of law and perceives each of these premises to be correct, it may be possible to construe the actions (in participating in targeted violence) or inaction (in failing to prevent legally prohibited violence) of agents of the sovereign to be tantamount to commands of the sovereign. Therefore the *behavior* of state officials in pre-transition societies could be understood to "count" as law itself (or alter the content of law) within those societies.[26]

However, there are three reasons why Gray's account of "law as paradigm" seems inconsistent with most versions of the command theory. First, to illustrate his "law as paradigm" arguments, Gray points to examples of transitional societies in which the sovereign appears to be formally (at least initially) constrained by legal limitations. In other words, the command of the sovereign in these societies appears to be formally subject to conditions of legality—at least until a point of political crisis or regime changes appears to signal the abandonment of a previously accepted legal order. Second, the abusive norms that Gray identifies as part of the paradigm of law do not appear to bear directly on the question of who the rightful sovereign is in any given society, or the content of the sovereign's commands. Finally it is difficult to square Gray's account of the positive obligations created by law with a command theory of law. Each of these ideas is discussed in turn below.

The first way in which Gray's ideas about "law as paradigm" seems an uneasy fit with the command theory of law concerns the fact that in the period leading up to the execution of mass atrocities, most (if not all) of the pre-transitional societies that Gray identifies as examples seemed to have in place formal pre-commitments that constrained the legal power of the sovereign. Perhaps the easiest illustration of this lies in Gray's example of the Reconstruction-era South. It was certainly the case in the Reconstruction-era South that many officials' behavior evidenced an expression and extension of abusive norms that were widely held within that society regarding the appropriateness of lynching former slaves. Countless sheriffs, prosecutors, judges, and other state officials engaged in concerted action to both participate in targeted violence (often as members of the Ku Klux Klan) and to decline to enforce laws that prohibited targeted violence.[27] As a result, both state and private actors throughout the South committed acts of targeted violence with near impunity.[28] Could this widespread endorsement and enforcement of abusive norms by state officials be said to "count" as law in that society?

Legal systems may answer this question differently depending on social facts specific to each system relating to whether state officials can be described as "sovereign" in that system. In a constitutional democracy, such as in the United States, the sovereign is "the people" rather than any particular branch or arm of the government, but the people (as sovereign) must follow specific procedures to create norms that count as "law."[29] Thus social facts specific to our legal system make it impossible for the behavior of officials (in failing to enforce the law) to affect the content of the law. The fact that individual laws are ignored or flouted does not mean, in this system, that those laws no longer "count" as law, because, here, laws are only altered by processes consistent with our rule of recognition.[30] Thus, in the instance of the Reconstruction-era South, our legal system has ultimately concluded that even the ubiquitous disregard of (or aggressive contravention of) law fails to nullify or amend those laws that have been created in a manner consistent with our rule of recognition.[31]

Thus, an evaluation of Gray's claim that the behavior of officials can be said to "count" as law (or alter the content of law) in some pre-transitional societies turns on specific facts about each of the societies in question as well as the version of positivism that one embraces. It may be the case that Gray embraces the command theory of law, and that his claims implicitly posit that some pre-transitional societies vest in their officials a kind of unconditional sovereignty (i.e., a sovereignty that is not conditioned on legal limitations) and therefore the concept of "law" in those societies consists of the command of the sovereign backed by sanction.[32] An analysis of whether legal pre-commitments formally constrained the legality of actions by the sovereign in each of the societies that Gray cites (or in most pre-transitional and transitional states) stands outside the scope of this chapter, but for the purposes of this brief exploration of Gray's idea of "law as paradigm," it is sufficient to say that it is not obvious that the content of "law" in each of these societies can be accurately described as the command of the sovereign backed by sanction.

However, even if this were the case, there is a second point of discontinuity between Gray's idea of the "paradigm of law" and the command theory of law. For the abusive norms that Gray identifies to affect the content of law within a command theory understanding of law, they would have to elucidate either *who* is empowered to give commands or the *content* of those commands.[33] In the examples that Gray raises, the former seems unlikely and the latter seems redundant.

Gray's narrative of German Nazism and the Holocaust provides an instructive example.[34] When the Nazis came to power in the early 1930s, a pronounced undercurrent of anti-Semitism existed in Germany, as in much of Europe.[35] The Nazi regime did not introduce anti-Semitism to Germany, nor did the abusive norm of anti-Semitism serve to identify or define who the sovereign was during the Nazis' twelve-year reign.[36] Instead, the Nazi party assumed authority to govern Germany first through mechanisms consistent with the rule of recognition established by the Weimar Republic, and later by a seizure of power that represented an abandonment of the parliamentary republican system of government that was in place prior to Nazi seizure of power.[37] As central as anti-Semitism was to the Nazis' political identity and agenda, the norm of anti-Semitism did not serve as an accepted criterion that fundamentally identified the Nazi party as the sovereign of Germany as distinguished from other plausible claimants. Of course, without question the Nazi regime exploited, amplified, participated in, encouraged, codified, and ultimately compelled anti-Semitism in Germany, in part by defining moral and patriotic imperatives through the lens of an almost preternatural hate.[38] However, the norm of anti-Semitism did not aid in identifying who, in Germany, commanded the obedience of the governed.

Further, were we to pursue the command theory from the alternative angle, the norm of anti-Semitism also did not serve to identify the sovereign's command. The Nazis codified the norm of anti-Semitism and used the abusive paradigm to perpetuate and justify the atrocities committed in the Holocaust.[39] However, to the extent that it is accurate to describe the Nazis' regime as a "legal system" and Nazi commands as "laws"—a point to which we will return later—the explicit "black-letter law" of the Nazi regime codified the abusive norm into a formalized set of rules.[40] To describe the paradigm of abuse as an unexpressed part of the law is superfluous: the paradigm of abuse was explicitly defined by the "law."[41] The parameters of authorized atrocity were expressly detailed by law and while it can certainly be said that abusive norms were therefore expressed and reinforced by the law, it is not the case that abusive norms *identified* the law. The "legality" of an order that incorporated abusive norms was identified by its source, not its content.[42] Even to the extent that officials or non-officials engaged in abuses that were consistent with the prevailing paradigm of abuse but not expressly authorized by "law," they did so because they took the attitude of the government to be such that extralegal atrocities consistent with the prevailing paradigm of abuse would be tolerated (and perhaps even rewarded)—not because the boundaries of the abusive norm had itself come to define the parameters of "lawful" activity. Therefore, under the command theory it is difficult to find grounding for Gray's argument that abusive paradigms affect the content of law in pre-transitional societies. The types of norms he identifies serve to neither identify the rightful claimant to sovereignty, nor to identify the sovereign's command.[43]

B. The Rules Make the Sovereign

Another way to understand Gray's claim that abusive norms affect the content of law is to hypothesize that Gray embraces the more widely held understanding of the concept of law in which social facts (here, officials' conduct in embracing and extending abusive paradigms) are relevant to the content of law insofar as they relate to a particular society's rule of recognition.[44] However, the basis for this claim is less clear. Generally we think of social facts that relate to the rule of recognition in a given society as those facts that indicate that "officials" in that society recognize that a particular rule (or set of rules) identifies what constitutes valid law in that society, and that officials understand this rule itself to be valid and to be binding on each official in the society.[45] Thus facts that relate to the rule of recognition generally shed light on the fact that such recognition exists among officials in the society.[46]

However, Gray is clear that the norms that comprise the "abusive paradigm" precede the abusive regimes that he identifies. While Gray contends that law functions to extend abusive paradigms and "grant leave" to individuals to act upon abusive norms, the "truth" that underlies abusive regimes—that is, the "truth" that one group is inferior to another—may have its origin in colonial occupation, political ideology, religious doctrine, or any number of other sources that are exogenous to the abusive regime.[47] In other words, Gray does not maintain—nor does it seem to be a fair extension of his argument to maintain—that the abusive norms that lie at the foundation of targeted violence originate in (or are themselves a fundamental form of) law *qua* law. In Gray's account, law functions to amplify, exploit, normalize, and more deeply entrench existing abusive identity-based lines of opposition, but it is not the case that these abusive paradigms provide *criteria for identifying legality* in a given society.

Much has been written about the rule of recognition in transitional and pre-transitional societies and a full discussion of the subject exceeds the scope of this chapter, as the norms that Gray describes as "part of the law" do not seem to bear on questions of the criteria for legality within the pre-transitional societies that he discusses. However, it is worth noting that secondary rules in transitional and pre-transitional societies may be more difficult to identify, particularly where the regime of interest—here Gray's "abusive regime"—represents a departure from a preceding form of government.[48] Where the rise of an abusive regime follows a war or other political event that represents a sharp or dramatic break with past forms of government, it may be difficult to identify settled secondary rules and in some instances it may be more accurate to identify these breaks with past forms of government as a departure from legality—a point which we will return to in the final part of this chapter.

II. The *Role* of Law: Law as Constitutive Agent and Participant in Social Practice

Much in Gray's arguments turns on his conception of the functioning of "paradigms" and particularly "abusive paradigms" within pre-transitional societies.[49] Gray aptly observes that "Paradigms draw and maintain the boundaries of society and designate the roles and positions of individuals within society. In addition, because paradigms regulate the terms of acceptable conduct and describe the content and categorization of social identity, they are both the subject and the object of social action. That is, in addition to generating their own subjects, paradigms enter into contest with competing paradigms."[50] Thus "paradigms," in Gray's view, seem to be sets of interdependent and mutually reinforcing social rules that are sufficiently accepted within a relevant community (or "group"), such that they can be described as "entrenched" for that community—meaning that the *fact* that a rule exists within the relevant community becomes a *reason* for each member of the community to adhere to the rule.[51] *Abusive* paradigms would seem to be those paradigms in which the organizing norms constitute hierarchical rules concerning the inherent superiority of one group and inherent inferiority of another.[52] Gray further describes the potential of abusive paradigms to render acts of targeted violence "pregnant with 'moral meaning.'"[53] Gray masterfully and successfully details the power of an abusive paradigm to transform garden-variety hierarchical preferences (e.g., "my group is superior to their group") into genocidal beliefs (e.g., "their group is subhuman and deserves to die"; or "the existence of their group threatens the existence of mine") that impose on the believer significant and affirmative ethical desires and obligations.[54]

Regardless of whether one accepts his idea that abusive paradigms comprise part of the "law" of some pre-transitional states, it seems clear that Gray is absolutely correct that abusive social norms play a central role in the construction and execution of genocide and other mass atrocities. But if we do not accept the idea that these broadly accepted abusive norms succeed in birthing abusive regimes (which ultimately engage in mass atrocities) or otherwise instigating targeted violence by affecting the *content* of law, what then is the relationship between law, abusive norms, and mass atrocity? Implicit in this question are really three questions: (1) What impact do abusive norms have on the role of law in a given society? (2) What impact does the law have on abusive norms? and (3) What role does the law play in ushering in abusive regimes or otherwise transforming abusive norms into targeted violence? The first two of these questions are addressed in the sections that immediately follow, while the final question is grappled with in part III of this chapter.

A. The Role of Law and Abusive Norms: Enforcement, Perception, and Enablement

Whether the participation in and sanctioning of mass violence by state officials "counts" as law (or alters the content of the concept of law in a given society) says nothing about the relationship between the "paradigm of abuse" embraced by those officials (and the broader society) and the role that law plays within that society. Thus, if it is the case that the "paradigm of abuse" that Gray describes cannot be said to constitute or affect what "law" *is* in a given state, this account certainly does not alter the impact that officials' (and/or non-officials') sanction-free lawlessness has on the manner that victims or perpetuators of targeted violence experience and interact with "law." Abusive norms may be embraced systemically or by individual officials and private citizens and may thereby fundamentally affect the degree to which law is enforced and experienced, and consequently the manner in which it is perceived. More significantly, where the adoption of abusive norms prompts officials to decline to protect victims of targeted violence, the abusive paradigm literally enables the perpetuation of targeted violence. The technical understanding that officials are behaving "illegally" in failing to protect victims does little to diminish the fact and impact of targeted violence.

In this sense, Gray is correct that by "sustaining an environment in which targeted violence is tolerated or encouraged" abusive norms affect the enforcement of law in pre-transitional societies such that perpetrators of violence have "license" to act with impunity.[55] However, Gray errs in stating that "these official acts [of tolerating and encouraging violence] form part of a paradigm of *law*."[56] Certainly the behavior of officials (in failing to enforce the law or directly participating in criminality) and the prevalence of abusive social paradigms (which provide moral motivation and justification for atrocities) both assume some manner of causal roles in the existence and extension of mass violence. But they do not contribute to the fact of mass violence by infiltrating and altering the content of law itself. The key point here is that regardless of the undeniably powerful impact that Gray's "abusive paradigms" have on the enforcement and perception of the law and the degree to which the consequent lack of enforcement enables atrocities, acts of violence by officials and non-officials that are not authorized by the law *qua* law of the state remain fundamentally extralegal or *lawless* acts.

For example, from the perspective of the victims and perpetrators of violence in the Reconstruction-era South it may have appeared as though widespread acts of lynching bore the shape and heft of "law." Undoubtedly the widespread adoption of abusive norms by state officials dramatically affected the *role* that law played in the lives of both the governing and the governed. Abusive norms greatly undermined the role that state actors played in delivering the substantive guarantees of the Fourteenth Amendment to southern African Americans, and yet the content of the law itself was not altered by the fact that state officials failed to enforce it (and indeed acted in contravention to it).[57] Instead, due perhaps in part to our system's internalized commitment to the rule of law, where state actors failed to enforce state and federal law (or directly participated in criminal activity) their conduct, although undeterred, was nonetheless understood as "lawless" even by the standards of the time.[58]

In this light it becomes clear that the *role* of law in a given society must be carefully distinguished from the *content* of law within that same society. Thus, Gray is undoubtedly correct that prevalent abusive norms within a society transform the role that law plays within that society, and the role that law plays in a pre-transitional society in the thrall of an abusive paradigm determines in part whether opportunity exists to transform abusive norms into abusive actions.[59] The fact that abusive norms affect the role that law plays in pre-transitional societies does not mean that abusive norms have become *part of* the law of those societies. Instead, it is more accurate to say that abusive paradigms succeed in overpowering and dissolving any conflicting concomitant commitment to legality itself on the part of officials and non-officials who participate in targeted violence. Rather than affecting "law," abusive paradigms affect adherents' sense of their obligation (whether it issues from a Hartian sense of positive duty or an Austinian fear of sanction) to follow the law—a point we will return to in the final part of this chapter.

B. The Constitutive Force of Law

A particularly persuasive aspect of Gray's argument holds that "'[l]aw' has a significant role in the construction, extension, and expression of abusive paradigms."[60] While much of this point is closely tied in Gray's chapter to the role that law plays in enabling targeted violence, implicit in this statement is the keen insight that apart from the impact that abusive norms have on "law" (or, more accurately, the role of law, as previously discussed), law has a significant impact on the construction and content of abusive norms. Law serves as one of the many (and perhaps one of the most potent) of the "public institutions" that develop, establish, and extend the identity norms that can form the basis of abusive paradigms.[61] In other words, the law plays an important constitutive role in the construction of social norms. The fact and degree to which law applies constitutive force to social norms has been the focus of much study, yet it is a phenomenon of particular significance in the context of mass identity-based atrocities, and so it warrants independent attention here.[62]

Law can operate with either "soft" or "hard" constitutive force on the development of social norms. Law operates with "hard" constitutive force in situations in which the law serves as a constitutive *rule* (rather than merely a guide or an influence) because the law is empowered to act as the definitive authority as to composition of a given class or category.[63] Generally, when we speak about a rule bearing constitutive force, we mean that the rule determines what does and does not "count" as falling within the extension of a particular concept or the boundaries of a particular practice.[64] Constitutive rules *enable* us to engage in certain practices by defining our activities as falling within the boundaries of those practices.[65] The paradigmatic constitutive rules are the rules of a game.[66] For example, the rules of baseball tell us what counts as a "ball" and what counts as a "strike" and only by abiding by those rules of baseball am I *able* to engage in the practice of baseball. Similarly, law operates as a constitutive rule when it serves to distinguish which practices, objects, or people fall within a legally defined category. So, for instance, in the United States, the law operates as a constitutive *rule* when it determines who counts as a "man" for the purpose of state marriage statutes that limit marriage to a "man" and a "woman."[67] A person who fails to meet the law's criteria is disabled, authoritatively, from not only *engaging* in the legally authorized practice (here, marriage), but from *being* or belonging within the legally constructed category (here, "man"). When the law operates with "hard" constitutive force there are no criteria by which one can contest the content of the rule, because authoritative constitutive rules do more than define boundaries—they themselves *are* boundaries.

Law operates with "soft" constitutive force when it does not serve as the definitive authority with respect to a contested class, but the law nonetheless interacts with and influences background social norms with respect to that class. For example, the law is not empowered to authoritatively determine whether a postoperative female-to-male transsexual individual is recognized as a "man" by his community, but the degree to which the law treats that individual as though he were a "man" may either substantially reinforce and entrench (or, alternatively, challenge and undermine) background norms regarding real or genuine "maleness." When the law operates with "soft" constitutive force in this manner, an individual may still employ a variety of other bases for validly claiming "maleness" within his community, but depending on the community, the law may serve as a significant influence on the development of social norms concerning "real" maleness.

Thus, the law has the potential to employ both "hard" and "soft" constitutive power in the context of the construction of identity-based norms, and this is particularly so in the context of abusive paradigms of identity-based norms such as Gray discusses. For example, the "law" of the Third Reich clearly exerted hard constitutive force on the construction of norms concerning the identity and character of German Jews.[68] In the 1930s, the Nazis promulgated a series of laws that identified "Jewish" as a racial category and defined in great detail the ancestral criteria by which individuals were designated "Jewish."[69] In so doing, these laws, sometimes called the Nuremberg Laws, eliminated the legal possibility of competing criteria of Jewish membership and identity (such as religious, cultural, or self-identified criteria), and imposed ancestry as the definitive and irrefutable boundary of the legally constructed (and consequential) Jewish identity.[70] Of course the Nuremberg Laws exerted soft constitutive force as well, as they necessarily served to reinforce and entrench existing background anti-Semitic norms within German society. The fact that the law authoritatively defined German Jews as "other" and as definitionally unentitled to German citizenship, rights, and privileges served to, as Gray observes, "normalize" and encourage existing anti-Semitic norms within German society.[71]

However, much of the soft constitutive force of law in constructing identity-based norms in pre-transitional societies exists outside the context of laws that formally identify racial classification. In the course of interpreting the distribution and application of rights and privileges in a society, law tacitly passes upon background judgments about what constitutes identity within that society and what consequences should follow from the designation of "other." In determining what justice requires in the context of equality and discrimination, law implicitly approves or disapproves of sets of background assumptions about the content of the concept of "other." Therefore, Gray's chapter presents an essential insight: insofar as transitional justice is concerned with preventing future atrocities, the project must be cognizant of the constitutive force that law applies to the shape and strength of existing abusive norms within transitional societies, and the ways in which law could be structured to exert a positive constructive influence on these background norms.

So if we embrace Gray's insight that law embodies tremendous constitutive potential in the context of abusive paradigms, yet we question his claim that those same abusive norms affect the content (rather than the enforcement or role) of law, where does this analysis leave us with respect to Gray's claim that the conventional emphasis on the "rule of law" in transitional justice literature is misplaced?[72] A consideration of this question follows.

III. The *Rule* of Law and Abusive Paradigms

If we take the behavior of abusive regimes to be distinct from the content of law, but we embrace the idea that abusive legal regimes largely rely on (and usually further entrench) existing abusive norms in order to execute genocidal goals, what, if any, role does the "rule of law" play in perpetuation of the violence that follows?

The argument that has been presented here holds that the content of the concept of "law" matters within a given society because "law" plays an indispensable role in distinguishing lawfulness from lawlessness, even where abusive norms within that society have succeeded in blocking the enforcement of legal protections, manipulating popular perception of the bounds of lawfulness, and even enabled the perpetration of mass violence. The content of law matters even in the absence of meaningful enforcement because departures from "law" mark the moments in which a commitment to the strictures and pre-commitments of the legal system would have generated an alternative, possibly atrocity-avoiding, result. In other words, the concept of law within a pre-transitional society allows us to determine when and how legality was incrementally discarded and ultimately abandoned on the road to the unimaginable.

Much of the time, the departure from legality in pre-transitional societies seems to take the form of an abrupt or violent political break with a previous legal order, as was in the case in Gray's examples of the Rwandan genocide and the Reconstruction-era South.[73] In each of these cases, an existing legal system was displaced and an abusive regime assumed power using methods that were inconsistent with the rule of law under the old regime. Insofar as the new abusive regimes lacked basic indicia and structures of a "legal system"—that is, minimally, that the sovereign itself is subjected to legal limits—the departure from legality can be located in the displacement of the previous legal order (if indeed it qualified as a legal system), or in the construction of a new abusive political order that lacks a system of "laws."[74]

Of course, it is not always the case that abusive regimes arise following a violent departure from an established order. For example, Hitler assumed power in a manner that was consistent with the rule of law under the Weimar Republic.[75] Even the major mechanisms by which Hitler began consolidating power in preparation for dismantling the republic and establishing a totalitarian regime were "legal" maneuvers within the Weimar legal system.[76] The Reichstag Fire Decree of February 1933, for instance, which suspended most of the Weimar constitutional civil liberties, was issued as an emergency order by Reich president Hindenburg pursuant to Article 48 of the Weimar Constitution, which allowed the president to take "emergency measures" without the consent of the Reichstag—a provision that had been used over 250 times to suspend rights prior to the Nazi seizure of power.[77] Similarly, the Enabling Act of March 1933, which transferred legislative powers to Hitler's administration, was passed by the Reichstag and signed by President Hindenburg.[78] Thus, it was not the case that the Nazis overthrew or violently destroyed the legal order that preceded their regime. Instead the Nazi takeover was encased in an existing legal framework and democratic institutions were imploded from within.[79] At some point in the transformation from the Weimar Republic to the Third Reich, the political order in Germany abandoned structures critical to a legal system. Yet, as the "rule of law" provides less of a bright line between a "legitimate legal system" and an "abusive regime" in this instance, it also seems to hold less promise as a means of preventing the rise of abusive regimes.

The Nazi example seems to underscore Gray's contention that a robust commitment to the rule of law is an insufficient safeguard against the rise of abusive regimes.[80] To prevent the rise of abusive regimes, Gray contends, law must provide support for the "diversification of groups and group affiliation" by, among other things, providing civil space within which groups and associations may compete with one another, supplying alternative routes to violence, and erecting barriers to claims of group superiority or entitlement.[81] A legal system that succeeds in creating these structures should be positioned to promote and protect the cross-associational "dynamic stability" that is, in Gray's view, essential to preventing the rise of abusive regimes within pre-transitional and transitional societies.[82]

However, in the absence of a robust commitment to the rule of law, it would seem that the types of legal structures and institutions that Gray prescribes would be of little use in situations in which the adoption of abusive norms by officials obstructs the enforcement (or equal enforcement) of laws, as was the case in the Reconstruction-era South. Such protections would also seem to be of limited utility in circumstances in which a politically ambitious group exploits (or creates) a political crisis to seize control and dismantle existing legal institutions, and uses abusive norms to justify the takeover or to silence opposition, as was the case in Nazi Germany, the Argentine Dirty War, and the Rwandan genocide. In each of these cases, for legal rules and institutions to provide protection against atrocity, they must be preceded by and ensconced within a minimal commitment to "the rule of law."[83] Where this is not the case, legal structures that serve to protect and promote diverse associations and construct barriers to the hierarchical ordering of those associations remain vulnerable to threat of abandonment in times of political crisis. It would seem that for the law to provide any degree of protection against atrocity, it must be attended by a minimal commitment to follow the law when those protections are most required.

Conclusion

Although Gray presents key insights about the significance of the constitutive force of law and the importance of fostering dynamic cross-associations within transitional societies, he draws broad conclusions about the impact that abusive norms have on the content of law in pre-transitional and transitional societies. In focusing holistically on the "multidimensional" role that law plays in pre-transitional societies, distinctions between the role and content of law become blurred. However, a closer parsing of these distinctions reveals that the rule of law serves as a necessary (but not sufficient) bulwark against catastrophic human rights abuses both in preventing the establishment of abusive regimes and in ensuring that legal protections and the positive constitutive force of law are engaged within a given legal paradigm.

Notes

1. David Gray, "Transitional Disclosures: What Transitional Justice Reveals about 'Law,'" in this volume.

2. Gray suggests that the particular "multidimensionality of 'law'" that he illuminates in this chapter is present, too (if overlooked), in "stable states where the central distraction frequently is black-letter law." Ibid., 149.

3. Ibid., 161.

4. Ibid., 170; 172.

5. Ibid., 161.

6. Ibid., 149.

7. Ibid., 150.

8. Ibid., 150–51.

9. Ibid., 149.

10. Similarly, in addition to theories that address the relationship between social norms and legal *content,* those who employ pragmatic approaches to legal *meaning* advance the proposition that legal meaning is derived from norms internal to legal practice. See, e.g., Karl Llewellyn, *The Case Law System in America* (Chicago: University of Chicago Press, 1989). Dennis Patterson has argued that in the wake of the collapse of legal formalism, it was proto-legal pragmatist Karl Llewellyn who first articulated the idea that the practice of law is the "ultimate source of legal meaning. Practice or 'way of acting' not rule or principle is primary." Dennis M. Patterson, "Law's Practice," *Columbia Law Review* 90 (1990): 577. For Llewellyn and other thinkers who apply pragmatic methods to questions of legal meaning, knowing what law is means knowing how to "do" law, and norms that guide the "doing" (i.e., practice) of law both justify and create legal meaning. Llewellyn, *The Case Law System in America,* 577.

11. Jules L. Coleman and Brian Leiter, "Legal Positivism," in *A Companion to the Philosophy of Law and Legal Theory,* ed. Dennis Patterson (Oxford: Blackwell Publishing, 1999). But see Kevin Toh, "An Argument Against the Social Fact Thesis and Some Additional Preliminary Steps Towards a New Conception of Legal Positivism," *Law and Philosophy* 27 (2008): 5. The analysis presented here is limited to legal positivist accounts of the relationship between "law" and social norms because I take Gray's position to be more closely aligned with that tradition than other plausible alternatives (such as natural law theories).

12. See, e.g., Jeremy Bentham, *Of Laws in General,* ed. H. L. A. Hart (London: Athlone Press, 1970); John Austin, *The Province of Jurisprudence Determined* (Cambridge: Cambridge University Press, 1995).

13. H. L. A. Hart, *The Concept of Law* (Oxford: Oxford University Press, 1961), 100–110.

14. Gray, "Transitional Disclosures," 149 (emphasis added).

15. Hart, *The Concept of Law,* 100–123.

16. Gray, "Transitional Disclosures," 157.

17. Ibid.

18. Ibid.

19. Ibid.

20. See John Austin, *The Province of Jurisprudence Determined* (Cambridge: Cambridge University Press, 1995); see also, Anthony J. Sebok, "Misunderstanding Positivism," *Michigan Law Review* 93 (1995): 2061–2066 (describing the major tenants of command theory positivism).

21. Sebok, "Misunderstanding Positivism," 2061–2066.

22. Ibid.

23. Gray, "Transitional Disclosures," 157.

24. Ibid.

25. See generally Thomas Hobbes, *Leviathan,* ed. Edwin Curley (Indianapolis, IN: Hackett Publishers, 1992). Many modern positivists do not recognize a system of rules that consists only of commands backed by the threat of sanction to be a "legal system." See Hart, *The Concept of Law,* 100. But see, Frederick Schauer, "Was Austin Right After All? On the Role of Sanctions in a Theory of Law," *Ratio Juris* 23 (2010): 1–21.

26. That is, if state officials could be said to be "sovereign" in those societies.

27. See *Monroe v. Pape,* 365 U.S. 167, 174–176 (1961) (discussing the congressional history of the Ku Klux Klan Act that was passed in 1871 to redress what was perceived to be widespread acts of violence against former slaves in the Reconstructive-era South. The court stated, "[The Act] was passed by a Congress that had the Klan 'particularly in mind.' The debates are replete with references to the lawless conditions existing in the South in 1871. There was available to the Congress during these debates a report, nearly 600 pages in length, dealing with the activities of the Klan and the inability of the state governments to cope with it . . . . It was not the unavailability of state remedies but the failure of certain States to enforce the laws with an equal hand that furnished the powerful momentum behind this 'force bill.' Mr. Lowe of Kansas said: 'While murder is stalking abroad in disguise, while whippings and lynchings and banishment have been visited upon unoffending American citizens, the local administrations have been found inadequate or unwilling to apply the proper corrective. . . . Immunity is given to crime, and the records of the public tribunals are searched in vain for any evidence of effective redress.'" "State official" is used broadly here to indicate individuals acting under the authority (or color) of state, local, or even federal law.

28. Ibid.

29. Scott Shapiro, "What is the Rule of Recognition (and Does it Exist)?" in *The Rule Of Recognition and the U.S. Constitution,* ed. Matthew Adler and Kenneth Himma (Oxford: Oxford University Press, 2009).

30. See generally, Matthew Adler and Kenneth Himma, eds., *The Rule of Recognition and the U.S. Constitution*(Oxford: Oxford University Press, 2009).

31. Reasonable minds disagree as to what, exactly (if anything), constitutes the rule of recognition in the United States. See generally, ibid.

32. See Austin, *The Province.*

33. Hart, *The Concept of Law*, 50–78.

34. Gray, "Transitional Disclosures," 158.

35. Daniel Jonah Goldhagen, *Hitler's Willing Executioners* (New York: Alfred A. Knopf, 1996), 49–79.

36. Ibid.

37. Ibid.; Joachim C. Fest, *Hitler* (New York: Harcourt Brace Jovanovich, 1974), 387–416.

38. Fest, *Hitler*, 80–128; see also, William Sheridan Allen, *The Nazi Seizure of Power* (New York: Franklin Watts, 1965), 218–232.

39. Goldhagen, *Hitler's Willing Executioners*, 131–163.

40. An example of this was the Law for the Restoration of the Professional Civil Service, enacted in April 1933, which required (with some exceptions) that Germans of Jewish descent and other non-Aryans retire from civil service. First Regulation for Administration of the Law for the Restoration of the Professional Civil Service, v. 4.11.1933 (RGB1. I S. 195). ("A person is to be regarded as non-Aryan, who is descended from non-Aryans, especially Jewish parents or grandparents.")

41. Goldhagen, *Hitler's Willing Executioners*, 89–111.

42. Fest, *Hitler*, 391.

43. Moreover, it is difficult to reconcile the command theory of law with Gray's description of abusive paradigms of law forming "positive expressions of ethical commitments to self and to the world as it ought to be." Gray, "Transitional Disclosures," 153.

44. Hart, *The Concept of Law*, 100–110.

45. Ibid.

46. Ibid.

47. Gray, "Transitional Disclosures," 158.

48. See Hart, *The Concept of Law*, 97 (discussing the emergence of secondary rules as marking the transition from pre-legal to legal society).

49. Gray, "Transitional Disclosures," generally, but particularly at 167–70.

50. Ibid., 154.

51. For a discussion of the entrenchment of social rules, see Frederick Schauer, *Playing by the Rules* (Oxford: Clarendon Press, 1991), 42–52.

52. Gray, "Transitional Disclosures," 155–156.

53. Ibid., 156.

54. Ibid., 167.

55. Ibid., 157.

56. Ibid., 157 (emphasis added).

57. See note 27, *Monroe v. Pape*, 365 U.S. 167, 174–176 (1961) (and accompanying text).

58. This understanding was expressed in the floor debates surrounding the passage as codified (and thereby itself became part of the corpus of American law) in 1871 when Congress passed the Ku Klux Klan Act in an effort to redress lawlessness on the part of southern officials. Ibid.

59. Abusive norms may even affect the enforcement and perception of law to the extent that the legal system ceases to bear any indicia of legality—but (depending on the version of positivism one embraces) this phenomenon, too, is generally best described as a departure from legality (or more precisely the abandonment of a legal *system*) rather than an enrichment or revision of the content of the concept of law itself. See Hart, *The Concept of Law*, 112–117. Hart understands that for a legal system to exist two conditions must be met: (1) the rules of behavior (or laws) that are valid according to the system's rule of recognition must be generally obeyed; (2) officials must accept the validity of the rule of recognition. Ibid.

60. Gray, "Transitional Disclosures," 157.

61. Ibid., 154.

62. See, e.g., Austin Sarat and Jonathan Simon, "Cultural Analysis, Cultural Studies, and the Situation of Legal Scholarship," in *Culture Analysis, Cultural Studies, and the Law*, ed. Austin Sarat and Jonathan Simon (Durham, NC: Duke University Press, 2003), 14–15 ("[Law] enters social practices and is, indeed, 'imbricated' in them, by shaping consciousness, by making law's concepts and commands seem, if not invisible, perfectly natural and benign. Law is, in this sense, constitutive of culture. . . . Law has played, and continues to play, a large role in regulating the terms and conditions of cultural production."). See also, Meredith M. Render, "Gender Rules," 22 *Yale Journal of Law and Feminism* (2010) 133.

63. For a discussion of constitutive rules, see Schauer, *Playing by the Rules*, 6–7.

64. Ibid.

65. Ibid., 6.

66. Ibid.

67. See, e.g., *Kantaras v. Kantaras*, 884 So. 2d 155 (Fla. Dist. Ct. App. 2004) (holding that a postoperative female-to-male transsexual person did not count as "male" and, therefore, could not marry a woman in Florida because the term "male" within Florida's marriage statute refers to an immutable trait determined at birth; therefore, no surgery could transform a person not born with

this trait into a person who counts as "male" for the purpose of the marriage statute); *accord Littleton v. Prange*, 9 S.W.3d 223 (Tex. App. 1999).

68. See Cecilia O'Leary and Anthony Platt, *Bloodlines: Recovering Hitler's Nuremberg Laws* (London: Paradigm Publishers, 2005) (discussing the Nuremberg Laws).

69. Ibid.

70. Ibid.

71. Goldhagen, *Hitler's Willing Executioners*, 89–128.

72. Gray, "Transitional Disclosures," 148.

73. See Gerard Prunier, *The Rwanda Crisis* (New York: Columbia University Press, 1995), 192–206 (describing the political events that led up to the death of President Habyarimana and the beginning of the Rwandan genocide).

74. See Hart, *The Concept of Law*, 100–110 (describing the fundamental structures necessary for a legal system); see also, Jeremy Waldron, "The Concept and the Rule of Law," *Georgia Law Review* 43 (2008): 19–37 (offering an account of "the essence of a legal system").

75. In the earliest part of Hitler's reign (January 1933–March 1933), the legality of an order by his government was determined by the criteria of legality (i.e., rules of recognition) of the Weimar Republic, which included in most instances that an act of law was passed by the Reichstag, was consistent with the provisions of the Weimar Constitution, and bore the signature of Paul von Hindenburg, then president of Germany. See Fest, *Hitler*, 387–391.

76. Ibid.

77. See Sanford Levinson and Jack M. Balkin, "Constitutional Dictatorship: Its Dangers and Its Design," *Minnesota Law Review* 94 (2010): 1811.

78. Fest, *Hitler*, 391.

79. Ibid., 391.

80. Gray, "Transitional Disclosures," 151.

81. Ibid., 170.

82. Ibid., 161.

83. See Waldron, "The Concept and the Rule of Law," 5 (describing the rule of law as the "requirement that people in positions of authority should exercise their power within a constraining framework of public norms, rather than on the basis of their own preferences, their own ideology, or their own individual sense of right and wrong").

5
Global Transitions, New Perspectives on Legality, and Judicial Review
Ruti Teitel

Introduction

After the Second World War, the legacy of Nazism and the context of social and political transition awakened a vigorous debate in the world of
Anglo-American jurisprudence about the relationship of law to morality,
and, especially, of lawmaking or legislation to adjudication and interpretation. H. L. A. Hart and Lon Fuller argued over whether considerations
of morality should be relevant to what counts as law for purposes of application by the judiciary. Hart claimed against Fuller that it is for politics and legislatures, not judges, to determine the moral content of legal
rules. Later in his probing *The Concept of Law*, Hart would observe that it
is in moments of transition—that is, the creation of new states—that illuminate the complexity of international law's sources of legitimacy. As he
pointed out, if ex ante state consent were the sole basis for international
law's legitimacy then it would be incomprehensible how a new state could
be automatically bound by preexisting customary law, to the creation of
which it obviously had no opportunity to consent or contribute.[1]

The question of what gives international law its authority is either explicit or implicit in debates today over the role of international law in global
politics and about how law shapes globalization. At the same time, the
traditional state-centric view of international law, dominant since West-
phalia, is under challenge, with many other actors and institutions now
the subjects and objects of international law (individuals, corporations,
peoples, etc.). Analogies are being drawn between international and constitutional law. In a 2009 piece in the *Harvard Law Review,* Jack Goldsmith and Daryl Levinson observe affinities between international and

constitutional law as forms of public law.[2] "[L]egal regimes that both constitute and govern the behavior of states and state actors . . . . The respects in which both international and constitutional law differ from ordinary domestic law follow from the distinctive aspiration of public law regimes to constitute and constrain the behavior of state institutions and the distinctive difficulty these regimes face of not being able to rely fully on these same state institutions for implementation and enforcement."[3] While these scholars' contribution is useful for its consideration of international law not as sealed off from the rest of law, its approach would seem to see the issues presented as static and hence does not register that there are significant changes underway in international law that go to its relation to global politics here in particular, its status and role vis-à-vis actors beyond the state, and its dependence on judicial lawmaking.

In this chapter I explore the entanglement of international law jurisprudence with transitional rule of law and the role of new judicial institutions in guiding the emergent global order. My claim is that there are forces of change relating to global changes that help illuminate the role of law, particularly at a time when political authority is itself fragmented and often weak. Hence, a look at contemporary international jurisprudence regarding state practice may well inform the question of meaning of legal norms. One might also ask about the role of the expanded international judiciary in the legitimation of international law, through interpretation based on human-centered interests and values—with implications for constitutionalism as well. Judicial interpretation is proving well suited to making sense of diverse normative sources, under conditions of political conflict and moral disagreement. Courts are inherently in dialogue with other courts and institutions that also play interpretive roles, and their decisions in individual cases give meaning to law without purporting to give "closure" to normative controversy in politics and morals.[4]

This seems consonant with the views articulated in *The Concept of Law*, where according to Hart, "It is a mistake to suppose that a basic rule or rule of recognition is generally a necessary condition of the existence of rules of obligation. The rules of the simple structure are, like the basic rule of the more advanced systems, binding *if they are accepted and function as such*."[5]

Today, from the vantage point of recent transitions, we are in a better position to see the "actual character" of these rules.[6] In this chapter, I suggest a new understanding that addresses a key anxiety in contemporary international legal scholarship regarding the proliferation of tribunals, or, more generally, the proliferation of sites of interpretation and application of international law, that is, regarding customary law, which goes to the role of state practice in relation to judicial determination of the existence of customary rules. I conclude by offering some thoughts on the implications of international law moving from state- to human-centric normativity.[7]

The Emerging Legal Framework

Globalization and the end of the Cold War have set the scene for a renewed debate on the meaning of law, rooted in and reminiscent of the debate that occurred at the end of that century's great conflict, World War II. At the same time, the growing density and extended reach of international law via the proliferation of tribunals and judicial review on both regional and international bases have led to controversy and confusion concerning international law's role in global order. In particular, there are developments in various legal orders, many of which had hitherto seemed apparently autonomous of one another; that is, an increasing overlap and interconnection between international and other levels, that is, regional and domestic legal orders, and between the regimes regulating public and private spheres. For example, within the doctrinal structure of international law as such, scholars have observed the growing convergence of human rights and humanitarian law. Thus, Theodor Meron has written of the humanization of international law, while other critical scholars have observed on humanitarianization of international human rights law. Yet, a third strand, post–Cold War, is the revival of legal discourse concerning the justice of war itself.[8] While humanitarian norms originated in settings of interstate conflict, at present contemporary developments challenge accepted understandings of war and peace, international and internal conflict, state and private actors, combatant and civilian.

What characterizes the now-emerging legal order is that it is addressed not exclusively to states and their interests and perhaps, not even primarily so. Post–Cold War politics has fueled the demand for a more sweeping universalizing rights regime. Persons and peoples are now at the core, and a nonsovereignty-based normativity is manifesting itself, which has an uneasy and uncertain relationship to the inherited discourse of sovereign equality. This, too, has had consequences for the vitality of earlier state-centric views of what gives international law its force. (In a larger book project, this new normativity I term "humanity-law"—the lens and discourse through which many of the key controversies in contemporary law and politics come into focus.)[9]

The core question is, what does this normative direction represent? Here, it may be useful to recall the historical transitional debates as to the role of law and morals in the postwar period. In the aftermath of the Second World War and the transition out of Nazism, there was a vigorous debate in the world of Anglo-American jurisprudence about the relationship of law to morality and politics. Leading legal philosophers H. L. A. Hart and Lon Fuller argued over what counted as law. Should an immoral law be recognized and enforced by judges as "law," leaving to politics the task of aligning positive legal rules and moral truth? Or, should an immoral law be eschewed as in tension with the very idea(l) of rule of law?

Today, international legal scholars debate the sources for international law's authority: front and center is the issue of customary international law, where formal state consent, based on written agreement, is absent.[10] This seems to parallel controversies in constitutional theory about sources of authority and legitimacy beyond and perhaps in tension with popular sovereignty.

With obvious affinities to constitutionalism based on judicial review (particularly in the postwar transitions), today the judicial enforcement of international norms is heralded as a sign of universal citizenship in the offing; this is ironic, perhaps, or somewhat circular since the ascendancy of global judicial power has largely occurred in the absence of—and arguably to fill the gap created by an absence of—political consensus. This gap is often finessed by the recourse to constitutional language. Thus, in Jürgen Habermas's words: "Following two world wars, the constitutionalization of international law has evolved along the lines prefigured by Kant toward cosmopolitan law and has assumed institutional form in international constitutions, organizations and proceedings."[11] For cosmopolitans, the move to an ethical human rights law discourse is construed as somehow opposite and superior to the classic or traditional language of state interest.[12] Thus, what is shaping up is a "new dispute . . . over whether law remains an appropriate medium for realizing the declared goals of achieving peace and international security and promoting democracy and human rights throughout the world."[13] Indeed, for some, this is their main virtue—that a global system offers plausible transpolitical standards for judging and delimiting the state from above. One might see this as one side of the polarized debate over the potential of the law in the contemporary political context.

As intense as these differences over the authority of law have been in the last decade, one cannot help but wonder about the rather simplistic framing of the relevant question at stake in terms of a debate about the law—that is, whether for or against—as it would abstract from much else that is going on in the world whether politically or legally. Admittedly, the debate has been enriched by an essential part of the cosmopolitan claim, which depends on the law for its normative logic. While the cosmopolitan perspective effectively captures the spirit behind the proliferation of the law, because cosmopolitanism tends to essentialize this spirit as a timeless moral truth, it ignores or is blind to the range of historically contingent factors that *explain* the law's normative direction in the present moment. More problematic still is the cosmopolitan position's dependence on the capacity of the law to function effectively as an authoritative ordering of individual rights and duties. This implies a universal ground of legitimacy that does not depend on political agreement or compromise between diverse multivariate political and moral claims.

Here, the cosmopolitan perspective cannot do justice to the complexity of the current situation, which throws up independent and conflicting individual—and group humanity—rights claims, all interrelated with the state and statehood. The advent of new processes and regimes allows not only for a greater multilateralism, but also, for one of a fundamentally different kind, made more complex by the current expansion in the available representation of diverse state—and non-state—interests in international affairs. This is seen, for example, in the conflict over the protection of preservation rights of persons and peoples in the Balkans, as well as tensions over the human rights costs of humanitarian intervention.

The most intransigent critics of the cosmopolitan view are those whom one might characterize as the "law skeptics," including realist scholars of international relations and law. These skeptics downplay the significance of the changes the cosmopolitans highlight: instead, they see the post–Cold War moment merely in terms of a reassessment and realignment of state interests and interstate power relations. For those who see law in state-centric terms, the developments discussed above concerning the meaning of legalism as an international matter bear little relevance because there would remain only one measure of the basis for legality, that is, one that is largely postulated in state-centric terms; namely, in terms of the possibility of state compliance with rules to which states have consented. The analogy is clearly to the positivist account of domestic law, which gives primacy to the efficacy of command as a characteristic of legal order; thus, international law is meaningful to the extent to which it is a set of effective commands to the states that are bound.[14]

Indeed, there is a growing revival of this view, with interest in retrieving empirical support regarding indicia of state behavior. As the state continues to be the main actor in international relations, sovereigntists question the degree to which there may be significant substantive transformation in the relation international law bears to the state-citizen relationship (for example, changes relating to the judicialization of the state) or to any other citizen-collective relationship. This position, associated with the Bush administration and closely aligned with realism, or law skepticism, known by some as "neo-sovereigntism,"[15] expresses a view of law that seems highly reductive and does not appear to recognize even the receptivity of the old common law to customary international law; for example, *Paquete Habana*[16]—where the United States Supreme Court declared that "international law is part of our law, and must be ascertained and administered by the courts of justice of appropriate jurisdiction, as often as questions of right depending upon it are duly presented for their determination . . . resort must be had to the customs and usages of civilized nations; and, as evidence of these, to the works of jurists and commentators, who by years of labor, research and experience, have made themselves peculiarly well acquainted with the subjects of which they treat. Such works are resorted to by judicial tribunals, not for the speculations of their authors concerning what the law ought to be, but for trustworthy evidence of what the law really is." Theirs is an arcane originalism simply not adequate to the current phenomena. As we have seen, in its American incarnation, this perspective espouses a distinctive republican view on what it is that gives law its legitimacy. Neo-sovereigntists view popular sovereignty as the central and indeed by some exclusive source of legal legitimacy, for example, Goldsmith and Levinson, translated to the international level this position is unrelentingly state-centric, as for them it is only within states that republican popular sovereignty can be exercised and thus it is state consent to international legal rules that becomes the essential proxy or vehicle for the democratic legitimization of (binding) international legal order.

At the very same time, the long-held sovereigntist view of international law is seriously challenged by various changing political realities: that is, the hollowing out of the state with ramifications for the interstate system, particularly for the development and interaction of the public and private spheres. There is also the increasing globalization of capital and labor as well as a half century of self-determination and movement of peoples—which again goes to the sovereigntist claim, as it implies a level of attenuation as to the meaning and force of political community and state consent as a plausible basis for the authority of constitutional or international law. Understanding the prominence of weak and failed states and the evident pressures upon and the attenuation of state sovereignty as traditionally understood may help to explain the puzzling seemingly paradoxical developments that are our present global context: greater international interconnection yet without greater consensus or integration. It is in precisely these circumstances that political conflict has been shifted to adjudicative institutions, the criminal tribunals and the International Criminal Court (ICC) being prominent examples.

Lessons from the Postwar Debate

In this light, let us reconsider the frequent characterization of Hart's position in the Hart/Fuller debate as one of arch positivism, his apparent view of rule of law solely in terms of the "command of a sovereign."[17] Were Hart a crude positivist, this would position him today as an ally of the skeptical camp in the current post–Cold War debate about the status of international law in regards to its contribution to rule of law. However, when one turns to Hart's considered view on international law developed later—in his subsequent seminal work, *The Concept of Law,* Hart rejects such a narrow understanding of legality—he expressly distances himself from the view that enforcement by a sovereign authority is what defines a legal system, distinguishing coercive enforcement from bindingness in the law.[18]

When Hart turns to international law, as he does at the end of his *Concept of Law,* he elides the straightforward positivist answer; all the while seeking to avoid the pitfall of essentializing about international law in natural law direction, Hart argues that even where law lacks a centralized command structure, as does international law, that it, nevertheless, can be distinguished from morality, because it operates through a distinctive set of rules of juridical communication with legal sources, arguments, and claimsmaking.[19]

So, for example, consider the many debates over the sources of international law today, such as regarding the ongoing meaning of the "law of nations" or "ius gentium,"[20] defined as the law that arises between nations. As legal philosopher Jeremy Waldron put it, "the law of nations is often used as a synonym for international law. But it once had a broader meaning, comprising something like the common law of mankind, not just on issues between sovereigns but on legal issues generally"—in the United States context this has been subject of litigation, notably under the historical Alien Tort Claims Act,[21] where the tradition of ius gentium has informed a federal tort cause of action since the days of the country's founding. The question today is, to what extent should this cause of action be confined to its original understanding in the late eighteenth century? For example, Scalia, in *Sosa v. Alvarez-Machain*,[22] where in the case of a detention claim brought under the Alien Tort Act, the U.S. Supreme Court (USSC) would reject the notion that a detention rises to the degree of violation assumed in the eighteenth century and yet recognized the ongoing authority of the law of nations, in the act, as well as the ongoing necessity of interpretation.[23] As a majority of USSC would find, the term hardly has just one meaning, but instead, evolves and therefore remains in part indeterminate—and yet determined by way of reference to the human and to analogous human practices. In *Sosa*, in the majority's words, "considerations persuade us that the judicial power should be exercised on the understanding that the door is still ajar subject to vigilant doorkeeping."[24]

As modern customary law appears to be directed more and more at arriving at the intentions of state actors—as opposed to measuring state practices, for example, the focus in *Paquete*—then we can see again the ways this points to a greater role for courts and for interpretation. Raising questions regarding guiding principles: Even with respect to treaty law, to what extent are the existing rules of interpretation—such as those set out in the Vienna Convention—aimed at conventional interstate law—an adequate basis for the interpretative activity of the proliferating judiciary? The question of interpretation has increasingly been on the table in diverse judiciary, for example, in *LaGrand, Bosnia v. Serbia*, where various courts have asserted their prerogative of interpretation of international law; that is, taking on the *Marbury* moment as it were.[25] Moreover, given the apparently increasing number of such fora, to what extent can normative pluralism and/or conflict be addressed via interpretation? This a challenge often associated with transitional times. Or, another instance, occasioning guiding normative principles, concerns the growth of international law and its interactions with domestic law, particularly where human rights are at stake. Hence, we see a belated recognition of the new grundnorm by the International Court of Justice, in decisions such as *LaGrand, Bosnia v. Serbia*, and the Security Fence advisory opinion, all of which were shaped more or less adequately, by the norm of protection of "humanity."[26]

At this juncture, human rights treaties have been subject to interpretation in a range of fora, including the European Court of Human Rights, the Inter-American Court, the UN Committee on Civil and Political

Rights, and other domestic, regional, and international courts. While their discussion in the International Court of Justice has been the subject of some scholarly writing,[27] human rights law jurisprudence in the deepest sense is still in many ways in its infancy. This is seen in that international law itself lacks a theory of interpretation. For the basic texts on the interpretation of treaties, see, for example, the Vienna Convention and the International Law Commission Articles on State Responsibility are inadequate regarding guidance on key interpretive choices.[28] These seem inapt to the present because these didn't anticipate the role of the courts in regular adjudication and judicial review in this area, nor the role of nonstate actors as claimants in a variety of fora where international law being applied, and hence ultimately as deeply enmeshed in lawmaking, perhaps, offering an inkling into the likely normative direction of the interpretive principles.

Interpretation responds to the challenge of the proliferation and fragmentation of legal orders, which renders immediately elusive the search for an original contextless "intended" meaning to the "law." Hence, one might say we are already and always in the mode of interpretation. Judicial interpretation is well suited to making sense of diverse normative sources, under conditions of political conflict and moral disagreement. Courts are inherently in dialogue with other courts and institutions that also play interpretive roles, and their decisions in individual cases can give meaning to law without purporting to give "closure" to normative controversy in politics and morals.[29]

The contemporary global order and in particular the framework constituting humanity-law in hermeneutic terms fits well with current legal and political conditions. Given the complexity of globalization (including legal globalization), the messy relationship of these forces to all levels of governance, and the related proliferation and fragmentation of legal regimes that are decentralized (that is, not ordered hierarchically), the exercise of adjudication simply cannot be framed in terms of the application of a rule based on the divination of the common will of the states that consented to that rule.

Rather, the pursuit of norms that are now reinforced by transnational parameters is governed by interpretive principles, as the norms are often at a distance from any "original" national origins. So what one can see today is that increasingly interpretation is not taking place solely within a given political community or culture as has often been assumed within American constitutional theory. This goes to interpretation without Hartian rules of recognition in the strong sense. One way of viewing this is in terms of "confirmatory principles."[30] Particularly, since humanity-law encompasses interests and norms of various cultures and political traditions, its application must allow for a form of pluralism, while at the same time being capable of resolving concrete controversies about rights and duties. Thus, humanity-law, as an interpretative lens, navigates the narrow strait between the *Scylla* of difference and the *Charybydis* of the claim to shared values. But, since interpretive practice arises in real cases of individual rights, this ensures that this is not about an essential ideal, but rather concerns the evolution of a norm to guide and manage conflict.

The inquiry is delimited by interpretation as *praxis*—especially the practice in adjudicative fora, where the parameters of state-citizen, citizen-society, and citizen-citizen relations are regularly contested. The subjects of the law are always linked up to the normative legal regime, with the potential for tension, and the demand for the reconciliation of a multiplicity of values elucidating what one might conceive as a guiding principle of interpretation.

What is at stake is nothing less than the ongoing meaning and authority of international law—in apparent transformation to a globalizing order—today, and how to respond to the demand for a guiding "rule of recognition"—a principle that sets, as the basis for the sources and bases for law's authority and significance, some means of managing or resolving normative conflict.[31] This goes to the weight of the relevant and diverse legal norms, and, finally, to what concerns or values might legitimately guide the decision making that informs the global rule of law.

Tribunalization's Proliferation and Contemporary Legality

Among the most remarked trends internationally is the increase in the number of courts and tribunals, international, regional, hybrid, and the greater uses of such bodies not only to interpret and enforce international law, but also to guide and resolve disputes between states and other actors in the international system. Supporters of international law have long had to deal with judgments that international law is not really law, or at least not an effective legal system, because it lacks the routine adjudicative mechanisms characteristic of domestic systems. This skeptical viewpoint may exaggerate or distort the extent to which adjudication relative to other institutions—political, social, and economic—is responsible for the effective realization of domestic legal norms, or more generally their impact on behavior broadly understood. It has nevertheless dogged those who would make the case for international law as an important and influential form of legal ordering.

Returning to Hart in his *Concept of Law* where he concluded that the lack of authoritative adjudicatory institutions in his time did not prevent international law from being real law, because its rules were "accepted and function as such" by the relevant community of states.[32] Today, however, while this lack is being remedied, it is also true as discussed above that international law seeks to bind and guide even non-state actors, and therefore arguably the law's authority or pedigree as law may not be so easily established through the notion that rules are "accepted and function as such" among states. Of course, the mere increase in the numbers of tribunals and the frequency of their use, while it is what seems most to impress casual observers, would not itself make international law seem more like a domestic legal system, as Hart observed in the *Concept of Law*, but for qualitative changes as well—changes that have been uneven across different areas and even within specific regimes but which point to shifts in "dispute settlement" along a court-like direction.[33]

A common narrative of tribunalization is that it signifies a shift from a power—to a rules-based international system. Seen this way, tribunalization is often thought to mean depoliticization. This view goes hand in hand with the perception or assumption of the qualitative change above. Yuval Shany has written of a "greater commitment to the rule of law in international relations, at the expense of power oriented diplomacy."[34] Yet, the depoliticization hypothesis is too simple as evaluation of how tribunalization has occurred in different regimes, and particularly in its relationship to shifts in the normative substance of the law. Indeed, posed this way this threatens to morph into another iteration of the "law-morals" debate, above. In fact, the dynamic relationship between tribunalization and shifts in normative substance has led to moments where tribunals rather than operating in isolation from or above the politics on the ground have become deeply entangled with it, in some ways arguably leading to the emergence of a new politics of international order, itself shaped by tribunalization, where tribunals become the most evident sites of the new global politics of contestation between multiple actors, NGOs, individuals, corporations, communities, and not just states.

Moreover, beyond its influence upon politics as such, the actual practices of interpretation tell us something that emerges regarding overlapping legal materials with authoritative weight that appears to be a human-centric norm—an emerging telos on a par with state sovereignty, which appears relativized in the contemporary political context. Moreover, this norm has weight across state borders and within domestic constitutionalism as well;[35] in this sense, it can be understood as genuinely global.

Just as the optimistic hypothesis of tribunalization as a full shift from a power-based to a law-based international order is likely too simplistic and misleading, so, too, is the countervailing anxiety that the contemporary proliferation of international tribunals in an uncoordinated and decentralized global legal order will only exacerbate "fragmentation," actually undermining the integrity and coherence (and implicitly the legitimacy) of international legal order, that is, in normatively speaking dis-order. Hence, there are those, like Koskenniemi, who write about present legality in terms of norm conflict.[36] Instead, one might well need to inquire further to see how tribunalization is actually operating today and, above all, consider the possibility of sustained attention to the interpretative sensibilities and practice of these regimes.

Here, one regime that lends itself to such study is that which appears to be playing a more significant role within transitional contexts; namely, international criminal justice. In this regard, to begin, one might observe that in the immediate postwar transitions, despite significant political flux, a recourse to similar fora (e.g. Nuremberg) was widely perceived to afford rule of law values such as generality and continuity of the law. The drive to normalize and generalize international criminal responsibility of individuals reflects a faith in the potential of international law to reflect and realize foundational social morality. From Nuremberg through the International Criminal Tribunal for the former Yugoslavia (ICTY) to the International Criminal Court, this drive has been intimately and indissolubly associated with tribunalization. Largely through tribunalization, criminal justice has become central to the normative understanding of political conflict, with important implications for international politics. Increasingly, international tribunals and processes are becoming the international society's demonstrable response to, and indeed, lens upon, foreign affairs crises. Instances of this institutional response are evident in the ongoing international adjudication of violations of humanitarian law in ad hoc tribunals regarding the Balkans and Rwanda,[37] as well as the more recent establishment of other more site-specific fora, such as in Sierra Leone and East Timor.[38] The high-water mark is arguably the establishment of the International Criminal Court.[39]

Tribunalization has normative consequences as it expands the aegis of international criminal justice. Indeed, the changed jurisdictional reach also has substantive implications, as by extending the concept of "international" jurisdiction beyond national borders and situations of conflict, to penetrate within states even during peacetime; the new normativity begins to ambiguate the hitherto-recognized differences between international and internal conflict.[40] In some regard, the charters that form the bases of the new international tribunals aim to simplify modern understandings of the law of war. Historically, protections under the law of war were accorded to individuals on the basis of particular status—nationality and citizenship. Today, the tendency is to evolve these protections in a more universalist direction, inspired by the idea of international human rights, with corresponding implications for individual responsibility.[41]

An obvious and dramatic flashpoint for the "fragmentation" anxiety concerning tribunalization was the pronouncement of the post–Cold War International Criminal Tribunal for the former Yugoslavia Appeals Chamber in the *Tadic*[42] case, where the court rejected the prevailing International Court of Justice's interpretation of certain of the rules of state responsibility: "International law, because it lacks a centralized structure, does not provide for an integrated judicial system operating an orderly division of labour among a number of tribunals, where certain aspects or components of jurisdiction as a power could be centralized or vested in one of them but not the others. In international law, every tribunal is a self-contained system (unless otherwise provided)."[43]

Of course, the current tribunalization did not create what the anxious have labeled "fragmentation."[44] But, the decentralized and specialized work of diverse functionally oriented international legal regimes, run by very different technical and bureaucratic elites with their own cultures, need not have given rise to great anxiety about fragmentation as a specific shortfall of international legal order: rather such a phenomenon might well be seen as a parallel to the increasing specialization and differentiation of governance functions within post-industrial capitalist democracies, for instance, a tendency frequently observed in social theory.

One might have supposed that, once there is a commitment to legality as in the Hart/Fuller debate, that the case of adjudication entails a requirement to fidelity to certain values, that is, that the commitment is not just to order itself as Fuller puts it "unless it is good for something."[45] In domestic legal systems, these cross-cutting values might be thought of as positivized or entrenched in the rules of the constitution—written or unwritten— and confided to the high courts for guardianship, assuring a coherent legal order. In international law, by analogy one might have imagined that the equivalent would be structural norms concerning responsibility, personality, sovereignty, territory, jurisdiction, and so forth, as reflected in custom, the "codification" work of the ILC in the UN Charter; and here one might imagine the International Court of Justice as the guardian of this "constitution," analogous to the domestic high or constitutional court. It is precisely in shattering this last element of the analogy that the *Tadic* Appeals Chamber ruling represents such a flashpoint for the anxiety of fragmentation: as even structural rules such as those concerning state responsibility take on their authoritative meaning within each self-contained system and the meaning assigned to them by what many might have conceived as the prevailing international law's high court, the International Court of Justice (ICJ), nevertheless has no clear, much less predominant, normative force.

Another reading of *Tadic* here is possible; namely, that there is a shift in the grundnorm, or ultimate value of international legality, from sovereign state equality, where states are not subject to any higher authority, whether natural or divine law, than to humanity and its protection.[46] Here one might say that the post-Cold war ICJ, insofar as it avoided humanity in its understanding of the structural rules and privileging the older state-centric grundnorm (for example, in upholding traditional political immunities in the *Arrest Warrants* case), appeared to concede the *Marbury v. Madison* moment of the new "humanity law" order to more contemporary post–Cold War tribunals such as the UN-established ICTY. One sees, albeit, dim or belated recognition of the new grundnorm by the ICJ in decisions such as *LaGrand, Bosnia v. Serbia,* and the Security Fence advisory opinion, as well as in other regional decisions, which are shaped (admittedly, often in a timid and subterranean way) by what I term the law of humanity or "humanity-law."

Indeed, the potential can be seen in the ways these precedents in particular in regard to their remedies pull in human-centered normative directions—for example, consider *LaGrand*. There, the world court goes beyond the traditional state-centric approach found in Bosnia v. Serbia and also eschews collective reparations to recognize systematic rights violations. And in the Security Fence advisory opinion, which in assuming jurisdiction over ongoing occupation/conflict sites where, insofar as the norm figures in jurisdiction, its anticipated scope often going beyond traditional interstate,[47] and recognizing the simultaneity of duties owed states under international humanitarian law as well as to humans under international human rights law, again reflecting the way the humanity norm is actually working in interpretation, case by case.

While, of course, there is the obvious pessimistic hypothesis, that the expansion of the rule of law through tribunals will simply continue to intensify incoherence and tension in the international legal system, undermining the "majesty of the law" and playing into the hands of those who are international law critics or skeptics—who may see the only clear and concrete order at the global level as the actual relationships between "states," determined by the hard or harder laws of power and interest. These critics can say: the more so-called international law there is, the more lawyers and justices there are, even less clear and certain does this purported law become.

In this regard, the views expressed here are neither straightforwardly optimistic nor pessimistic. First, because this chapter questions—as did Hart in an earlier moment of transition—whether the actuality and significance of international law as "law" should be determined by comparison against a benchmark itself drawn from a stereotype of a "domestic legal system"—one based on a historically contingent project, that of building the modern state with its monopoly on legitimate coercion, a project which itself is challenged by the apparent rise of normativity of international law, among other tendencies in emergent global orderings.[48] In this regard, the perspective here is praxis driven, as it views interpretation as central to the construction and evolution of legal order, whether domestic or international. Interpretation responds and normalizes in a sense the proliferation and fragmentation of legal orders, which renders immediately elusive the search for an original contextless "intended" meaning to the "law." Hence, one might say we are already and always in the mode of interpretation. Judicial interpretation is well suited to making sense of diverse normative sources, under conditions of political conflict and moral disagreement. Courts, whether domestic or international, are inherently in dialogue with other courts, institutions, and actors that also play interpretive roles, and their decisions in individual cases can give meaning to law without purporting necessarily to give "closure" to normative controversies in politics and morals. The humanity norm is realized through the interpretation of diverse positive legal rules in multivariate contexts, and is often entangled in politics. This understanding is developed in recent work reflecting changes implied by an increasing amalgamation of the law of war, human rights, and humanitarian law.[49]

Tribunalization has sometimes been accompanied by an expectation of the reinforcement of law as a self-contained system, protected from an "outside"—whether politics or other cultures, for example technocratic, that challenge the purity of the particular legal order. But, tribunals have found themselves always reaching to and entangled with the "outside," resisting collapse into or subordination to the outside, but always maintaining a dynamic engagement through interpretation. Looking at how tribunalization has unfolded in relation to the evolution of the regimes themselves, within a context of rapidly shifting political, social, and economic realities, in each case, there is little evidence of "self-containment," only a sense of non-subordination or assimilation of other normative orders or institutional actors that match the nonhierarchical reality. Again, through interpretation, tribunals are always engaging with the supposed "outside," the relevant "other," and address it, but without engaging in a struggle for dominance or supremacy. Interpretation implies normative communication—not unconstrained conflict or clinical isolation. This does not imply stable agreement or harmonization on the one hand nor delegitimating incoherence—nihilistic or radical indeterminacy—on the other.

War and Peace: Global Rule of Law

One can see there is an increasing overlap and interconnection between the law of war and the law of peace, between international and other levels of legal order, and between the regimes regulating public and private spheres. Indeed, this blurring or ambiguity between the ordinary and the exceptional, between war and peacetime, was already evident in the postwar period: where the question of fidelity transcends the "affairs of everyday life."[50] Here, one might consider affinities in the U.S. constitutional context with precedents, from *Youngstown* to *Hamdan*, on what constitutes constraints on such ostensibly exceptional moments, for example, United States constitutional and public law jurisprudence concerning war powers, executive authority, detainees, and so on. Even in the midst of the war on terror and counterterror the aim is to situate within constitutional regime. In *Hamdan*, the United States Supreme Court held that the sweeping executive scheme under challenge violated both domestic justice and the law of war,[51] finding the military tribunals created by presidential order to try enemies captured in the "War on Terror" legally in violation of the U.S. Uniform Code of Military Justice, as well as the Geneva Conventions. In establishing courts of law, the United States executive must coordinate with Congress, *and* abide by international law. In then-Justice

Sandra Day O'Connor's words, "a state of war is not a blank check for the President." Within the doctrinal structure of international law as such, there is an apparent fusion between human rights and humanitarian law as well as the tradition of just war, which even instill values of justice into the initiation of conflict.

On the contemporary rule of law question regarding the legality of the use of force—that is often characterized in terms of the dilemmas of humanitarian intervention—there is a rising demand for the involvement of courts in making sense of this fusion of legal regimes, as it involves interpretation of the evolving normative developments regarding the role of custom concerning human protection.[52] Hence, as in *Tadic* where the ICTY appellate chamber declared: "[T]his is however an area where opinion juris sive necessitates may play a much bigger greater role than usual was a result of the aforementioned Martens Clause. In the light of the way states and courts have implemented it, this Clause clearly shows that principles of international humanitarian law may emerge through a customary process under the pressures of the demands of humanity . . . *opinio necessitatitis,* chrystallizing as a result of the imperatives of humanity, may turn out to be the decisive element heralding the emergence of a general rule of humanitarian law."

The present impetus to expand upon and generalize international criminal justice via individual enforcement reflects a belief in the possibility of international law to reflect and realize foundational social morality. Under the expanding legal framework, by extending the concept of "international" jurisdiction beyond national borders and situations of conflict, to penetrate within states even during peacetime, the new normativity itself begins to ambiguate the hitherto recognized differences of international and internal conflicts, challenging relatred understandings of human security and bases for responsibility for protection.[53] In some regard, the charters that form the bases of the new international tribunals aim to simplify modern understandings of the law of war, where protections over time had been accorded to the particular status of persons (along the lines of state nationality and citizenship) moving now instead to a more global view of rights protection and related responsibility.[54] Here, illustrative is constitutional case law relating to counter-terrorism, in particular detention policy where rights, as a constitutional matter, have been accorded largely without regard to state-centric nationality. Consider that in the same year the House of Lords issued an opinion leveling the principle of treatment on detention for British citizens and foreigners;[55] in the United

States in one of the very first high court evaluations of the war on terror in the case of *Hamdi v. Rumsfeld,* one can see a similar instance of a leveling approach, reflecting the complex implications of a humanity—rather than citizen-based—standard of treatment. As the USSC declared "there is no bar to this Nation's holding one of its own citizens as an enemy combatant,"[56] while, at the same time, holding "alleged enemy combatants" to be entitled to habeas rights and special processes guaranteed to hear challenges to their status. Thus, many of the developments in humanity-law aim beyond the categorical framework that has been quintessential to the humanitarian protections of the last half century as well as to the fragile rule of law in the international system.

The critical juncture point in the regimes here, postwar, where the international trials at Nuremberg may be understood to represent a unique historical juncture or convergence of the three regimes that today can be seen to make up a legal framework of protection—humanity-law. For while the international military tribunal was understood at the time primarily for its condemnation of the aggressive war via the sanctioning of "unjust war," other humanitarian norms also emerge at that time, reflecting the court's newfound extension over other human relationships, such as rights protections, and related duties. While their avowed purpose was to protect the prevailing interstate system, particularly its security framework, these landmark trials also display the concern for humanity, for persons, otherwise left unprotected by the state. One might say that these trials perform the paradigm shift. Over time, we see the critical tipping point whereby at some point, Germany's aggression and expansionism begin to pale compared to the trials' vindication of persecuted persons and peoples.[57]

Another site where one can see an expanded set of aims for criminal justice is in the mandate of the post–Cold War International Criminal Tribunal for the former Yugoslavia established at the time hardly to ratify the gains of a hard won peace but rather in the midst of conflict, convened by the UN Security Council to hold war criminals to account with the aim that this would advance the peace: "the prosecution of persons responsible for serious violations of international humanitarian law . . . would contribute to the restoration and maintenance of peace."[58] With the revelations of massacres in the context of a political impasse, the ICTY's asserted mission was somehow to transform the conflict in the Balkans into a matter of individual crimes answerable to the rule of law. While this appeared as an attempted apoliticization or depoliticization at the same time, the aims were also political: peace and reconciliation in the region. Thus, the scene was set not for tribunalization to operate as judgment detached and insulated from politics but rather, deeply (re)entangled with it.

In its landmark decision asserting its jurisdiction under the UN Charter (that is, *Tadic),* the ICTY stated that the crimes at issue "could not be considered political offenses, as they do not harm a political interest of a particular state." As in *Marbury v. Madison,* the tribunal is saying it has "kompetenz kompetenz," that is, genuine authority to determine its own jurisdiction and the scope of its operations—and in this moment, becomes more than a creature of the UN political system and the "norms prohibiting them have a universal character." Presently, identifying violations of the "law of nations" is one of the ways the humanity-law regime is now defining the subject and impact of globalization in terms of its affected personality, transcending state borders to protect diverse peoples and persons. Such identifications can be seen in adjudicating this normative offense whose meaning is evolving, whether in domestic civil litigation in regard to tort reparations, for example, *Sosa,* where USSC asserted, "It would take some explaining to say now that federal courts must avert . . . their gaze entirely from any international norm intended to protect individuals,"[59] or, in the vindication of violations via international criminal fora, for example, Kupreskic, where state sovereignty concerns yielded to the enforcement of international humanitarian law.[60]

In this regard, consider that in its reach beyond the state and beyond interstate conflict, one can see that the Nuremberg tribunal's jurisdiction over atrocities was always tied to the conduct of a war conceived of as unjust within the understanding of the prevailing classical interstate system.[61] The ICTY by contrast was to address persecution during an armed conflict that was only partly international if at all in the classic sense of interstate conflict, with a conceded focus on the protection of civilians regardless of the nature of the conflict.[62] Indeed, by the time of the Rwandan genocide and the extension of "international" jurisdiction in the International Criminal Tribunal for Rwanda's (ICTR) charter, there is an added explicit change in jurisdictional reach: although the genocide of approximately one million Tutsis and Hutu moderates in Rwanda was committed within the country's borders, nevertheless, its charter clearly provides for the first time such violations are deemed subject matter appropriately before an international forum, and therefore a reinterpretation of the purview of international jurisdiction.

With the establishment and now-ongoing operation of the International Criminal Court, we can now see that international criminal justice is increasingly enmeshed in managing conflict and regular regime change, both internationally and internally, characterizing justice on a global basis. Thus, in jurisprudence relating to recent conflict, the long-prevailing distinction between international and internal conflict is "more and more blurred, and international legal rules have increasingly been agreed upon to regulate internal armed conflicts."[63] Just as the classical international legal regime premised on state sovereignty and self-determination was inextricably associated with the growth of modern nationalism,[64] conversely, one might see the present developments in the emergent humanitarian law regime as bound up with the contemporary loss of political equilibrium, political fragmentation, weak and failed states, and globalization. These political realities have also sparked efforts at UN reform, with endeavors to reconcile the archetypal statist norm of territorial sovereignty with the mounting justifications for greater international humanitarian intervention based on evolving duties of protection to vulnerable persons and peoples; for example, the new "Responsibility to Protect" (R2P), which now contemplates complementary responsibilities for addressing the gravest threats to human security to vulnerable persons and peoples.[65] The charters of international criminal tribunals reflect a mandate that transcend any one aim or value: as these tribunals are engaged in a dynamic reconstruction of the understanding of international security in terms of humanity-based subjects. So, we can see that tribunalization is not a form of heightened rule of (existing) law, but rather, deeply entangled with the change in the law itself. It is not a suppression of political conflict by "rules" but is enmeshed in the reordering of normative argument—both justificatory and constraining—in relation to violence. This would appear a constitutional moment inasmuch as criminal accountability for violence has become a norm affecting constitutionalism in important ways, especially as we have seen in transitional contexts, for example, South Africa,[66] where vital questions concerning transitional accountability were enmeshed with and legitimated by the new constitutionalism.

The "law of humanity" has clearly moved beyond its association with the politics of specific conflicts, as epitomized by the exceptional 1990s tribunals, instead, to the standing International Criminal Court with the potential of general application.[67] The greater normativity and authority of the humanitarian regime is seen in the consensus in the charter incorporating an understanding of humanity that reflects the dynamic tension discussed, in the appeal to the universal, together with the contradictions posed by contemporary politics. Indeed, for the first time in history, an international institution has been established that is committed to security and peacemaking and yet intended to operate significantly independently of the UN system, notably, independently of both the conditions and nexus of interstate conflict, but also, of the related prevailing supervisory multilateral institutions.

Of even greater significance are the ongoing political and normative implications of a standing international tribunal that is concededly available where all else fails—a court, in the words of Chief Prosecutor Luis Moreno Ocampo, "of last resort."[68] Indeed, consider the everyday implications of a court, which, according to its charter at its preamble and statements of ongoing purpose, is aimed at managing conflict worldwide: "recognizing that . . . grave crimes threaten the peace, security and well-being of the world, . . . determined to put and end to impunity . . . and thus to contribute to the prevention of such crimes." Consider the role judicialization is expected to play in current politics.

So far, the court has implicated itself in a number of conflict situations, often involving conflicts in Africa, for example, the Congo and Sudan. One of the first, a situation "referred" to the ICC, against key members of the brutal Ugandan rebel group, the Lord's Resistance Army,[69] while following state referral, nevertheless, raised a profound dilemma for the court, illustrating the potential tensions regarding the assumption of jurisdiction over a situation, which, at the same time, demanded a political resolution, which some assert might well be jeopardized by the judicial intervention.[70] This may be true as well of other hot spots. Yet, despite the "peace versus justice" dilemma, it appears that the resolution that has for the moment been reached in that region involving bargaining in the shadow of the law reflects a political resolution that nevertheless was structured by and built in the justice dimension. Though this posits a counterfactual, it may well have not been achievable in a different context.

In another more recent illustration, the Security Council's failure to come up with a resolution regarding Darfur led to the referral of the situation to the ICC—highlighting its clearly complementary role (as basis for authority)—a referral that may give an inkling as to how the court will operate going forward, as the pattern appeared to emulate the ad hoc's in a number of ways, such as the establishment of courts in conditions of apparent political impasse. The exercise of such Security Council referral points to a plausible contemporary connection between punishment and international security and reflects how the new institutions of judgment connect up to the prevailing interstate security regime. One can see that in the case of Libya, the consensus on referral appeared to lay the basis for greater international consensus on military intervention.

The above explorations of the evolution of international criminal justice in the present post–Cold War transition point to the ways the emergence of humanity law has been constitutive of—that is, shaped—by tribunalization. Faced with the lack of a comprehensive criminal code, and a complex mandate extending beyond "ordinary" criminal justice in many respects, the tribunals to discharge their mandate so far could not but bring in or confront through interpretation a wide variety of legal material. To the extent that this exercise brought the tribunals into engagement with or in conversation with the interpretations of other tribunals, domestic or international, the terms of such engagement, given the decentralized non-hierarchical system, have been those of equality. Hence, the statement of the *Tadic* court concerning "self-contained systems," where engagement through interpretation is consistent with and in some sense depends on separateness and equality of diverse tribunals, as does a respectful conversation between individuals that crosses over between their two separate lifeworlds.

One might conclude that there are a number of interpretative practices afoot—both within regimes and without—that is dialogic as to the evolution of the humanity-norm. Here there is a growing jurisprudence, on issues like state responsibility, attribution, and so forth, where one can actually see the humanity-norm working interpretatively at the concrete level.

Conclusion

In the wake of the transition from fascism following World War II, the debate between legal philosophers H. L. A. Hart and Lon Fuller has been depicted as one pitting positivism against idealism with the argument conceived as one claiming the strict separation of law and morals. Yet, when we turn to the post–Cold War debate about the status of international law as a legal system, one might assume that Hart would be an ally of the skeptics, who often impugn the authority of international law based on such features as the absence of centralized application and enforcement of the law. However, in the original Hart/Fuller debate, the argument on Hart's side was not really for the strict separation of law and morals, but rather more of a political theory with an institutional claim that legislatures rather than judges ought to be the appropriate institutional actors for aligning morality and positive law, a conclusion that would seem to be all the more true for international law. So, understandably, when we turn to Hart's later seminal work, *The Concept of Law*, he distances himself from the view that the sine qua non of a legal system is commands backed by threats and coercive sanctions; and this leads him to consider again what distinguishes law and morality. The answer, as I argue above, is one that provides a window into crucial contemporary debates about the nature of contemporary global rule of law: namely, what distinguishes legal from moral controversy in international relations is that disagreement and discourse in international law is distinguished by certain particular sources of a legal nature-precedents, treaty texts, and the like. Here we have seen what I have termed "crossjudging" going on,[71] where constitutional courts across cultures grapple with international and transnational material, amounting one might say to a virtual interpretive community—one thinner than that imagined by Dworkin and others, but, also, one that is not isolated and autonomous, that benefits from greater richness of sources, and that has greater potential for a claim to global legitimacy.

This is a crucial insight where in the context of yet another wave of political transition, the turn has been largely away from constitutionalism to international law as a guiding form of legality. Or, rather, one can see that constitutionalism in the first instance is being shaped via transnational or regional review, as we are seeing from Latin America, to Africa as above, instances where because of the overlapping subject matter, protection of justice in the transition is shaping critical understandings of what process and other rights are owed.[72]

Thus, illuminated by the postwar philosophical debate, we can see that a system characterized by diffused and decentralized interpretation, nevertheless, can be considered to have the requisite coherence and integrity of a legal system, because there is a common idiom, one recognizable by lawyers as legal and therefore distinguishable from other modes of normative discourse, such as religion, morality, and so forth.

This chapter has explored this insight by addressing a key anxiety in contemporary international legal scholarship and practice—(with implications for constitutional law, at least in the United States) that of fragmentation—the notion that the multiplicity or multiplication of tribunals, or more generally, sites of interpretation and application of international law, threaten its integrity and legitimacy as a legal system. Here, one might further observe that the role of interpretation in law's normative evolution—despite the plethora of legal orders and adjudicative fora and in the absence of hierarchy—may well address the anxieties surrounding the law/morality debate associated with the earlier postwar transitions. Given multiple actors engaging in normative conversation where there may well be no clear line between the is and the ought, the interpretive project is nevertheless bounded by the parameters of the adjudicative enterprise, that is, the need to resolve conflicts, the associated aim of the preservation of the state, as well as of other actors, and the absence of normative hegemony in the global order.

Notes

1. See H. L. A. Hart, *The Concept of Law* (Oxford: Claredon Press, 1961), 221.

2. Jack Goldsmith and Daryl Levinson, "Law for States: International Law, Constitutional Law, Public Law," *Harvard Law Review* 122 (2009): 1791 (claiming similarities between these areas of public law across axes of uncertainty, enforcement, and sovereignty).

3. Ibid., 1795.

4. See generally Cass Sunstein, *One Case at a Time: Judicial Minimalism on the Supreme Court* (Cambridge, MA: Harvard University Press, 1999); Cass Sunstein, *Legal Reasoning and Political Conflict* (New York: Oxford University Press, 1996).

5. Hart, *Concept of Law*, 229.

6. Ibid., 230.

7. On interpretation generally, see Michael Walzer, *Interpretation and Social Criticism* (Cambridge, MA: Harvard University Press, 1987). For discussion of the potential role of interpretation in the ongoing conceptualization of justice, see Georgia Warnke, *Justice and Interpretation* (Cambridge, MA: MIT Press, 1993).

8. See Ruti Teitel, "Humanity's Law: Rule of Law for the New Global Politics," *Cornell International Law Journal* 35 (2002): 356.

9. Ruti Teitel, *Humanity's Law* (New York: Oxford University Press, 2011).

10. Regarding customary international law, compare Harold Koh, "The Obama Administration and International Law," speech given at the Annual Meeting of the American Society of International Law (March 25, 2010), available at http://www.state.gov/s/l/releases/remarks/139119.htm, with Jack L. Goldsmith and Eric A. Posner, *The Limits of International Law* (New York: Oxford University Press, 2005).

11. See Jürgen Habermas, *The Divided West* (Cambridge, MA: Polity Press, 2006), 115.

12. Ibid., 116.

13. Ibid.

14. See Goldsmith and Posner, *The Limits of International Law,* 192. For a discussion of the drift toward compliance as a central preoccupation, see generally Robert Howse and Ruti Teitel, "Beyond Compliance: Rethinking Why International Law Really Matters," New York University School of Law, Institute for International Law and Justice, International Legal Theory Colloquium (March 6, 2008) (draft article) available at http://www.iilj.org/courses/2008iiljcolloqium.asp. See generally Edith Brown Weiss, ed., *International Compliance with Nonbinding Accords* (Washington, D.C.: American Society of International Law, 1997).

15. For discussion of this phenomenon, see generally Peter Spiro, "The New Sovereigntists: American Exceptionalism and Its False Prophets," *Foreign Affairs* (November/December 2004); Jeremy Rabkin, *The Case for Sovereignty: Why the World Should Welcome American Independence* (Washington, D.C.: The AEI Press, 2004).

16. See *The Paquete Habana,* 175 U.S. 677, 700 (1900) (on the relevance of customary law to U.S. law).

17. Lon L. Fuller, "Positivism and Fidelity to Law—a Reply to Professor Hart," *Harvard Law Review* 71 (1958): 631.

18. Hart, *The Concept of Law,* 212.

19. Hart, *The Concept of Law,* 223.

20. On the evolution of ius gentium, see Jeremy Waldron, "Foreign Law and the Modern Ius Gentium," *Harvard Law Review* 119 (2005): 130–132.

21. See Judiciary Act of 1789, providing federal district courts "shall have original jurisdiction of any civil action by an alien for a tort only, committed in violation of the law of nations."

22. See *Sosa v. Alvarez-Machain,* 542 U.S. 692, 720–721 (2004) (opposing "discretionary power" in the federal judiciary to create causes of action for the enforcement of international-law-based norms).

23. Ibid., 730.

24. Ibid., 729.

25. LaGrand Case *(Germany v. United States of America),* Judgment 2001 I.C.J. 466 (June 27, 2001); Application of the Convention on the Prevention and Punishment of the Crime of Genocide *(Bosnia and Herzegovina v. Serbia and Montenegro),* 2007 I.C.J. 108 (February 26, 2007); Legal Consequences of the Construction of a Wall in the Occupied Palestinian Territory, Advisory Opinion, 2004 I.C.J. 136 (July 9, 2004).

26. Compare post–Cold War transition rulings along these lines, e.g., German Border Guard case ruling on humanity grounds. Berlin State Court,

Docket no. (523), 2 Js 48/90 (9191) ("Justice and humanity were explained and pictured as ideals in the then GDR.").

27. See Joseph Weiler, "Prolegomena to a Meso-theory of Treaty Interpretation at the Turn of the Century," New York University School of Law, Institute for International Law and Justice, International Legal Theory Colloquium (February 14, 2008) (draft article), available at http://www.iilj.org/courses/2008IILJColloqium.asp.

28. E.g., see LaGrand Case *(Germany v. United States of America)*, Judgment 2001 I.C.J. 466 (June 27, 2001).

29. See generally Sunstein, *One Case at a Time*; Sunstein, *Legal Reasoning and Political Conflict*.

30. See *Lawrence v. Texas*, 539 U.S. 558, 574–577 (2003).

31. See Hart, *The Concept of Law*, 228–231.

32. Ibid.

33. Ibid., 212–213.

34. Yuval Shany, *The Competing Jurisdiction of International Courts and Tribunals* (New York: Oxford University Press, 2003), 3–4.

35. See Ruti Teitel, "Transitional Justice and the Transformation of Constitutionalism," in *Comparative Constitutional Law*, eds. Rosalind Dixon and Tom Ginsburg (New York: Edward Elgar, 2011); see Jeremy Waldron, "Foreign Law and the Modern Ius Gentium" *Harvard Law Review* 119 (2005): 129.

36. See Martti Koskenniemi and Paivi Leino, "Fragmentation of International Law? Postmodern Anxieties," *Leiden Journal of International Law* 15, no. 3 (2002): 553–579.

37. See Security Council Resolution 827, 1, U.N. Doc. S/Res/827 (May 25, 1993), and Security Council Resolution 955, 2, U.N. Doc. S/RES/955 (November 8, 1994) (establishing ad hoc international criminal tribunals for the former Yugoslavia and Rwanda, and noting "that the establishment of an international tribunal and the prosecution of persons responsible for the above-mentioned violations of international humanitarian law will contribute to ensuring that such violations are halted and effectively redressed").

38. See Agreement Between the United Nations and the Government of Sierra Leone on the Establishment of a Special Court for Sierra Leone, January 16, 2002, available at http://www.unhcr.org/refworld/docid/3fbdda8e4.html (last visited July 11, 2011); U.N. Transitional Admin. in E. Timor, Regulation No. 2000/15 on the Establishment of Panels with Exclusive Jurisdiction Over Serious Criminal Offences, UNAET/REG/2000/15 (June 6, 2002).

39. Rome Statute of the International Criminal Court (Rome, July 17,

1998) UN Doc. A/CONF.183/9 of July 17, 1998, entered into force April 10, 2002 (hereinafter Rome Statute) (governing the establishment and mandate of the ICC). As of March 24, 2010, 111 countries are States Parties to the Rome Statute, available at http://www.icc-cpi.int/asp/statesparties.html (last visited April 27, 2010).

40. On the current challenge to and evolution of the differentiation of international and internal conflicts, see Rome Statute art. 7 (regarding jurisdiction for crimes against humanity); *Prosecutor v. Tadic,* Case No. IT-94-1, Decision on the Defence Motion for Interlocutory Appeal on Jurisdiction (International Criminal Tribunal for the Former Yugoslavia, October 2, 1995): 128–142 (October 2, 1995); see also Ruti Teitel, "Humanity's Law: Rule of Law for the New Global Politics," *Cornell International Law Journal* 35 (2002): 373–374 (arguing that the expanded application of international criminal law has blurred previous distinctions between state and non-state actors, and war and peacetime situations). The ICTR reflects another instance of expansion of international criminal jurisdiction as the international tribunal prosecuted solely intrastate crimes committed in the Rwandan genocide. See Statute for the International Criminal Tribunal for Rwanda, art. 4.

41. See "Developments in International Criminal Law," *American Journal of International Law* 93 (1999): 1–2.

42. *Prosecutor v. Tadic,* Case No. IT-94-1, Appeal on Jurisdiction, Appeals Chamber (International Criminal Tribunal for the Former Yugoslavia, October 2, 1995).

43. Ibid.

44. See Koskenniemi and Leino, "Fragmentation of International Law?" 553–579.

45. Fuller, "Positivism and Fidelity to Law," 657.

46. This shift and its implications are set out in Teitel, *Humanity's Law.*

47. See Palestinian Authority referral to the ICC, Letter to the UN High Commissioner on Human Rights from the Office of the Prosecutor of the International Criminal Court, January 12, 2010, available at http://www .icc-cpi.int/menus/icc/structure%20of%20the%20court/office%20of%20the %20prosecutor/comm%20and%20ref/palestine/12%20january%202010%20 _%20letter%20to%20the%20un%20high%20commissioner%20on%20human %20rights.

48. See Howse and Teitel, "Beyond Compliance."

49. Teitel, "Humanity's Law," 355.

50. Fuller, "Positivism and Fidelity to Law," 634.

51. See *Youngstown Sheet & Tube Co. v. Sawyer*, 343 U.S. 579 (1952)(limiting power of president to seize private property during emergencies); *Hamdan v. Rumsfeld*, 548 U.S. 557 (2006).

52. See *Prosecutor v. Tadic*, Case No. IT-94-1, Decision on the Defence Motion for Interlocutory Appeal on Jurisdiction (International Criminal Tribunal for the Former Yugoslavia, October 2, 1995): para 99, 527.

53. On the current challenge to and evolution of the differentiation of international and internal conflicts, see Rome Statute (regarding jurisdiction for crimes against humanity); *Prosecutor v. Tadic*, Case No. IT-94-1, 128–142; see also Ruti Teitel, "Transitional Justice: Postwar Legacies," *Cardozo Law Review* 27 (2006): 1615–1631 (arguing that the ICTY expanded the international criminal jurisdiction first established at the Nuremberg Trials to cover "crimes against humanity" even when they occur wholly within the state). The ICTR reflects another instance of expansion of international criminal jurisdiction, which while an international tribunal prosecuted solely intrastate crimes committed in the Rwandan genocide. See ICTR Statute, at Art. 4.

54. See "Developments in International Criminal Law," *American Journal of International Law* (1999): 1–2.

55. See *A (FC) & Others (FC) v. Secretary of State for the Home Department*, [2004] UKHL 56 (December 16, 2004), paras. 54–73 (holding law incompatible with the European Convention on Human Rights because it discriminated between British and foreign nationals in not providing for the potential detention of British terror suspects).

56. See *Hamdi v. Rumsfeld*, 542 U.S. 507, 519 (2004) ("no bar to this Nation's holding one of its own citizens as an enemy combatant"). See also Neil Katyal and Laurence Tribe, "Waging War, Deciding Guilt: Trying the Military Tribunals," *Yale Law Journal* 111 (2002): 1259, 1300–1301; James B. Anderson, "*Hamdi v. Rumsfeld:* Judicious Balancing at the Intersection of the Executive's Power to Detain and Citizen-Detainee's Right to Due Process," *Journal of Criminal Law & Criminology* 95 (2005): 689.

57. See Judith Shklar, *Legalism: Law, Morals and Political Trials* (Cambridge, MA: Harvard University Press, 1986).

58. United Nations, Security Council, United Nations Security Council Resolution 827 on Establishing An International Military Tribunal for the Prosecution of Persons Responsible for Serious Violations of International Humanitarian Law in the Territory of the Former Yugoslavia Since 1991, S/Res/827 (May 25, 1993).

59. See *Sosa*, 542 U.S. at 730.

60. See *Prosecutor v. Kupreskic*, Judgment, No. IT-95-16-T, (January 14,

2000): para. 558 ("crimes against humanity need be committed with a discriminatory intent only with regard to the category of 'persecutions' under Article 5(h).").

61. See Agreement for the Prosecution and Punishment of the Major War criminals of the European Axis, Charter of the International Military Tribunal, August 8, 1945, Art. 69 (c) 2 U.N.T.S. 279.

62. The resolution that formed the ICTY stated specifically: "The Security Council, expressing once again its grave alarm at continuing reports of widespread and flagrant violations of international humanitarian law . . . [d]ecides hereby to establish an international tribunal for the sole purpose of prosecuting persons responsible for serious violations of international humanitarian law." Security Council Resolution 827, U.N. Doc S/RES/827 (May 25, 1993).

63. *Prosecutor v. Tadic,* Case No. IT-94-1, Decision on the Defence Motion for Interlocutory Appeal on Jurisdiction (International Criminal Tribunal for the Former Yugoslavia, October 2, 1995): para. 97; see also *Prosecutor v. Tadic* Appeal Judgment, Case No. IT-94-I-A, Int'l Criminal Tribunal for the Former Yugoslavia (App. Chamber, July 15, 1999, 38 I.L.M. 1518 [1999]); reprinted in *American Journal of International Law* 94 ([2000]: 571, available at http://www.un.org/icty/ind-e.htm); see also Ruti Teitel, "Nuremberg and Its Legacy, Fifty Years Later," in *War Crimes: The Legacy of Nuremberg,* ed. Belinda Cooper (New York: TV Books, 1999), 44–54.

64. See Stephen Krasner, *Sovereignty: Organized Hypocrisy* (Princeton, NJ: Princeton University Press, 1999), 182–183.

65. UN Charter, Article 52. But see ibid., Article 2, para. 4 ("All members shall refrain in their international relations from the threat or use of force against the territorial integrity or political independence of any state, or in any other manner inconsistent with the Purposes of the United Nations"). See Louis Henkin, "NATO's Kosovo Intervention: Kosovo and the Law of 'Humanitarian Intervention,'" *American Journal of International Law* 93 (1999): 824, 827–828 (suggesting that a "living Charter" would support an interpretation of the law and an adaptation of UN procedures). Contra see Christine Gray, ed., *International Law and the Use of Force* (New York: Oxford University Press, 2008). Regarding R2P, see United Nations 2005 World Summit Outcome Document, U.N. Doc. A/60/L.1 (2005): paras. 138–140.

66. See Ruti Teitel, "Paradoxes in the Revolution of the Rule of Law," *Yale International Law Journal* 19 (1994) (discussing post–Cold War constitutional court rulings on accountability and rule of law); see also Teitel, *Transitional Justice,* 11–26; see also Teitel, "Transitional Justice and the Transformation of

Constitutionalism," in *Comparative Constitutional Law Handbook*(discussing current Argentine context of cases regarding disappearances).

67. See Rome Statute.

68. "International Criminal Court prosecutor says first Darfur cases are almost ready," UN News Centre, December 14, 2006, available at http://www.un.org/apps/news/story.asp?NewsID=20989&Cr=sudan&Cr1=.

69. See "Uganda Asks Sudan to Arrest Rebel Leader Accused of Atrocities," *New York Times,* October 8, 2005, at A7; Evelyn Leopold, "Global Court Targets Uganda cult in first case," *Reuters,* October 6, 2005.

70. For a current update on the ICC docket, see http://www.icc-cpi.int/cases.html.

71. See Ruti Teitel and Robert Howse, "Cross-Judging: Tribunalization in a Fragmented but Interconnected Global Order," *New York University Journal of International Law and Politics* 41 (2009): 959.

72. See, e.g., *Azanian Peoples Organization (AZAPO) and Others v. President of the Republic of South Africa and Others* (CCT17/96) [1996] ZACC 16 (July 25, 1996).

Commentary on Chapter 5

Daniel H. Joyner

Professor Ruti Teitel, a leading scholar in the areas of transitional justice and human rights, has contributed to this volume a chapter that, as she describes it, explores "the entanglement of international law jurisprudence with transitional rule of law and the role of new judicial institutions in guiding the emergent global order." In commenting from the perspective of an essentially jurisprudentialist public international lawyer, Professor Teitel and I will on some points be largely "talking past each other." By this I mean that my response to her work may not be formed within the same theoretical lines as those within which she has expertly framed her arguments. However, I think that there is value in seeing how international legal theorizing based in transitional justice dialogue is perceived by someone whose work is more rooted in the classic sources, doctrines, and principles of international law.

I see Teitel's chapter, at its essence, as a critique of state-centric positivism, and in particular the "neo-sovereigntist" brand of positivism that she identifies as being present in some current academic literature. In summary, Teitel appears to argue that we should increasingly look to judicial decisions at both the domestic and international level to see which rules of law should be considered valid or legitimate rules of law. In essence she argues that courts should in some measure supplant the political branches of state governments as the positive source of legal validity, that is, as the forum for positivistic rule validation. According to Teitel, courts effectively and properly perform this role of rule validation through the process of rule interpretation.[1]

On a normative level, Teitel posits that there is a newly ascendant Kelsonian grundnorm in the international legal system, which can best be distilled through an examination of judicial decisions. This new grundnorm is the protection of humanity. Teitel juxtaposes the ascendance of this new grundnorm with the descent of an older grundnorm, which she identifies as state-centrism. On this normative point, I think that Teitel is correct. I think that the ascendance of this human-centric grundnorm can be illustrated by the development of modified substantive rules, and even new *sui generis* legal regimes, in the post–World War II decades, which represent, as Theodor Meron has written, a "humanization" of international law.[2] These new sources of law include the 1949 Geneva Conventions on the law of war, along with their associated 1977 Additional Protocols; the entire edifice of international human rights law, beginning with the 1948 Universal Declaration on Human Rights and developing through the landmark 1966 multilateral treaties and the many subsequent treaties covering more discrete issues of human rights concern; and finally the rules and institutions of international criminal law, establishing individual liability for the most heinous violations of human rights law and the law of war.

However, on a process level I must say that I disagree with Teitel's view that judicial bodies, as opposed to states, have been the primary facilitators of this normative phenomenon.[3] Nor do I think that judiciaries can, or should, in the future play the primary role in promoting the further establishment of this new grundnorm.

On the historical question of where to locate the primary forum for or source of rule validation and grundnorm evolution in the international legal system, I think it is necessary to bear in mind that in all of the cases to which Teitel cites to forward her argument regarding the centrality of tribunals to this enterprise, the international or domestic tribunals in question were applying law that was itself created by states. The judicial decisions that she cites as instrumental in creating "humanity law" are decisions applying, *inter alia,* conventional and customary international human rights law and international criminal law. The treaties and rules of customary law that comprise the substance of the law applied by tribunals were invariably created through the actions of the political bodies of state governments, as recognized in Article 38(1) of the Statute of the International Court of justice (ICJ).

Indeed, the international tribunals that decided the cases Teitel cites as the prime facilitators of the ascendance of the humanity law grundnorm were themselves created by state political bodies. Here also, Article 38(1) of the ICJ Statute provides insight. After listing the sources of international law to which the court should have reference in its decisions (i.e.,

treaties, custom, and general principles), Article 38(1) provides that judicial decisions should be considered by the court as a "subsidiary means for
the determination of rules of law." Judicial decisions are thus recognized
in the classic listing of the sources of international law, not as a source of
law *per se*, but rather only as law-determining mechanisms. This ascription
of a subsidiary, law-determining function for the judiciary is very much in
keeping with the civil law judicial model upon which international tribunals have always been based. It is also, I would argue, in keeping with the
mechanics of judicial interpretation, and what we should expect judicial
interpretation to accomplish.

As stated above, Teitel sees the act of judicial interpretation as having a rule-validating force. The ICJ Statute, however, fairly clearly does
not conceive of international tribunals fulfilling the role of rule validation
through the exercise of their interpretive function, but rather conceives of
the judicial interpretive role as a rule-clarifying and -applying force. The
difference is that in Teitel's model, the interpretive role of courts has a re-
flective effect back onto the rules of law the court is applying, which serves
to either validate or invalidate the rule. The ICJ Statute, rather, sees the
validation of the rule as occurring through its creation by state political
bodies in the form of a treaty or rule of customary law, and views the judicial interpretation function of tribunals simply as a "subsidiary means"
for clarifying the scope and meaning of the rule through its application to
disputes.

Thus, I would argue, in harmony with the orientation of rule validation mechanics recognized by the ICJ Statute, that if there has been an ascendance of a new humanity-centric grundnorm in the international legal system—and again I think that indeed there has been—this evolution
has primarily been facilitated, and the pursuant substantive rules of international law validated, by the states which both created those substantive
rules and created the international judicial bodies to apply those rules to
international conflicts. I am thus of the opinion that, by vaunting to primary status the role of international tribunals in performing the functions
of rule validation and grundnorm evolution in the international legal system, Teitel has unduly marginalized the primary role that states' political
bodies have played in performing these functions.

Turning from the historical and descriptive to the future and prescriptive, I must confess that I do not myself see how judges have a better claim
to knowledge of truth and possession of wisdom than do state political
leaders, such that we should accord the intent and judgment of courts

more weight than the intent and judgment of state political leaders as the source of positivistic rule validation. My students know well my American Realist views on the independence and objectivity of judges. I think that judges are just as susceptible to bias of all kinds as are state political leaders. Additionally, what judges even more importantly lack in most legal systems, in comparison to political leaders, is any meaningful claim to a democratic mandate or democratic representative role. In my first-ever published article, I addressed issues of democratic deficit present in judicial validation of rules of law in the specific context of the role of judges in formally incorporating rules of international law into a domestic legal system.[4] Public international law suffers from democratic deficit criticisms already under the classic state-centric rule validation model recognized by the ICJ Statute. I think that these criticisms would only intensify were the system to move toward an increased emphasis on judicial validation of rules, as Teitel argues for.

In addition to these future prescriptive comments based in legitimacy, I must also say from a more practical perspective that I do not see a systemic change toward judicial rule validation and away from state-centric rule validation, as necessary in order to continue to advance the new grundnorm of protection of humanity. Again in harmony with the conception of the role of the international judiciary contained in the ICJ Statute Article 38(1) listing of the sources of international law, I see the judicial cases that Teitel cites as evidence for her theory of the rule-validation role of courts, to rather establish the conclusion that the classic state-centric system of rule validation is working as it should and is not in need of systemic change. Again, in all of the cases that Teitel cites in which international law is being applied, whether by the International Court of Justice, by international criminal tribunals, or by domestic tribunals, in my view the court is applying rules of law that have been validated through the positivistic processes of their creation as treaties or rules of customary international law. Inasmuch, therefore, as these cases in totality demonstrate that there is a newly ascendant grundnorm of protection of humanity, in my view that grundnorm and the rules implementing it have been successfully validated through the state-centric source creation methods recognized in the ICJ Statute. Thus, inasmuch as we laud the creation of the newly ascendant grundnorm and its implementing substantive rules, we should be satisfied that this result has occurred through the processes of the classic, state-centric rule validation and grundnorm evolving system.

Let me make a provocative suggestion in closing. It has been my experience that much argumentation in academic literature on human rights appears to be principled ends driven instead of jurisprudential means driven. By this I mean that in the literature on human rights, academic commentators are often willing to sacrifice jurisprudential theory for the sake of principled results—that is, in order to have human rights law of a substance that they approve of. I have seen this most notably in the turn to natural law justifications in human rights scholarship, in order to avoid dealing directly with the positivist deficit that some substantive rules or principles face.[5] These ends-driven arguments do frequently place greater emphasis upon the authority of courts to either interpret or outright make the law in what is seen by such commentators to be a more correct image. I think there is a confidence that legal academics promoting human rights place in judges that they do not place in politicians, that the judges will "get it right on the substance"—right, of course, being the way that the academics think it should be. Judges, after all, are kindred lawyers of a frequently liberal academic bent, particularly in the context of judges of international tribunals. Human-rights academics, I believe, are more confident that judges will share their values and priorities on certain human-rights rules and principles than will state political leaders.

In making this observation, I do not mean to be critical. There is nothing necessarily professionally or morally wrong with seeking ends at the expense of means. In fact, in the area of human-rights law quite the opposite is likely true. However, and again here my jurisprudentialist bent will come through, for those commentators who take process and jurisprudential theory seriously, it is a concern.

I see in Teitel's research an undercurrent of such a principled ends-driven analysis—that is, the noble desire for the furtherance of a grund-norm of protection of humanity in the international legal system.[6] However, as with other human-rights scholars, I wonder whether theoretical and practical problems with the court-centered validation approach that she argues for are overlooked or marginalized in their significance for the sake of these legitimate ends?

Notes

1. Ruti Teitel, "Global Transitions, New Perspectives on Legality, and Judicial Review," 227: "In this regard, the perspective here is praxis driven, as it views interpretation as central to the construction and evolution of legal order, whether domestic or international. Interpretation responds and normalizes in a sense the proliferation and fragmentation of legal orders, which renders im-

mediately elusive the search for an original contextless 'intended' meaning to the 'law.' Hence, one might say we are already and always in the mode of interpretation. Judicial interpretation is well suited to making sense of diverse normative sources, under conditions of political conflict and moral disagreement. Courts, whether domestic or international, are inherently in dialogue with other courts, institutions, and actors that also play interpretive roles, and their decisions in individual cases can give meaning to law without purporting necessarily to give 'closure' to normative controversy in politics and morals. The humanity norm is realized through the interpretation of diverse positive legal rules in multivariate contexts, and is inevitably entangled in politics."

2. Theodor Meron, "The Humanization of Humanitarian Law," *American Journal of International Law* 94, no. 2 (April 2000): 239–278.

3. As Teitel states, 234: "The above explorations of the evolution of international criminal justice in the present post–Cold War transition point to the ways the emergence of humanity law has been constitutive of—that is, shaped—by tribunalization. . . . One might conclude that there are a number of interpretative practices afoot—both within regimes and without—that is dialogic as to the evolution of the humanity-norm. Here there is a growing jurisprudence, on issues like state responsibility, attribution, and so forth, where one can actually see the humanity-norm working interpretatively at the concrete level."

4. Daniel H. Joyner, "A Normative Model for the Integration of Customary International Law into United States Law," *Duke Journal of Comparative & International Law* 11 (2001): 133.

5. See, e.g., Louis Henkin, "Human Rights and State 'Sovereignty,'" *Georgia Journal of International & Comparative Law* 25 (1996): 32.

6. As Teitel states, 222: "What is at stake is nothing less than the ongoing meaning and authority of international law—in apparent transition to a globalizing order—today, and how to respond to the demand for a guiding 'rule of recognition'—a principle that sets, as the basis for the sources and bases for law's authority and significance, some means of managing or resolving normative conflict. This goes to the weight of the relevant and diverse legal norms, and, finally, to what concerns or values might legitimately guide the decision making that informs the global rule of law."

Contributors

Akhil Reed Amar is Sterling Professor of Law and Political Science at Yale University, where he teaches constitutional law at both Yale College and Yale Law School. He received his B.A, summa cum laude, in 1980 from Yale College, and his J.D. in 1984 from Yale Law School, where he served as an editor of the *Yale Law Journal*. After clerking for Judge Stephen Breyer, U.S. Court of Appeals, First Circuit, Professor Amar joined the Yale faculty in 1985. Along with Dean Paul Brest and Professors Sanford Levinson, Jack Balkin, and Reva Siegel, Amar is the coeditor of a leading constitutional law casebook, *Processes of Constitutional Decisionmaking*. He is also the author of several books, including *The Constitution and Criminal Procedure: First Principles, The Bill of Rights: Creation and Reconstruction*, and most recently, *America's Constitution: A Biography*.

William L. Andreen is Edgar L. Clarkson Professor of Law at The University of Alabama. Professor Andreen received his B.A. in 1975 from the College of Wooster, where he was a member of Phi Beta Kappa and was awarded the college's prize in history. He holds a J.D. from Columbia University School of Law (1977). At Columbia, Andreen was the Special Projects Editor of the *Columbia Journal of Transnational Law* and a Harlan Fiske Stone Scholar. After two years of litigation practice with the Atlanta law firm of Haas, Holland, Levison & Gibert, he was appointed Assistant Regional Counsel of the U.S. Environmental Protection Agency, Region 4. In 1983, Andreen joined The University of Alabama law faculty where he presently serves as the Edgar L. Clarkson Professor of Law and Director of the Joint Summer School Project with the Australian National University (ANU). During the summer of 2008, Andreen was a Visiting

Professor at Lewis & Clark Law School; during the fall of 2005, he was a Fulbright Senior Scholar and a Visiting Fellow at the ANU's National Europe Centre; during the spring of 2005, he was a Visiting Professor at Washington and Lee University School of Law; and during the spring of 1991, he was a Visiting Fellow in the law faculty at the ANU. He has also served in a number of other capacities: legal advisor to the National Environment Management Council of Tanzania (1994–1996); Research Associate, Law Faculty, Mekelle University, Ethiopia (2001; 2003; 2004); past Chair, Environmental Law Section, American Association of Law Schools; Scholar, Center for Progressive Regulation; Environmental Law Commission, World Conservation Union (IUCN); past President and currently Of Counsel, Alabama Rivers Alliance; and Co-Chair, Enforcement and Administrative Penalties Stakeholder Committee, Alabama Environmental Management Commission. Andreen teaches Environmental Law, International Environmental Law, and Administrative Law and publishes widely in the area of water pollution law.

Jack M. Beermann is Professor of Law and Harry Elwood Warren Scholar at Boston University School of Law where he has previously served as Associate Dean for Academic Affairs. He has published articles in *Aspen Law & Business; Northwestern University Law Review; Boston University Law Review; Boston University Public Interest Law Journal; San Diego Law Review;* and *North Carolina Law Review.* He was a contributing author to *Administrative Law in a Changing State: Essays in Honour of Mark Aronson.*

Heather Elliott is an Associate Professor of Law at The University of Alabama. She is a former law clerk to U.S. Supreme Court justice Ruth Bader Ginsburg. She joined the law school after serving as Assistant Professor at Catholic University's Columbus School of Law. Previously, Professor Elliott served as a law clerk for Judge Merrick B. Garland of the U.S. Court of Appeals for the D.C. Circuit as well as an appellate litigation associate at Wilmer Cutler Pickering Hale & Dorr LLP. Her recent scholarship includes an article published in the *Stanford Law Review* and a chapter in the third volume of *Comparative Perspectives in Portuguese and American Law.*

Joshua Alexander Geltzer earned his J.D. from Yale Law School, his A.B. from Princeton in 2005, and his Ph.D. from King's College London in 2008.

David Gray is an Assistant Professor of Law at the University of Maryland. He teaches criminal law, criminal procedure, and jurisprudence. His scholarly interests are eclectic, but focus on transitional justice, criminal law, criminal procedure, and constitutional theory. His recent publications have appeared in the *Vanderbilt Law Review*, the *California Law Review*, the *Alabama Law Review*, the *Washington University Law Review*, the *Stanford Law Review*, *Law & Contemporary Problems*, the *Fordham Law Review*, and in prominent volumes edited by leading scholars. In addition to his own scholarship, Professor Gray works closely with students to develop and publish their work. Recent work written by or with his students has appeared in the *Federal Sentencing Reporter*, the *Vermont Law Review*, the *Maryland Law Review*, and in edited collections. Consistent with the law school's mission as a public educational institution, Gray frequently provides expert commentary for local and national media outlets. Prior to joining the School of Law Faculty, Gray practiced law at Williams & Connolly LLP, was a Visiting Assistant Professor at Duke University School of Law, clerked for the Honorable Chester J. Straub, U.S. Court of Appeals for the Second Circuit, and for the Honorable Charles S. Haight Jr., U.S. District Court for the Southern District of New York.

Paul Horwitz is Gordon Rosen Professor of Law at The University of Alabama. He teaches law and religion, constitutional law, and legal profession. He received his B.A. in English Literature from McGill University in Montreal in 1990; M.S., with honors, in Journalism from Columbia University in 1991; LL.B. from the University of Toronto in 1995 where he was coeditor-in-chief of the *University of Toronto Faculty of Law Review;* and LL.M. from Columbia Law School in 1997. Horwitz clerked for the Honorable Ed Carnes of the United States Court of Appeals for the Eleventh Circuit. Before joining The University of Alabama, Horwitz was an associate professor at the Southwestern University School of Law in Los Angeles. He has also been a visiting professor at the University of Iowa College of Law, the University of San Diego School of Law, and Notre Dame Law School. In addition to having written and spoken widely on issues of constitutional law, Horwitz is a member of the popular legal blog Prawfsblawg.

Daniel H. Joyner is an Associate Professor of Law at The University of Alabama. Joyner received a B.A. in Japanese from Brigham Young University, his J.D. from Duke Law School, an M.A. in political science from the University of Georgia, and a Ph.D. in law from the University of Warwick School of Law in the United Kingdom. Prior to joining The University of Alabama law faculty in 2007, Joyner taught for four years on the faculty of the University of Warwick School of Law. During Michaelmas Term 2005, he was also a Senior Associate Member of St. Antony's College, Oxford University. Joyner teaches Public International Law, International Trade Law, and Contracts. Professor Joyner's research interests are focused in public international law, with particular interest in the area of WMD proliferation, including nonproliferation treaties and regimes, issues of international trade and export control law, use of force law, and international legal theory. Joyner's first monograph, *International Law and the Proliferation of Weapons of Mass Destruction,* was published in 2009. Professor Joyner's current research project is a book on the 1968 Nuclear Non-proliferation Treaty.

Nina Mendelson is a Professor of Law at the University of Michigan. Mendelson's research and teaching interests include administrative law, environmental law, statutory interpretation, and the legislative process. Prior to joining the Michigan faculty in 1999, she served with the Department of Justice's Environment and Natural Resources Division, litigating and advising on legislative matters and environmental policy initiatives. She also participated extensively in federal legislative negotiations. She earned her A.B. in economics, summa cum laude, from Harvard University, where she was Phi Beta Kappa. Her J.D. is from Yale Law School, where she was an articles editor of the *Yale Law Journal.* After law school, she clerked for Judge Pierre Leval in the Southern District of New York and for Judge John Walker Jr. on the Second Circuit. Professor Mendelson has served as a fellow to the Senate Committee on Environment and Public Works and practiced law with Heller, Ehrman, White & McAuliffe of Seattle, when she also won the Washington State Bar Association's Thomas Neville Award for outstanding pro bono service. Her work has been published in prominent law reviews, including the *Columbia Law Review,* the *New York University Law Review,* and the *Michigan Law Review.* In addition, she currently serves as one of three U.S. special legal advisers to the NAFTA Commission on Environmental Cooperation. She is also a member scholar at the Center for Progressive Reform.

Meredith Render is an Assistant Professor of Law at The University of Alabama. Render earned her B.A., magna cum laude, from Boston College and J.D., cum laude, from Georgetown University. After graduating from Georgetown University Law Center, Render clerked for the Honorable George W. Lindberg of the United States District Court for the Northern District of Illinois and the Honorable Fortunato Benavides of the United States Court of Appeals for the Fifth Circuit. She taught law at Stanford Law School and was an associate in the Litigation Department of Goodwin Proctor LLP in Washington, D.C. Professor Render teaches civil rights legislation, property classes, and gender and the law.

Austin Sarat is William Nelson Cromwell Professor of Jurisprudence and Political Science at Amherst College and Hugo L. Black Visiting Senior Scholar at The University of Alabama School of Law. Sarat is author or editor of more than seventy books, including *When the State Kills: Capital Punishment in Law, Politics, and Culture; Something to Believe In: Politics, Professionalism, and Cause Lawyers* (with Stuart Scheingold); *Cultural Analysis, Cultural Studies and the Law: Moving Beyond Legal Realism* (with Jonathan Simon); *Looking Back at Law's Century* (with Robert Kagan and Bryant Garth); *Law, Violence, and the Possibility of Justice; Pain, Death, and the Law; The Blackwell Companion to Law and Society; Mercy on Trial: What It Means to Stop an Execution;* and *Imagining Legality: Where Law Meets Popular Culture.* He is currently writing a book titled *Hollywood's Law: Film, Fatherhood, and the Legal Imagination.*

Ruti Teitel is Ernst C. Stiefel Professor of Comparative Law at New York Law School. She is also Chair of Comparative Law & Politics Discussion Group and Founding Co-Chair, American Society of International Law, Interest Group on Transitional Justice and Rule of Law. An internationally recognized authority on transnational law, comparative law, international human rights, transitional justice, and comparative constitutional law, Ruti Teitel is the first Ernst C. Stiefel Professor of Comparative Law at New York Law School. Her pathbreaking book, *Transitional Justice,* examines the twentieth-century transitions to democracy in many countries. Her extensive body of scholarly writing on comparative law, human rights, and constitutionalism encompasses articles is published in some of the country's most prestigious legal journals, including the *Yale Law Journal, Cornell Law Review, Columbia Human Rights Law Review, Michigan Journal of International Law, Cornell International Law Journal,* and the *Harvard Law Review.* In addition, she has contributed dozens of book chapters to published volumes relating to law and politics, including *Taking Wrongs Seriously: Apologies and Reconciliation; Rethinking the Rule of Law After Communism; History: A Watershed Moment;* and *Transnational Legal Processes: Globalisation and Power Disparities.* She also writes on human-rights issues for a broader audience, having published in the *New York Times,* Legal Affairs, Findlaw.com, and Project Syndicate.

Lindsey Ohlsson Worth is Board of Visitors Fellow, Pepperdine University School of Law. She earned her A.B. from Harvard in 2002, and her J.D. from Yale in 2009.

Index

AAA (Argentine Anticommunist Alliance), 150
abolition, 10, 101–2, 119, 122
abortion rules/regulations, 4, 24–25, 30–31, 35n17, 54, 74n2, 80n66
abusive legal paradigms: law as justification of violence, 169–70; and misconceptions of role of law, 161–62; nature of, 155–61, 182n51, 195, 198–99; position of within the law, 11–12; and role of law in society, 200–202; role of litigation in avoiding development of, 171–72; state officials in, 198–99
abusive regimes: and Argentine Dirty War, 11, 150–51, 159–60, 179n11, 179n13, 207; in Balkan states, 156, 172, 217, 224, 230–31, 238n37; and collapse of dynamic stability, 177–78; legal justification for targeted violence in, 157–61, 169–70, 194, 205–7; and multidimensionality of law, 149–50; position of within the law, 148; in Reconstruction-era American South, 102n27, 193, 196, 205, 206; religion as source of abuse, 172–73; role of law in, 192–94; role of state officials in, 195–99; and rule of law, 192–94, 205–7; and segmented nature of societies, 162, 190–91; in South Africa, 134, 137, 159–60, 232; violence as response to crisis, 167–69. *See also* Nazi crimes; Rwanda Massacre

abusive social norms, 195–200, 202–4, 208n10, 211n59, 211n62
Accardi v. Shaughnessy, 93n19
accountability of agencies, 46, 56, 58–59
Ackerman, Bruce: on consequences of constitutional amendments, 5; on distinction between ordinary and extraordinary lawmaking, 140–42; on legitimacy of Fourteenth Amendment, 132–33; "Revolution on a Human Scale", 144n16; *We the People, Vol. 1: Foundations*, 125n6, 125n7, 126n27, 127n33, 143n3, 143n5; *We the People, Vol. 2: Transformations*, 15n27
"active liberty," Justice Breyer's use of term, 172
Adamson v. California, 127n36
Additional Protocols (1977), 244
Administrative Procedure Act (APA), 24, 46, 94n29
administrative state, 8, 55–59, 60–62, 91
admission of states, 108, 109, 110
Africa, conflicts in, 11, 134, 137, 150, 156, 158, 159–60, 168, 179n9, 190, 205, 207, 212n73, 224, 231, 233–34, 235, 238n37, 239n40, 240n53
African Americans. *See* race and racism; slaves and slavery; voting rights
agencies: accountability of during late-term periods, 84; Congress as source of democratic values of, 8–9; congres-